The History
of
LOS GATOS

The History of
LOS GATOS

Gem of the Foothills

BY

GEORGE G. BRUNTZ

Western Tanager Press
Santa Cruz 1983

THE HISTORY OF LOS GATOS

Printed and bound in the United States of America

Library of Congress Catalog Card Number 79—174678

ISBN Number: 0-934136-30-0

Western Tanager Press (Valley Publishers)
1111 Pacific Ave., Santa Cruz, CA 95060

Table of Contents

Foreword

If history is the recorded pilgrimage of the soul of man as expressed by his words and deeds, this volume is truly a journey---and a fascinating one--- through more than a century and a half of existence of this spectacular foothill area that is now Los Gatos. It is narrated by Dr. George G. Bruntz, who is pre-eminently qualified for such an undertaking. As the author of five other books and numerous articles in periodicals and pamphlets, he has established himself as a research student and a writer. As a resident of Los Gatos for more than 40 years, a teacher in the local high school for 16 years and a college professor for nearly 20 years, Dr. Bruntz has the feel of local history and the qualities needed by a good writer of history.

Officially, the history of Los Gatos began with its incorporation as a Sixth Class city in 1887, but incidents recorded herein predate that era, beginning with the early Indians, then through 1776 when Captain Juan Bautista de Anza and his men camped near where the Main Street bridge is now.

Dr. Bruntz traces the story of the early founders and builders---their achievements and disappointments---from the beginning to the advent of a village, then a town---and a TOWN it has remained because the people wanted it so.

Over the years other writers have turned out snatches of history on Los Gatos, but usually the accounts were brief and in generalities, or about specific phases in the life of the town. But none is known to have attempted, and accomplished so well, such a complete history as this book, which starts with the beginning and ends with the present. It covers location, climate, beauty; it tells of the struggles of the pioneers to bring about industries or expand horticulture and agriculture; and the building of mountain roads; advent and demise of railroads; and finally the arrival of today's freeways. Early government and politics are described; the several newspapers the town boasted since 1881 are enumerated. Schools, churches, service clubs and cultural activities all are given their fair share of attention. In fact the entire spectrum of life comes under the purview of the writer in this absorbing story. No one who reads it can deny that Los Gatos has had a most fascinating history. This volume will forever be the reference that present and future historians and scholars will use to seek out the realities of what happened. They will, that is, if they want an account of history that tells it like it was.

Lloyd E. Smith

Los Gatos, California
1971

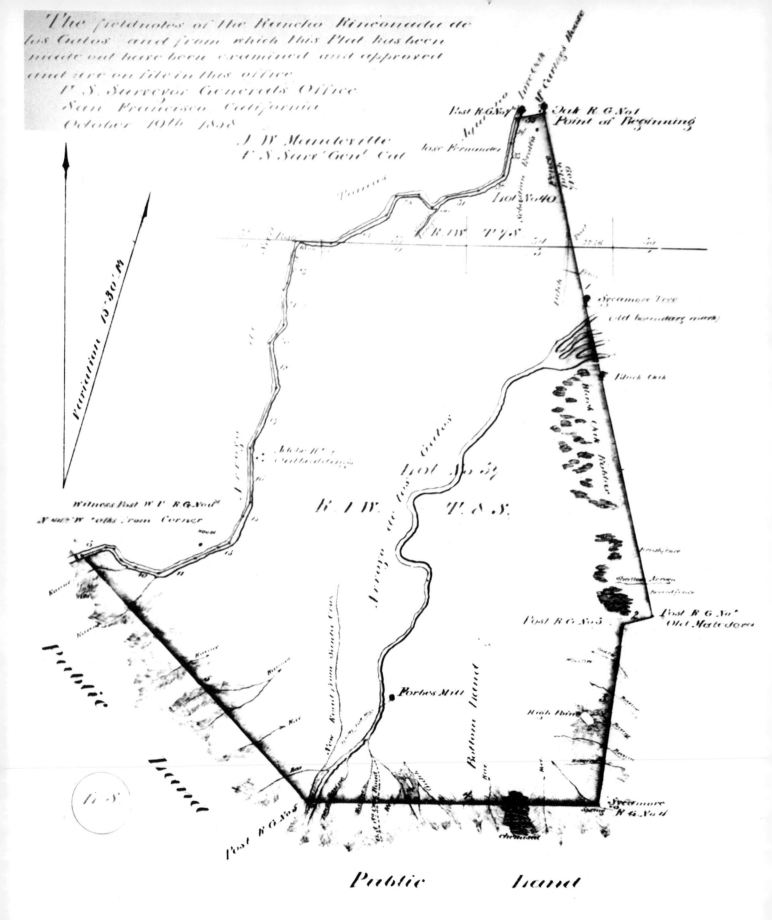

Plat of the *Rancho Rinconada de Los Gatos* granted by the Government of Mexico to Jose Hernandez and Sebastian Peralta and certified in 1860 by the United States Government. *(Santa Clara County Recorder)*

Introduction

This new edition of *The History Of Los Gatos* is presented in response to popular demand. The earlier editions have long since been sold out.

As indicated in the Introduction to the earlier editions we make no pretense of covering every minute detail of the story of Los Gatos. Many will no doubt feel that the writer should have covered this or that, or given more space to some event or person. But no history can be absolutely complete, and we would not want it so, lest we lose sight of the forest for the trees.

However, in this new printing we should point out some inadvertent omissions in the original edition. For example, in the section on "Early Stores" we neglected to mention the Templeman Hardware Store at 24 North Santa Cruz Ave. This was, for years, the only hardware store in our town. Owned originally by Mr. Arthur W. Bogart, it was purchased by Arthur W. Templeman in 1917. Mr. Templeman had worked for Mr. Bogart for a number of years. Mr. Templeman owned and operated the store until his tragic death by an automobile accident in 1954.

After the death of Mr. Templeman, Mr. Bernard Hardwicke, Mr. Templeman's son-in-law, took over the management of the store. Mr. Hardwicke operated the business until 1966 when he retired. The premises are now occupied by an antique shop.

In the first edition we also neglected to mention Dr. Horace Jones who was the physician for almost every person in Los Gatos for many years. Besides his medical practice Dr. Jones played an active part in community affairs. He was a member of the High School Board of Trustees and served on the Town Planning Commission for a number of years.

Dr. Jones went into "retirement" after 68 years of community service. However, he still had many old-timers who depended on him for medical attention. He was, like other doctors in our town, much loved by everyone.

Many people have expressed interest in the story behind the huge statues of cats that guard the entrance to the former home of Col. Charles Erskine Scott Wood and his wife Sara Bard Field, two prominent American literary figures. The two statues were executed in 1922 by the sculptor Robert Paine. The Woods chose the cat as the subject, not because Los Gatos means "the cats" but because they believed that there is no more dignified and beautiful subject for sculpture than members of the feline family. Their reason for placing the cats where they now stand (the old Santa Cruz Highway passed in front of them before Highway 17 bypassed them) was to impress people with the fact that sculpture can be used to beautify our highways.

The statues were made of poured cement rather than bronze or marble or expensive stone. The sculptor, Robert Paine, spent a year making them, first studying wildcats at the San Francisco Zoo and making preliminary sketches. He lived at the Wood estate in a small shack, and accepted only a day laborer's wages rather than a high fee artists would command.

The cats are eight feet tall and ten feet in circumference, and stand on pedestals one and a half by four feet. The statues have stood the ravishes of time and the scars of vandalism for all these years, a monument to the foresightedness of Col. and Mrs. Wood. Although they are now partially hidden from public view, they stand in all grandeur and dignity today as they did when they were first completed.

Space will not permit the mention of all the good people who have helped with information, anecdotes of old times, photographs and artifacts of various kinds, but a few should be mentioned. Mr. W. R. Hamsher turned over to the Los Gatos Memorial Library the clippings and other items of historical interest that had been assembled over the years by his father Mr. Clarence F. Hamsher. Mrs. George Kretsinger and a crew of volunteers put these in chronological and topical order, and gathered them in loose-leaf notebooks and deposited them in the Reference Room of the library. These were good sources of information.

Mr. Lloyd Smith, former publisher of the Los Gatos *Times* saw the importance of assembling material on the history of our town and published photos and stories gathered from old-timers, which he made available to the writer. Mr. George Kane, publisher of the Los Gatos *Times-Observer* continued the practice of publishing pictures and stories.

To both of these men the writer is indebted for material they willingly supplied, and for their encouragement.

Others who were a great help include Mr. Leland Walker, the son of the publisher of the first newspaper in Los Gatos. He permitted the writer to study back issues of the Los Gatos Weekly *News* and supplied a number of interesting facts about Los Gatos. Mr. George Place was a fountain of information. Mrs. D. Lloyd Smith loaned her file of old newspapers, and Miss Hulda Erickson, an old-timer, was helpful in filling in details of the "olden days."

Mr. Henry C. Crall, another old-timer furnished many sidelights and kept the writer from making errors of fact. The Sewall Brown family, Mrs. Lyndon Farwell, Mrs. Martin LeFevre, and Mrs. Sheila Stanfield Heid supplied illustrations and information, Mrs. Mary Rugh and the Edward S. Yocco family were very helpful.

Bert Donlon, instructor in photography at the Los Gatos Union High School was most cooperative and to him and his students we owe thanks for reproductions of many old pictures. Mr. and Mrs. John Barnes gave every possible assistance in photo reproductions. Mr. T. P. Schweitzer of the History Department of the High School was helpful in finding elusive material. Miss Dora Rankin's contributions are cited in the footnotes, as are others who have contributed information, including Mr. John Lloyd on Montezuma School for Boys and Mrs. Natalie Wollin on Hillbrook School. Mr. and Mrs. Leo Frank volunteered information on the mountain communities and the Gymkana Association.

The author enjoyed several hours of conversation with Mr. John D. Crummy about the early days in Los Gatos and the development of the Food Machinery Corporation (FMC). Mrs. Jo Liebfritz, the Town Clerk and her staff, including Mrs. Lucille Beams and Mrs. Rose Aldag, were very kind in making the Town Board minutes and other documentary materials available. Mrs. H. D. Long, the Adult Librarian and staff, in particular Mrs. Phillip White and Miss Ruth Rigby were helpful in directing the writer to valuable sources of information.

Finally, the author owes a debt of gratitude to Mr. Charles Clough, the publisher of the first two editions. It was he who gave the final push that started the writer on this project.

Similarly, the Los Gatos Museum Association should be credited with taking the steps necessary for the production of this new printing of *The History of Los Gatos*. Thanks to Mr. Hal Morris, of Western Tanager Press, whose encouragement made this edition possible.

CHAPTER I

From Wilderness to Village

Beauty and Climate of Los Gatos

THE FAMOUS Greek Historian Herodotus tells us that the Ionians of Asia built their cities in a region where the air and climate "are the most beautiful in the whole world; for no other region is equally blessed with Ionia, neither above it nor below it, nor east nor west of it." In other words, Ionia was believed to have the best climate in the world.

Early settlers in Los Gatos and modern-day citizens alike would dispute that statement. To them, Los Gatos has the perfect climate and the most beautiful scenery. As early as 1868 Bayard Taylor, the world traveler, is said to have stood at the foot of the Santa Cruz Mountains and exclaimed: "How shall I describe a landscape so unlike anything else in the world--with the beauty so new and dazzling that all ordinary comparisons are worthless."[1]

In 1881 the writers of a History of Santa Clara County said of Los Gatos: "How this pleasantly situated village came to get the name 'The Cats' we are not in a position to say, but this we dare assert, that there are few spots in the broad county of Santa Clara, indeed we do not except the state, in its immense length, where we find so many charms of scenery and vegetation."[2]

Another source, dating to 1888 said, "Los Gatos where all the zones and all the seasons seem to have combined to crown this favored spot with the choicest of treasure of them all."[3]

In an issue of the San Jose Mercury in September 1887 the Los Gatos correspondent was eloquent in his praise when he said, "While beautiful pictures cost money and must be insured, the grand, ever-changing panorama of mountains, valleys, orchards, vineyards, country homes ... such as a resident of Los Gatos has always before him, costs nothing. Day after day it presents new features of beauty, new reasons for admiration."

The Los Gatos newspaper was not to be outdone, for on November 16, 1888 the Los Gatos News quoted a circular from W. Peck & Company as follows: "Here, amid delightful views of mountains and valley are found scenery for the artist, health for the invalid, investment for the capitalist, and many very attractive and remunerative homes." Eugene Sawyer, wrote in his History of Santa Clara County, "Los Gatos, the Gem City of the foothills, is in the most delightful part of the most delightful California county." He went on to say that Los Gatos has many commanding views, is sheltered from winds and fog. It is just the place for those "who want to withdraw from the heat and clamor of the city life, either permanently or at the end of the week, to enjoy the witchery of enchanting surroundings." Not only, said he, is the town located at the foot of the Santa Cruz Mountains, but it is situated at the mouth of a beautiful canyon, "part of the town lying on one side and part on another, of the Los Gatos Creek. The foothills and mountains form a delightful amphitheatre above the town opening out to the floor of the valley on the north."[4]

In 1915 Sunset Magazine issued a special pamphlet on Los Gatos in which it referred to our town as "a dream city among the picturesque foothills." It quotes from the columns of the San Jose Times as follows: "To see Los Gatos is to love the town. To enjoy the privilege of a few days' or weeks' stay within the gates of that beautiful city of 3,500 souls is to wish to come again, and to become a permanent resident there is to live in paradise, if such there be on this earth."[5]

Even today, experienced travelers, who have seen much of the world are taken with the beauty and climate of Los Gatos. In 1957 while the present writer was traveling in Spain, he met an Englishman who had been all over the world. We were sitting in the lobby of our hotel in Burgos, Spain waiting for the dining room to open when the Englishman remarked, "If I should ever retire there is one spot I think is the most ideal in all the world." Pressed for the location of this spot, he replied that I had probably never heard of the place. It was in California. When I informed him that I came from California he said, "You've probably never heard of the place. It is just south of San Francisco. It's a little town called Los Gatos." When I told him that Los Gatos was my

1

Los Gatos Creek ran full and beautiful in the early days as evidenced by this 1899 picture. Bunker Hill Park later flanked this. *(Library Collection)*

home town he was surprised but added, "I have been there many times. It fascinates me. The beauty, the climate, the entire setting of the place is so perfect."

Los Gatos has an elevation of slightly higher than 400 feet. The average temperature is about 58 degrees and the average rainfall is around 28 to 34 inches, although there have been winters when the rainfall was well over 45 inches. The wind, except in rare stormy weather, is gentle, having an average velocity of just over seven miles per hour.

All these facts make Los Gatos as near an ideal community, climate-wise and scenic-wise, as can be found anywhere. W. Drummond-Norie, a Los Gatos poet, wrote a poem praising Los Gatos. It was published as the frontispiece of the *Sunset* pamphlet referred to above.

L ying amid the green encircling hills,
O dorous with the perfumed breath of countless blooms:
S he basks in golden sunshine canopied with blue.
G em-like and beautiful, a hamlet wondrous fair,
A dorned with roses, bright with poppy flowers.
T o see her is to love her. She calls you from your toil.
O ut from the city's gloom, and desert's heat:
S he bids you rest within her heart of hearts."

However, one of the most eloquent praises of Los Gatos came from the pen of one of our own writers. Ruth Comfort Mitchell, who was born in San Francisco and came to Los Gatos when she was four years old, loved the Los Gatos foothills. So impressed was she as a girl that she made it the subject of the first poem she ever wrote. She was only 14 years old when she wrote the poem "To Los Gatos". It was originally published in the Los Gatos *News,* the first newspaper in Los Gatos, and reprinted in the Los Gatos *Mail News* on December 20, 1934. The first verse follows:

"The Rockies must be grander
And the Alps are more sublime,
And things are far more wonderful
In far-off foreign clime,
But for rich and natural beauty
And simple rustic grace
On all the earth's broad surface——
Los Gatos is the place."*

From its position in the foothills of the Santa Cruz Mountains Los Gatos faces the wide valley and the Mount Hamilton range on the east. Beyond it, fifty miles to the north, lies San Francisco, its great Bay visible from many points in the town. In the heyday of fruit growing in the valley, one

*Several years before her death in 1954, Mrs. Ruth Comfort Mitchell Young told how she had hinted to Mr. Walker, the publisher of the *News* that she would like some remuneration for this poem. He replied that her loyalty to Los Gatos and the publicity she got out of the publication of the poem, should be reward enough.

could see the orchards for miles around and in the spring blossom-time, the white and pinkish blossoms of prunes, apricots, peach and cherry trees perfumed the very air one breathed.

Besides being near to San Francisco, Los Gatos is only 18 miles from Palo Alto and Stanford University, 10 miles from San Jose and Santa Clara, and 52 miles from Oakland and Berkeley. It is only 20 miles from Santa Cruz and the beaches of the Pacific Ocean, less than 20 miles from the Big Trees; and Big Basin Park, with its massive Redwood trees is less than 30 miles away. Everything a person could want of beauty, culture, economic advantage, education, are in or near Los Gatos. Were Herodotus writing today he would no doubt compliment Los Gatos as he did the city the Ionians built.

How was this beautiful spot found? And where did it get its unique name? These are interesting questions and they have even more interesting answers. Fact and legend combine to make a fascinating story.

Early Background

The first inhabitants of the Santa Clara Valley were the Ohlone Indians, or Costanes. They are thought to have been descendants of aboriginal tribes that came to North America from Asia across the Bering Strait. These Indians were a fine looking people, tall with straight noses. In religion they were sun worshippers who cremated their dead. They were hunters and fishermen and lived on animal and vegetable foods, contrary to the California "Digger" Indians who lived on roots and shellfish.

It is estimated that about 5,000 Ohlones lived in the valley when the first white man arrived here. The Mission Fathers found these Indians of the West Valley very reliable, responsive and zealous converts. It was the Ohlones who found cinnabar of the Almaden Mines and used this bright red clay to paint their bodies which through long use poisoned their skin. A mural painted for the Los Gatos Union High School in the early 1930's depicts this tradition. The mural hung above the main entrance to the school library just opposite the south entrance to the building, but was removed in 1966 when the school building underwent extensive remodeling.

The Santa Clara Mission, founded in 1777, had between 1,500 and 2,000 Ohlone Indians in the Mission compound. They helped develop agriculture and assisted in the planting of crops and fruit trees. Dr. A. E. Osborne, a prominent Los Gatos physician, and one-time President of the Santa Clara Valley Historical Society, made a study of the early Indians of our valley and reported many of the facts recorded here.

The Spanish claimed all of California long before 1765 when Charles III sent Jose de Galvez to New Spain to act as Visitor-General. His chief purpose was to reorganize the finances of Spain's Pacific Empire. However, he also sought to strengthen Spain's hold on the Californias. He organized an expedition to the north which was led by Gaspar de Portola. Charles III had expelled the Jesuits from Mexico and Baja California and turned the Missions there over to the Franciscans. When Portola organized his expedition he asked Padre Junipero Serra, the head of the Missions in Mexico, to accompany him.

Arriving in San Diego in July 1769, Father Serra founded a Mission and remained there while Portola and his party went north in search of Monterey Bay. When they reached Monterey Bay on October 1, 1769 they failed to recognize it and started on north. Because of the rain and the illness of some of their party, they planned to camp a few

Sebastian Peralta's house built in the 1840's. Peralta with José Hernandez, received the Land Grant from the Mexican Government that included much of present day Los Gatos. This house, along the Creek on Roberts Road, was a convenient stopping place for the ox-driven freight wagons going from Lexington to San Jose. This house stood until 1920 when it was destroyed by fire. *(Library Collection)*

days at Point San Pedro. While the party was in camp two soldiers decided to go hunting deer. They climbed the northeastern hills and from the summit saw "a valley like a great inland sea, stretching northward and southeastward as far as the eye could reach." These two deer hunters, whose names are not recorded, stood on the summit of the western foothills on November 2, 1769 and were the first white men to see the beautiful Santa Clara Valley.[6]

In March 1776 Captain Juan Bautista de Anza, who was to select the site for the city of San Francisco, and his small expedition passed through the present Los Gatos area. With the Missions established all along the coast, the Pueblos founded, and the Presidios erected to protect the territory, Spain felt that her Pacific Empire in America was safe.

However, the people of Mexico rebelled and won their independence in 1821. All of the California territory came under Mexican rule. The Missions were secularized. Under Mexican law private citizens could petition for lands that had formerly belonged to the Missions. Hundreds of large land grants, in the form of Ranchos, were made, some containing more than 50,000 acres, while most were 4,500 acres or larger. In fact, Mexican law fixed the minimum size of a land grant at one square league or about 4,500 acres. By the time the United States took over California more than 8 million acres were owned by about 800 grantees.

After 1834, California saw a great influx of colonists from Mexico. Great landholders built luxurious residences after the Spanish style. The whole tenor of life was one of leisureliness and graciousness and has been accurately referred to as the romantic era of the Ranchos. What is today the Santa Clara Valley was known as San Bernardino Valley, and it had its share of large Ranchos. The Mission Fathers who founded a Mission in the Valley and named it Santa Clara, gave the name to our valley and county.

The United States Wins California

American interest in California was the result of commercial activities and fear of the growing influence of England and Russia on the Pacific Coast. Our New England whalers, sea-otter hunters, and fur traders came in contact with Russian and English activities. The Russians were pressing down from Alaska and had built Fort Ross just north of San Francisco. The British, it was believed, were interested in making California a British Protectorate and were actually taking steps to accomplish this. Confronted with the prospective separation of California from Mexico and the threat of English or Russian domination of this vast province on the Pacific, the United States tried to purchase the territory from Mexico. Mexican hostility to our government was such that our envoy, John Slidell, had to return to the United States empty-handed.

American settlers had come into the territory, helped by private colonizing companies. Because of the unsettled political condition of Mexico these American colonists staged a "revolution" and set up the "Bear Flag Republic" in June 1846. They were aided in this by Captain John C. Fremont, who had made several expeditions into California between 1843 and 1846. Later Fremont camped "near the road to Santa Cruz" on the night of February 21, 1856 and crossed the Santa Cruz Mountains at the gap made by Los Gatos Creek.

Even before war was officially declared against Mexico our naval forces under Commodore Sloat sailed into Monterey harbor and occupied it July 2, 1846. Mexico was no match for our army and navy, and the war ended with the Treaty of Guadalupe Hidalgo, February 2, 1848. Mexico surrendered all of the California territory to the United States and we thus became the heirs to the once vast Spanish Empire on the Pacific north of Mexico.

By the Treaty of Guadalupe Hidalgo the United States recognized the old Mexican and Spanish land grants. Since our government suspected some fraudulent land claims, it set up a commission to examine the grants and those found to be fraudulent were thrown out. But many large landholdings continued to thrive and the romantic era of the Ranchos continued.

But on January 24, 1848, two weeks before the treaty was signed ending the war with Mexico, gold was discovered by James W. Marshall on the South Fork of the American River. This spelled the end of the Rancho period of California history. People were plainly more attracted by gold than ranching.

A Village Is Born

Los Gatos was a part of the early Spanish and Mexican period of California. Rumors had reached Spain that a fine harbor, sheltered from winds, existed along the coast north of Monterey. Missionaries and military scouts came——the one to Christianize the Indians, the other to build military outposts.

Crossing the Santa Cruz Mountains the Missionaries and soldiers gazed upon a valley that seemed a paradise. Heavy grass covered the valley and trees for lumber crowded the hillsides. They got a glimpse of the bay which was the answer to their search for a "wind-free harbor."

Jose Hernandez and Sebastian Peralta were given a land grant of one and a half leagues by the Mexican Governor at Monterey on May 26, 1840. When the United States took over California, all claims to land had to be proven in court. Sebastian Peralta and Jose Hernandez presented their claims in the Federal Court in San Francisco in January 1853.[7] On March 9, 1860 the United States Government granted a patent to Hernandez and Peralta, recognizing their claim to La Rinconada de Los Gatos which comprised 6,631.44 acres of land. The town of Los Gatos was built on part of this grant. A later description of the property's boundaries was given as follows:

"Beginning at a point on the San Tomas Aquino Creek up in the hills back of and westerly from the present Withey Ranch, following the creek as the Westerly and northerly boundary to a point which would take in as the present Eastern boundaries including the E. N. Parr Subdivision, Sunny Oaks Tract, Mrs. W. J. Parr Tract, the Walker Partition (which lies West of the San Jose-Los Gatos Road) the National Tract, (National Avenue) turning southerly to and including the Cilker Farm, M. S. Gardner Estate Subdivision, now easterly on Kennedy Road and Shannon Road to a line of Frank Concklin's place, then turning south and passing east of H. G. Osborn's ranch, back of Wilder Hill, coming across to a point on the Santa Cruz highway back and south of what is the present Farwell home, thence to the point of beginning, passing south and a little distance

James Alexander Forbes, builder of Forbes Mill around which the town of Los Gatos grew. *(Museum Collection)*

away from the present Fairview Plaza Tract to the McCullagh Tract and all of the Withey Tract except a narrow strip."

In passing we might mention that the Sebastian Peralta adobe house stood 100 yards from Roberts Road near the bridge across the Los Gatos Creek.

Forbes Mill

Los Gatos Creek, which was once called Jones's Creek, became the focal point from which a town was to be born. The first person to see the economic advantage of this creek was James Alexander Forbes. Born of a wealthy family in Scotland and educated in Spain, Forbes had made several trips to California before being appointed Vice-Consul for San Francisco by the English

Forbes Mill, the first building in Los Gatos. Completed in 1854. *(Library Collection)*

5

San Jose Glee Club picnic at Forbes Mill in 1861. *(Museum Collection)*

Government. He visited the Santa Clara Mission and was there when California became a part of the United States. From this vantage point he saw the possible economic opportunities of the Valley.

During the Spanish, Mexican, and early American periods the Santa Clara Valley was a vast grain field. But there was no flour mill in the area to produce flour from the grain for the people of the valley. Flour was imported from South America at great cost. Why not build a flour mill amidst the grain fields? The valley needed a mill. A mill needed water-power, and the Los Gatos Creek could supply that power.

Forbes could see all these advantages and in 1850 he proceeded with his project of building a flour mill on Los Gatos Creek. He had purchased 3,000 acres of land in the area. His mill was a four-story building completed in 1854. The first three stories were of stone quarried from the canyon South of Los Gatos. The fourth story was of wood. The project cost over $100,000, financed mostly by an uncle, J. Alexander Forbes, who had financial interests along the Pacific Coast from South America to San Francisco. Much of the Old Stone Mill is still standing on the original site just below the Main Street Bridge in Los Gatos.

Forbes' original Mill was "an old-fashioned structure with over-shot wheels twenty feet in diameter." The water-head was only 20 feet and this did not give enough power. Poor management, together with poor power, spelled failure for Forbes' Mill. Always in debt, James was constantly asking his uncle to bail him out. But in 1855, when his uncle disposed of his vast American holdings and returned to England, James no longer had anyone to call upon to pay his debts. Despite his debts he continued his carefree style of living. A luxurious home in Santa Clara with rock crystal chandeliers imported from France, dumb waiters to carry food and drink from the kitchen, and well-stocked cellars were only some of the evidences of his high living. His debts kept piling up and when they reached more than $100,000 he

declared bankruptcy in December 1856. His only assets were a $24,000 mortgage on his land and an old, almost worthless carriage.[8]

In May 1857 the mill and dams passed to Gustav Touchard by foreclosure. Then in 1862 a French firm, V. Marzion & Company, got hold of the property but they could not make a success of the mill. A. Pfister & Company of San Jose leased the property for a while before it passed into the hands of Samuels and Fanner, who raised the water to a height of 30 feet. Finally, in 1866, W. H. Rogers & Company purchased the property and made a number of improvements, raising the water to 65 feet and putting in a turbine water wheel of great power. In 1870 they raised the headwater to 200 feet, forming a joint stock company with W. S. McMurtry and J. W. McMillan getting half interest in the company. They now had enough power and the mill began to prosper. The mill and its various activities are discussed further in a later chapter.

James A. Forbes did very little for Los Gatos directly. He tried to introduce citrus trees but had no luck. His chief contribution was the starting of a settlement. First called Forbes Mill, or Forbestown, it was some time later that it became Los Gatos. It can be said that in 1854 a village was born.

FOOTNOTES

1. Alley and Bowen, *History of Santa Clara County,* p. 30. Also Hamsher Notebook, #34. These will be referred to hereafter as Library *Collection* since they are only part of a larger library collection.
2. *Ibid,* p. 310.
3. Foote, H. S., ed. *Pen Pictures from the Garden of the World.* Lewis Pub. Co., Chicago 1888, p. 24.
4. Sawyer, Eugene T., *History of Santa Clara County,* Historic Record Co., Los Angeles, 1922, p. 289.
5. Irvine, Leigh H., *Los Gatos, Gem City of the Foothills.* Sunset, the Pacific Monthly, San Francisco, 1915, p. 17.
6. Shortridge, Chas. M., *Santa Clara County and its Resources.* A Souvenir of the San Jose *Mercury* 1895, p. 6.
7. From *Official Records,* Superior Court, San Francisco, 164ND, p. 5. Photo copies supplied by Mrs. Theo. W. Smith, a great granddaughter of Jose Hernandez.
8. Holdredge, Helen, *Mammy Peasant's Partner.* G. P. Putnam's, N.Y. 1954, p. 152 ff. Also Library *Collection,* Bk 34.

CHAPTER II

A Town Is Born

Slow Start

IT WAS 33 years from the establishment of Forbes Mill in 1854 to the incorporation of the town of Los Gatos in 1887. While Lexington and the other mountain areas were booming as a result of the lumbering industry, Los Gatos was only a stopping place for the teamsters. But the building of the Los Gatos Turnpike road placed it on the route of travel between San Jose and Santa Cruz. People started coming to the area, some because of the beauty and climate, and others because they saw business opportunities. In 1852 there was only one adobe house in the area, and seven years later there were still no other houses except a few cabins for the workers in the mill. The first home in Los Gatos was located at East Main Street and Mill Road (Church Street). Built by Mr. Samuels, it was purchased later by Dr. W. S. McMurtry, who remodeled it. The house became known as the McMurtry house and remained a landmark on East Main Street for many years.

By 1868 Los Gatos consisted of the Mill, a blacksmith shop, a stage depot, a lumber yard, temporary school house, a hotel incorporating the post office and a few houses. Actually, Lexington, now submerged by Lexington Lake, was the business center for the people in the area. As one writer put it, "There was nothing grander than Lexington between San Jose and Santa Cruz."[1] Lexington owed its beginning to the sawmill built there in 1848 by Isaac Branham and Julian Hank.

When Zachariah "Buffalo" Jones bought the mill for $3000 he laid out a town and called it Jones Mill, also dubbing the stream "Jones Creek." In 1860 he sold the mill and 480 acres. John P. Hennings bought some of the property and built a sawmill, changing the name of the settlement from Jones Mill to Lexington, after his home town of Lexington, Kentucky. Lexington remained the industrial center throughout the 1850's.

In the early 1860's the saw mills moved back into the hills to be nearer the stands of timber. As a result, Lexington lost its importance and began to disintegrate, while Los Gatos began a period of growth.

It is interesting to note that the original business houses of Los Gatos, and even the residences, were, for the most part, located on the east side of the creek––the areas of the present Rex Hotel, Masonic Temple, and city offices. W. S. McMurtry and J. W. McMillan owned the first store and lumber yard. This was one of the few business establishments on the west side of the creek, where the Parkview (formerly Bank of America) building now stands. The Ten Mile House, owned by H. D. McCobb, was the first hotel in Los Gatos and it was located at the end of Front Street––now Montebello Way. McCobb, having been appointed the first postmaster in 1864, maintained the postal facilities in the rear of the hotel.

Forbes Mill in 1865. After it left Forbes' hands it continued as a flour mill until 1887. Then it became successively a power plant for the Los Gatos Ice & Power Co., the Los Gatos Gas Co. and the P. G. & E. It housed the P. G. & E. substation until 1955. *(Library Collection)*

How Los Gatos Got Its Name

When the area was still young, cattle and sheep raising was the chief industry, though horses were also raised for racing and show. The Mission at Santa Clara sent shepherds out with their flocks every day. This fact provided the background for several legends of how Los Gatos got its name. One story, and the one most acceptable, is told by Mr. C. F. Hamsher, an early banker interested in the history of Los Gatos. His pamphlet "How Los Gatos Got Its Name" tells the story.

According to this, Jose Hernandez left San Jose in 1839 to seek more land to support his growing family. Accompanied by his brother James, his brother-in-law, Gabriel Sabrian, and four Indians, he made his way across the mountains to Santa Cruz. They hacked most of their way through the chaparral and brush to make a path for themselves. Not finding what they wanted on the coast, they cut their way back over the mountains coming out north of their original trail and found an open field of grass. This was just the spot Hernandez wanted. But it needed water. The legend has it that while Hernandez and his party were discussing what to do, they heard the frightening noise of two wild-cats which were fighting nearby. Gabriel wanted to shoot the animals, but Hernandez restrained him saying, "There must be water near or there would be no wildcats." One of the Indians in the party said he smelled water and offered to search for it. They stripped him of implements and food, so he could not ambush them, gave him a machette to cut a path, and sent him forth.

After several hours the Indian returned, saying he had found water. He had evidently come across San Tomas Creek. There was much rejoicing over the find and Hernandez said they should call the area "Rinconada de Los Gatos," meaning "the corner of the cats," because the fighting of the wildcats had led them to water.

Another legend regarding the name of Los Gatos is told by George Place, an old-timer in Los Gatos. The Mission Padres were making their way from Monterey to the Santa Clara Mission by way of the Santa Cruz mountains. When dusk set in, being weary from their travels, they decided to make camp beside the creek for the night. When they arose early next morning one of the Padres, feasting his eyes on the magnificent panorama nature had spread before them, exclaimed, "Look! Look! Did you ever gaze on a picture so grand as we now behold?" Another of the Padres agreed, saying "In all my journeys I have never seen anything so beautiful, and I would call this place Paradise." The third Padre could not wax so

The Ten Mile House, 1875, built by H. D. McCobb in 1864 at the end of Front Street (Montebello Way). J. W. Lyndon purchased it in the early 1870's. When the S. P. Railroad needed the land for a depot and freight sheds, Lyndon gave them the land on condition that the hotel be moved across the street to Santa Cruz Avenue. It became known as the Los Gatos Hotel, and later, as the Lyndon Hotel. *(Library Collection)*

eloquent for he had been kept awake all night by the wildcats that periodically approached their camp in a threatening manner. He was kept busy throwing sticks of fire at them and keeping the campfire going as a precaution against their attack. "You may call this place Grand Vista or Paradise if you like," he said, "but I shall name it after the pesky varmints that kept me up most of the night, and call it 'The Cats'."

The most dramatic and least plausible explanation of how the town got its name is the legend of the baby killed by wildcats. According to this, one Pedro Vasques, a sheepherder, came from Mission Santa Clara and brought his wife and baby to the bank of the Los Gatos Creek near the present Main Street bridge. Heavy rains set in and the creek became a torrent. Having seen to it that his sheep on the other side were safe for the night, Pedro started across the stream on a small foot-bridge. He slipped and fell into the raging water and was drowned. After a terrible night alone with her baby, the wife started for help at Mission Santa Clara. Fearing that the little bridge was too danger-ous to cross she returned to the hut, and dis-covered to her horror that wildcats had killed and carried away her child. The mother was so grieved that she drowned herself in the Los Gatos Creek. This dramatic story was recounted often at the Mission and the locale of this event was always referred to as "Los Gatos"——the cats.[2]

Whether these stories are legends or not, they all have a common basis of fact, and that is, that wildcats played a part in giving Los Gatos its name.

8

Los Gatos Hotel, 1890. This was the old Ten Mile House moved to the Santa Cruz Avenue location when the Southern Pacific Railroad needed the land for a depot and freight sheds. *(Library Collection)*

Lyndon Hotel And Los Gatos

Among the pioneer business leaders of Los Gatos was John Weldon Lyndon. He came to California by way of Panama from Vermont in October 1859 when he was 23 years old, landing in San Francisco with 65 cents in his pocket. He came down to San Jose, and after a brief stay there, came to Lexington where he worked for H. M. Hervey, who operated a boarding house in that booming lumber town. After two months he quit his job and obtained work in Bernard Joseph's grocery store. He worked there for two years and showed his ability to make money by investing in land in the Willows (Willow Glen) near San Jose. (Incidentally, he paid $500 for the land and sold it a year later for $4000.) Tired of working for someone else, he started his own store and operated it for a year, when he and Joseph went into partnership in the grocery business under the name of Joseph and Lyndon. After a year and a half of this, Lyndon bought out Joseph and continued a prosperous business until 1868.

Selling his business, he went back to Vermont, only to return to California again in the fall of 1869. His brother, James H. Lyndon, ten years younger, came to Los Gatos from Ireland in 1869 and worked for John, who had purchased another store. Though James was not as enterprising as John, he dabbled in various activities and ran for county sheriff in 1894. Mr. John D. Crummey, in a conversation with the writer, recalled one of the slogans during James Lyndon's campaign for sheriff. It went as follows:

> "Rah, Rah, Rah, Biff, Biff, Biff,
> James H. Lyndon
> Our next Sher-iff!"

The Lyndon Hotel as re-built after the fire of 1898. Later additions retained the general style of architecture. *(Museum Collection)*

James was elected and served one term as sheriff of Santa Clara County, 1894–1898.

John W. Lyndon purchased 100 acres and the Ten Mile House Hotel, which had been owned by H. D. McCobb. Always the sharp trader, he paid $7,500 for it and sold it for $10,000 after two months. Four years later he bought it back for $8,500.

Lyndon rented the land on which the Wilcox House was later located. He also kept a lumber yard, supplying people throughout the valley with much-needed lumber.

When the railroad came in 1877 Lyndon divided part of his land into lots. He opened a second store in Los Gatos, being one of the first to foresee the future growth of the town. One of the original Town Trustees and a stockholder in the Los Gatos Fruit Packing Company in 1882, he organized the Los Gatos Gas Company, and was a stockholder in the Los Gatos Bank. His land holdings were such that they took in most of today's business district. In 1889 the local press reported that J. W. Lyndon was the second highest taxpayer in Los Gatos --- Just behind the Los Gatos Manufacturing Company. His taxes were $227.17 while the manufacturing company paid $294.45. Total taxes collected that year were $4,438. "It will be seen," said the news item, "that Mr. Lyndon pays nearly one-twentieth of the city taxes."

Since the Lyndon Hotel was to play such an important part in the development of Los Gatos, it is important that we give several of the basic facts relating to this famous hostelry. The first hotel, known as the Ten Mile House, was started in a cottage owned by H. D. McCobb, located a short distance from the place where the Southern Pacific Depot was later built---now the town plaza and the post office building. Lyndon bought it in 1868, then sold it to Morgan Covell, who operated it for

Los Gatos looking west, 1880's. *(Library Collection)*

Los Gatos, 1883, looking northwest. Main Street and old wooden bridge on right. *(Library Collection)*

Looking east from West Main Street about 1883. *(Los Gatos Museum)*

From Market Street (Loma Alta Avenue) looking westward, 1886. *(Library Collection)*

10

Los Gatos from the south about 1890. Santa Cruz Avenue runs horizontally just below the center of the picture. The Los Gatos Hotel at the right. *(Library Collection)*

View from above Broadway, 1890. *(Library Collection)*

Los Gatos from the west, looking down on Main Street toward the east in 1890. *(Library Collection)*

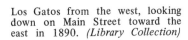

Pennsylvania Avenue 1901. House on right is on Glen Ridge. *(Library Collection)*

several years before selling it to Jacob Rich. In 1872 Lyndon repurchased the property, enlarging and improving it.

Old-timers told of the wooden watering trough that stood in front of the hotel where a traveler, for ten cents, could not only water his horses but also enjoy a drink of whiskey inside. Miss Dora Rankin, in her reminiscences of Los Gatos, tells us that in the 1890's one could hear the rumble "of the farmers' wagons as they came down from the mountains with their loads of apples, prunes, etc. Sometimes there would be six or seven of them lined up waiting their turn at the old wooden watering trough on Santa Cruz opposite the depot before going on to San Jose to sell their produce."[3] This trough was later replaced with a stone trough by the ladies of the Los Gatos History Club.

The hotel was almost completely destroyed by fire on May 26, 1898 while under the management of G. W. Gertridge. The fire started when a lamp exploded in room 64 on the first floor and spread rapidly, damaging furniture and personal effects worth more than $8,000 and eventually causing an estimated $15,000 loss. Also adding to the calamity was the injuring of two firemen, Al Williams and Arthur Bond, when a wall of the hotel collapsed.

After the fire, Lyndon took over the hotel again. He wanted to rebuild it as a frame building, but the town Trustees insisted on better fire-protective material. The matter went to court, and Lyndon completed the building. It is assumed that he satisfied the Trustees on the safety of the hotel.

Built in the New Orleans Colonial style, the hotel had a frontage of 177 feet on Santa Cruz

This was originally the Wheeler House on Church Street which catered to teamsters who drove loads of tan bark from the Santa Cruz Mts. to the tannery in Santa Clara. It was purchased in 1883 by Mary C. Knowles, who had come from Moline, Ill. with her son Dr. Frank Knowles and daughters Cynthia and Ella (later Mrs. E. C. Yocco). Notice the gas light in front. *(Photo and information from Mrs. Mary Yocco Rugh)*

Avenue and a depth of 100 feet. It stood 30 feet back from the property line. It became known as the Lyndon Hotel after it was remodeled in 1898. It was re-opened in early 1901 and became a mecca for travelers from all over the world. A President, governors, writers, royalty, big businessmen and stage and screen personalities all visited this famed hotel some time or other.

In June 1958 Ben Knuth purchased the historic hotel and made many improvements. It remained a Los Gatos landmark until it was torn down in 1963. The railroad stopped coming into Los Gatos and the new highway by-passed the town. The once proud Lyndon Hotel was forgotten. With its demise went a gay era in the history of Los Gatos.

Incorporation

When grain growing and grazing gave way to the orchardists, many new people came to Los Gatos. The beauty of the spot and its mild climate proved strong attractions to many people. By 1887 the town had grown to the point where many felt it should have its own government. As early as August 1881 the editor of the Los Gatos *News* advocated a city government. "Many matters need attention. Our streets are in a very poor condition, sidewalks we have none. As things are now all our public improvements and benefits must come from

Drug Store and News Depot before 1890, located at 5 North Santa Cruz Ave. On the left is a portion of the AOUW building which was later moved around the corner. *(Library Collection)*

12

individual subscription and in this way a few individuals have to pay it all or there will be nothing done." He pleaded for a sidewalk from the Los Gatos Hotel to the Coleman House. "In our humble opinion," he continued, "that would enhance the value of the property 25 per cent." He advocated a better drainage system "sufficient to carry off the filth and rubbish that now accumulates and rots and produces sickness."[4]

The newspaper carried other editorials and articles giving the *pros* and *cons* of incorporation. A letter to the editor from "A Taxpayer" argued for incorporation in the early part of 1887. Poor sidewalks seemed to be the big issue. "Surely a stranger walking through our town would say we have no regard for our wives and children to allow them to walk through the slush and mud week after week. The approaches to the bridge and especially in front of the Chinese house at the end, and around the depot are a living disgrace to every property owner in town." The remedy, the writer believed, was to incorporate. "Then our streets can be put in decent condition. Until this is done, lawlessness will also grow to such dimensions that it will hardly be safe for decent people to walk our streets." He concluded with "Blood thirsty scoundrels are now able to carry concealed death in their pockets, and will be until we are able to protect ourselves."[5]

Finally several leading citizens called a meeting to discuss the matter and decide on the boundaries of the proposed incorporated town. J. W. Lyndon was chairman of the meeting and W. H. Trantham was secretary. Mr. G. W. Lynch, who had been instrumental in calling the meeting, suggested that

Royal Shaving Parlors in the Arlington Hotel 1894. Arlington Hotel building was located on north side of West Main Street next to the old bridge. A restaurant downstairs overlooked Los Gatos Creek. Building destroyed by fire of 1901. *(Library Collection)*

the boundaries be one mile in each direction from the bridge. This met with opposition. It would cut into some property, putting part inside and part outside the city. Finally a committee was appointed to draw up suggested boundaries. F. H. McCullagh, A. E. Wilder, and C. F. Wilcox were appointed to this committee. Again their report was not accepted. Mr. McCullagh, a member of the committee, suggested that more time and thought be given to the matter. A committee of twelve was appointed with power to fix the boundary. Twelve good, solid citizens were designated and included F. H. McCullagh, C. F. Wilcox, A. E. Wilder, W. A.

Sketch of East Main Street in the middle 1880's, looking westward toward the bridge from Mill Street (Church Street). Practically all of the buildings on the right were destroyed by the great fire of 1891. Notice wooden sidewalks. *(Library Collection)*

Sketch of West Main Street before 1893 (upper) and picture of 1892 (lower). The artist obviously added numerous improvements which undoubtedly pleased the businessmen of the town. View is to the east. Right foreground in the sketch is the Los Gatos Hotel. *(Both Library Collection)*

Stidston, E. E. Dow, J. J. Groom, Palmer Perkins, H. Sund, L. A. Cole, F. M. Jackson, N. E. Beckwith, and Dr. W. S. McMurtry. J. W. Lyndon, the chairman of the meeting, was asked to serve with the committee.

For the information of the people at the meeting, Mr. Wilcox outlined the requirements for incorporation. Under the laws of the state of California, a town of 2000 could incorporate as a sixth class city. A governing board of five trustees whose terms expired alternately so that there would always be hold-over officers, was to be elected by the people. The two other elective officers were to be a Clerk and Assessor, and a Marshall and Tax Collector. As tax collector the Marshall was to receive for his service one per cent of the moneys collected. One of the Justices of the Peace for the township was to act as Recorder. According to state law, the tax limit was 65 cents on $100, but since the corporation was to get a rebate of 30 cents on state and county taxes, it could not increase taxes over 35 cents per $100 without a vote of the people. The Trustees could not incur any indebtedness in any year beyond the revenue for that year.

The boundary committee later reported on the proposed boundaries and the election was held with the eligible voters within the proposed boundaries permitted to participate. The boundaries were as follows:

Commencing at the corner of section 21, 22, 27, and 28, in Township 8 South, Range 1 West, Mt. Diablo Base and Meridian and running thence northerly along the line between said Section 21 and 22 and the same produced to the south line of lands of Levi Hill or the same produced thence northwesterly along said line of lands of Hill to the center of the Los Gatos Creek, thence down the center of said creek to its intersection with the continuation Easterly of the South line of what is known as the Daves Tract being also

14

IOOF Hall and store building located at 27 to 35 East Main Street at site later occupied by the Beckwith Building. These were destroyed by the big fire of 1891. *(Library Collection)*

The famous Lyndon Hotel in its hey-day in the early 1900's. *(Museum Collection)*

Above buildings on south side of East Main Street east of Pageant Way (previously Seanor Street) were on property taken over in 1913 for Town Hall and Park. Below is rear view of buildings with steeples of Methodist and Presbyterian churches in background. (*Both Library Collection)*

Mr. George Wilson, the depot agent in Los Gatos, standing in front of his home in 1890. The home was located near what is today the corner of University and Saratoga Avenues. *(Library Collection)*

Homes on Glen Ridge. Gracious evening in 1920's. *(Library Collection)*

the continuation Easterly of the North line of lands of Magnus Tait, thence Northwesterly along the Easterly line of the Los Gatos and Saratoga Road, thence Southwesterly in a straight course, passing through land of Massol, Bachman and McCullagh to the extreme Westerly point of what is known as Fairview Addition, and continuing in the same course to its intersection with the line dividing lands of McCullagh and P. Herold; thence southeasterly with the 1/3 section line running north and south between lands of J. W. Lyndon and Livermore, thence southerly along last-named line to the south boundary line of section 20 and 21 easterly to the place of beginning.[6]

On May 19, 1887 a petition with 100 names was filed with the Board of Supervisors for permission to incorporate. The petitioners included J. H. Pearce, Z. A. Macabee, W. H. B. Trantham, E. E. Place, C. C. Suydam, Dr. F. W. Knowles, W. S. McMurtry, Dr. R. P. Gober, F. H. McCullagh, and Grant Moore. On June 18 the County Supervisors granted permission, and the way was cleared for an election on the issue.

The election on incorporation was held on July 28, 1887 and incorporation carried by a vote of 126 to 44. The County Supervisors canvassed the vote, and on August 8 declared the town incorporated and the officers duly elected. Incorporation documents were filed with the Secretary of State in Sacramento on August 10.

The officers chosen at that first election were: *Trustees:* Palmer Perkins, J. W. Lyndon, George Seanor, D. D. Holland and H. Sund. *Treasurer:* George McMurtry (who held that office for over 40 years). *Clerk and Assessor:* A. E. Wilder. *Marshall and Tax Collector:* G. L. Gelatt.

The first meeting of the Board of Trustees was held on August 12 and Palmer Perkins was elected Chairman. They met again on September 15 and passed three ordinances. One gave the cannery the right to cross Santa Cruz Avenue with a spur track. Another fixed the bonds of the officers as follows: Clerk, $250; Marshall, $1000; Treasurer, $1000. The third ordinance fixed the time of meetings as the first Monday of every month at 8 o'clock, the Trustees to meet in the office of the Justice of the Peace.

The salary of the officers was set as follows:

The Town Clerk	$480 a year
The Marshall	$720 a year
The Policeman	$720 a year

Los Gatos was now incorporated, had its officers, and took its place as a Sixth Class city of the State of California.

FOOTNOTES

1. Addicott, James E., *Grandad's Pioneer Stories.* Los Gatos *Times* Printing, 1953, p. 40.
2. "The Legend of Los Gatos" Bank of Los Gatos Leaflet. (No date.)
3. Dora Rankin, "As It Was" Los Gatos *Times-Observer* March 1, 1965.
4. Los Gatos Weekly *News,* August 20, 1881.
5. Library *Collection,* Bk. 34.
6. Town Board *Minutes* August 10, 1887.

SCHEDULE "A"

Description Corporate Limits — Town of Los Gatos

Commencing at the common corner of Sections 21, 22, 27 and 28 in Township 8 South, Range 1 West, Mt. Diablo Base & Meridian and running thence Northerly along the line between said Section 21 and 22 and the same produced to the South line of lands of Levi Hill or the same produced thence Northwesterly along said line of lands of Hill to the center of the Los Gatos Creek, thence down the center of said creek to its intersection with the continuation Easterly of the South line of what is known as the Daves Tract being also the continuation Easterly of the North line of lands of Magnus Tait, thence Northwesterly along the Easterly line of said land of Houghton to its intersection with the north line of the Los Gatos and Saratoga Road, thence Southwesterly in a straight course passing through land of Massol, Badiman and McCullough to the extreme Westerly point of what is known as Fairview Addition, and continuing in the same course to its intersection with the line dividing lands of McCullough and P. Herold, thence Southeasterly along the last named line to its intersection with the one-eighth section line running North and South between lands of J. W. Lyndon and Livermore, thence Southerly along last named line of the South boundary line of Section 20, Township 8 South, Range 1 West, Mt. Diablo Base & Meridian, thence along the Southerly line of said Section 20 and 21 Easterly to the place of beginning. All in the County of Santa Clara, State of California.

The two cats, Leo and Leona, stand guard at the entrance to the former estate of poet Charles Erskine Scott Wood and his famous poetess wife, Sara Bard Field just south of town. These famous cats have become the trade mark for the town. (Story in the Introduction.) *(Courtesy Chamber of Commerce)*

Following page: Scenic view of modern Los Gatos, looking southwest up the highway toward Santa Cruz. *(Courtesy Chamber of Commerce)*

Bird's eye view, 1900, *left* and *below* Los Gatos looking eastward toward Blossom Hill, 1925. Note the changes from the previous pictures. *(Library Collection)*

17

CHAPTER III

Early Industries in Los Gatos

The Los Gatos Manufacturing Company

FORBES MILL continued to be the center of industrial activity even after the bankruptcy of James Forbes. The W. H. Rogers Company purchased it in 1866, raising the water head and making other improvements. In 1869 J. W. McMillan and Dr. W. S. McMurtry purchased half interest in the mill and shortly thereafter it was incorporated as the Los Gatos Manufacturing Company. Other members of the Corporation were W. H. Rector and C. C. Hayward. The corporation made extensive improvements in 1870, including raising the head to 200 feet and adding new machinery valued at $30,000. This gave plenty of power to the mill and made it "the most complete mill of its size on the Pacific Coast." It had a warehouse with a capacity of 30,000 centals.

The water power came from the creek three miles above Los Gatos. Two reservoirs, with over 100 million gallons each, supplied water during the summer season. Water was carried from the reservoirs to the pit through a 15 inch wrought iron pipe.

By 1881 the mill was doing a booming business. The Los Gatos *News* waxed eloquent in its August 13, 1881 issue: "While other cities and towns may boast of a larger population than ours, for the manufacture of the finest grade of flour known to the markets of the civilized world, Los Gatos Flouring Mills stand pre-eminent. Between the grim iceburgs of Alaska to the rugged headlands of Patagonia, and from the muddy waters of the Missouri River to the ocean-laved shores of this sunset land, it has no superior, and well may our little village be proud of its wonderful Flouring Mills, whose name and fame have gone abroad and are now becoming more familiar in the countries beyond the sea."

The mills, with a capacity of 100 barrels a day, produced Los Gatos Water Mill Flour which found a ready market in the east and elsewhere "because it has no superior." Mr. George McMurtry, one of the old timers of Los Gatos, recalled in 1931 that "It was a common sight to see a string of teams two and three blocks long waiting at the doors of the mills to be unloaded. Some of the farmers

brought their wheat and had it ground and the mill took a tenth of the grinding and the farmer got the rest."

An advertisement in the March 19, 1886 San Jose *Mercury* described the flour mill and its operation. The mill had just gone through another "retooling" period. Said the advertisement:

"Custom work will be done on the old-fashioned plan of taking toll; and wheat, rye, corn and buckwheat will be ground for one-sixth. Barley will be ground for one-fifth. Parties preferring to pay money will be charged the lowest cash rates; and large quantities ground by the barrel, on the most favorable terms."

Then it promised that each lot would be ground separately so that all customers could depend upon getting the flour from their own grain. All grains to be ground at the mill could be stored free of charge.

The Los Gatos Manufacturing Company expanded into other fields. In 1869 a separate building was erected for a woolen mill. But in 1872 the woolen mill burned and no further effort was made in that direction. With more power available than the mill could use, the company sublet some of it for other industries. In 1885 A. King and W. D. Tisdale, of the First National Bank of San Jose, organized the Los Gatos Ice Works in a separate building near the mill using its power for the operation. The Ice Works had 8 tanks with a capacity of 10 tons each. The first method of freezing was not very successful, but new methods were introduced and the business prospered, producing more than 25 tons of ice a day. The ice made life a bit more comfortable in Santa Cruz, San Jose and as far away as San Francisco. The ice, protected by a blanket of sawdust, was shipped in freight cars.

In January 1887 the Los Gatos Manufacturing Company merged with the Central Milling Company of San Jose. The milling machinery was sold to the Pacific Coast Milling Company and the local flour mill went out of existence. For a while

19

Forbes Mill and railroad track in the 1880's. It was operated by the Los Gatos Manufacturing Company at that time. Notice the flow of water in the Los Gatos Creek. *(Library Collection)*

the stone building was used as a brewery, with the local press reporting that the mill was now "dispensing ales instead of breadstuff to a hungry world." A large bottling establishment was operated in connection with the brewery. It was believed that the substantial character of the building, its situation in a deep cool place, "and the nearness to the Ice Plant and railroad transportation made it a desirable place for the bottling industry."

The mill seemed to have served its purpose. In addition to grinding flour, making ice and producing woolens, it formed the basis for a town. Until 1971 when it was brought to life as a Youth Activities Center, it stood abandoned, lonely and forgotten, a forlorn reminder of the good old days of the founding of the village of Los Gatos.

Lumber and Oil

The mountains behind Los Gatos vied with the Los Gatos Creek in the development of Los Gatos. The redwood timber very early attracted the attention of settlers. Lumber became the big industry during most of the 1850's and early 1860's. The trees in the gulches toward the south were cut by no fewer than eight sawmills which produced more than 60,000 board feet of lumber a day. It was a lucrative business. Miners even deserted the gold fields to take up lumbering. S. O. Houghton, who had worked in the mines, turned to lumber and paid his employees sixteen dollars a day—wages that reflected his returns from lumber.

Los Gatos was the stopping place for lumber haulers. Each day saw long lines of teams and wagons lined up to go into the mountains to bring the logs to the mills in Alma and Lexington. By 1880 the South Pacific Coast Railway was taking two heavily laden trains of lumber daily out of the mountains. All this was going on in the mountains while the valley was producing grains and feeding cattle.

It might surprise Los Gatans to know that at one time there was an oil fever in the hills above the town. On November 9, 1861 Joseph Smith discovered oil in the hills near Lexington. According to a news story in the San Jose *Mercury-Herald,* "The supply appears to be inexhaustible and of very pure quality." A letter, dated November 24, 1861, from a guest at the Lexington Hotel, stated that the Swain brothers had found cinnabar at the entrance to the canyon at Lexington, and that there was oil near Moody's Gulch about 100 yards from the Santa Cruz road. It also stated that Thomas Stevens had filed a "mining claim" notice dated November 6, 1861 for oil and that he had sold one-half interest to Henry McCobb.[1]

Los Gatos Manufacturing Co. and store. First owned by the Manufacturing Co. the store and buildings were later owned by G. S. McMurtry. They were destroyed by the fire of July 26, 1891. *(Library Collection)*

20

Oil was first discovered in small quantities floating upon the water in Moody Gulch and springs nearby. A well that had been dug for water at the Half-Way House at Moody Gulch was so polluted with oil that it was useless. This led to a mad search for oil and the development of oil fields. In 1865 a Mr. McLaren bored a well there and it was reported that oil was struck in October 1870 and that it "gushed up 85 feet." In 1878 William E. Youle drilled a well and struck oil at a depth of 800 feet. A second well struck oil at 765 feet, eventually pumping 30 barrels a day. The third well went to 1080 feet and produced both gas and oil, but later caved in and proved useless. A fourth well struck oil at three levels---at 980 feet, at 1040 feet, at 1085 feet, producing more than 100 barrels a day. During the first ten days this well produced 1025 barrels, making it one of the most productive wells in California at that time.[2]

Others drilled in the Moody Gulch area. Charles Felton, who later became a State Senator, and R. C. McPherson both bored near Moody Gulch in 1873. In ten years the wells produced more than 80,000 gallons. The property was sold to the Trigonia Oil Company which worked the wells until the 1920's. A pipeline was laid in 1879, extending two and one-half miles to the Southern Pacific Railroad track near Aldercroft Heights. The Los Gatos *Mail News* reported on December 16, 1920 that the Trigonia Oil Company's wells "are producing at highest capacity and new wells are being sunk." The wells were said to be producing from 10 to 50 barrels each a day, with a yearly net income amounting to $119,755.

At one time or another almost the entire mountain area from Alma to Wrights was in the

Woodhams' Carriage Shop on East Main Street, 1894. *(Los Gatos Museum)*

midst of an oil fever. The Santa Clara Petroleum Company bored wells near Lexington in 1910. The Shaw and Weldon Petroleum Company also had wells in Lexington. After boring to a depth of only 30 feet, said the Los Gatos *Mail News*, a "nice vein of oil of the finest quality was found." "There is no doubt," continued the article, "but California will some day excel by far the famed Pennsylvania petroleum region and Santa Clara County beat the State."[3]

Oil was also found on the H. H. Main ranch in April 1891. A well was sunk to 800 feet but oil was found at 300 feet. The pipe was cut at 300 feet and 125 barrels were pumped in less than two days. However, Mr. McPherson, who had charge of the work, left it to go to the Los Angeles Oil fields and no further work was done on this property.[4]

Lumbering above Los Gatos in the 1850's. Ox teams were used extensively for heavy work. *(Library Collection)*

THE TRIGONIA OIL FIELDS

The Trigonia Oil Co.'s oil field is no experiment. The wells there from the start have produced a high grade of parafine base oil (the only grade of this base found in the west) and it has only been the question of obtaining sufficient capital to develop the field and sink sufficient wells to operate it on an extensive scale and bring attractive returns to the investors.

Previous managements have either been hampered with lack of capital or lack of knowledge. The management of the Trigonia Oil and Gas Co., now controlling the oil field at Trigonia, are experts in oil field development matters and are backed with sufficient capital to make their work a success. Already the old wells are producing oil to their highest capacity and new wells are being sunk, the plan being to develop the property to its highest pro-ducing capacity in the shortest time possible.

Prospective investors are cordially invited to inspect the Trigonia Oil Co.'s fields. Mr. Rose, the superintendent, will be pleased to show you over the property and explain to you in detail the present plant—the oil wells now in operation and plant which is now busy manufacturing crude oil into high grade gasoline —and also the future development plans of the company.

The company wants its understood that their proposition is open and above board and that they have nothing to conceal, that they believe that the more information the public has concerning the property the more investors and friends will rally to them.

The wells now produce from 10 to 50 barrels each, and it is clear to figure the profit when it is known that oil is worth from $6 to $10 per barrel and it costs only from $6000 to $8000 to complete a well at Trigonia. The following are some interesting figures on possible net profit from wells per year at Trigonia:

Oil Struck Near Lexington

the Shaw & Weldon Petroleum Company near Lexington, and adjoining the Santa Clara Petroleum Company's lands have 'struck ile'. This is the first instance in the state, we believe, of oil being struck on ground where there was not a natural spring in the first instance.

"The Santa Clara Petroleum Co. have a natural petroleum spring on their land, and are now boring for a paying well. The Shaw & Weldon Company have commenced operations on the Evans ranch, adjoining, and about two hundred yards distant from the Santa Clara spring. There was no sign of oil on the surface anywhere on the ranch.

"They have not commenced to bore yet—are sinking a shaft preparatory to boring. They are only down 30 feet, and have struck a nice vein of oil of the finest quality. Lucky 'hombres.'

"There is no doubt but California will some day excel the far famed Pennsylvania petroleum region, and Santa Clara county beat the state."

* * *

High hopes were being held for oil development in the Los Gatos district. T. A. Piper had two wells "under the drill" for several weeks in a tract of 3500 acres which he has secured. One well was down 2000 [...] WELL. [...] ever drilled [...] ed at Bakers- [...] feet deep. [...] Ir. Piper said that it was [...] fact that oil was plenti- [...] reat chasm below which [...] entered."

Oil fever is reflected in the news article on the Trigonia Fields in the Los Gatos *Mail News* of December 16, 1920. (Yes, this was a news story, not an ad.) Other articles are from the San Jose *Mercury Herald* of Sept. 8 and 15, 1910. The profit figures were missing.

Main Street looking west about 1894. Los Gatos Hotel in background. Notice the *Mail* printing office. *(Library Collection)*

In 1910 T. A. Piper made one more last digging on the Main Ranch.

But oil was not to become a permanent part of Los Gatos and the valley, which was to remain an orchard economy. Perhaps few people will regret that the wells were plugged and the rigs removed. But as late as January 31, 1938 the San Jose *Mercury* reported that several of the oil wells, some of them with the rigs still standing, and dating back nearly a century, were buried by the big Moody Gulch fill on the New Los Gatos-Santa Cruz highway alignment.

The search for oil also led to the discovery of coal in the Lexington area. On May 15, 1865 coal deposits were found and a company was organized to develop it. In December 1877 a crew working in the summit tunnel uncovered a bituminous coal vein. For years some exploratory work had been going on attempting to locate coal deposits, and

Prune trees in bloom near Los Gatos before the days of sub-divisions and freeways. Old timers will, no doubt, look at this with nostalgia. *(Museum·Collection)*

some thought that there might be huge coal deposits in the Santa Cruz mountains.[5] But coal, like oil, was of very short supply and the mining of coal, like the drilling for oil, was short-lived and without a secure long-term profit.

Coming of the Orchards

The real basis of the economy of Los Gatos, like that of the Santa Clara Valley, was fruit. The soil and climate were well-adapted to the raising of fruits of all kinds. Water also was plentiful since artesian wells could be opened anywhere in the valley. As early as 1854 a writer waxed eloquent over artesian wells. Seeing "water surging up from the hidden depths to play and sparkle in the light of day," he wrote, "is much more valuable than the discovery of a dozen gold mines. Along with the genial climate and the rich soil, nature also supplied the valley with a sparkling element that can cause the fame of this land to spread like the light of the sun all over the world."[6]

John Erickson, 1915. Mr. Erickson was an early day blacksmith and a civic leader. Died in 1921. *(Courtesy Hulda Erickson)*

The Mission Fathers discovered the ease with which fruit trees grew. They planted peaches, pears, apricots, apples and some oranges, and all flourished. Even grapes from southern France and Italy did well, and olive trees produced in abundance. The Missions supplied many an orchardist with young trees or scions and gave advice on the care and nurture of the trees. With most fruit selling at 50 cents a pound and apples at one dollar apiece, the prospects for profit from fruit seemed limitless.

Rogers and McMurtry, who had taken possession of Forbes Mill in 1868, experimented with orange and lemon trees on their acreage, planting more than 400 citrus trees on the land bordering the Mill. Other orchardists put in citrus trees and when the products of the Los Gatos trees were shown at the San Jose Citrus Fair in 1887, great interest was shown in them. According to an item in the Los Gatos *News* the verdict was that the Los Gatos fruit was even finer than that of Florida and Southern California.

Figs, grapes and other semi-tropical fruits produced well also. The reports of their success soon spread and the people of Los Gatos found themselves in the midst of a land boom. Land that had been selling for $15 to $20 an acre, now sold for $40 to $60 an acre. Town lots were worth nearly as much per foot as they had formerly been per acre. What's more, land that had been considered worthless for grain, proved to be perfectly adapted to fruit growing. This land shot up to $200 and even $300 an acre. Land on the hillside behind Los Gatos which had been considered valueless proved to be excellent for horticultural development. Cleared of brush it was planted in fruit trees and vines and brought rich harvests to the owner. Lyman Burrell planted fruit trees in the mountains

Typical Prune Drying yard of the early 1900's. *(Museum Collection)*

above Los Gatos as early as 1856. In 1874, J. F. Kennedy planted a small orchard in the hills east of Los Gatos, while Harvy Wilcox planted 160 acres to oranges in the hills behind the town.

Gradually it became evident that the slopes of the hills were particularly well-adapted to fruits and vines. One news report explained proudly, "The cool winds from the bay are materially softened as they sweep down the valley and the differences in the temperature between day and night are not so marked. The air is mild and balmy and the nights agreeably cool and pleasant."[7]

It is interesting to note that citrus trees in the valley were not originally planted to produce for the market, but merely as an ornament and for home use. Citrus never became very important as an agricultural industry, not because the soil was unsuited, but because other fruits were more profitable.

Prunes

The most popular and profitable fruit grown in the valley was the prune. According to Carl J. Hansen' in the *Bulletin* of the California State Agricultural Service, Circular 180, a prune may be defined as a plum that can be satisfactorily dried whole without fermentation at the pit. Very few varieties of plums meet this requirement. The most successful in our valley was the *Petit Prune d'Agen* started by Louis Pellier in 1856.

Louis Pellier was a vine and fruit grower from France who had come to California during the Gold Rush fever of 1848–1849. After trying his hand at mining he came to San Jose in 1851. He purchased a tract of land and started a nursery and experimented with plants and flowers. When his brother, Pierre, came over from France in 1853 he brought with him, at Louis' suggestion, cuttings of five varieties of grapes. These did so well that Louis decided to bring samples of the best fruits in France and transplant them in the valley. In 1854 he sent Pierre back to France with instructions to select cuttings and scions from the best fruits in France and bring them back to California.

Pierre and his brother Jean, who had not yet immigrated, spent two years collecting a variety of select samples from all parts of France, for Louis' nursery. They brought scores of cuttings and scions back in potatoes buried in sawdust. Louis developed the *petit* prune and the *gros* prune in his nursery and sold young trees to orchardists in the valley.[8] Since fruit drying had not yet developed, the smaller *petit* prune did not go over well. The orchardists preferred the larger *gros* prune. As a matter of fact, the undried prune—large or small—did not go over well with the public. Only when fruit drying became popular did the prune come into its own. It soon ranked first among the products produced in the valley.

Fruit Drying

Prunes were originally harvested after they had dropped from the tree and were then dipped in lye and put on flat trays out in the sun to dry. The area in and around Los Gatos was filled with "drying yards" with their wide open spaces for fruit trays. As the ripe prunes dropped, or were shaken from the trees, they were picked from the

24

ground. Families picked prunes, often forcing schools to open late because the prune harvest was not completed by early September. The prunes when picked were put into large dipping pails with perforated bottoms and dipped into a solution of lye which punctured the skin. After a thorough washing they were placed on trays in the sun to dry. The fruit required no pitting or paring and all work was done by unskilled labor. It was an interesting sight to see the acres and acres of prune trays in the sun drying. The rich odors from drying purple plums reminded one that fruit was a big industry in the area.

The original method of dipping prunes was slow and awkward. In the spring of 1889 Luther Cunningham invented a machine for dipping prunes that revolutionized the process. He manufactured the machine in San Jose and soon took into partnership Mr. Barngrover, the firm becoming known as the Cunningham and Barngrover Company. Manufacturing practically all of the machines used in the dried fruit industry, this was one of the industries that later became a part of the huge Food Machinery Corporation.

Among the larger drying yards in the area were the Hume Company yard in the Glen Una district, the H. D. Curtis Company yard, the Los Gatos Cured Fruit Company and the Gem City Packing Company. J. D. Farwell, who later became one of the leading businessmen of Los Gatos, was, for years, the manager of the 700 acre Glen Una Prune Ranch which yielded as high as 1,100 tons of prunes in one season.

The fruit from our foothills was considered better than the valley fruit. The amount of green fruit sun-cured on trays at Los Gatos amounted to more than 7 million pounds a season. The H. D.

Some of the labels on canned fruit processed by the Los Gatos Canning Company in the 1890's and early 1900's. *(Courtesy Charles Torrey)*

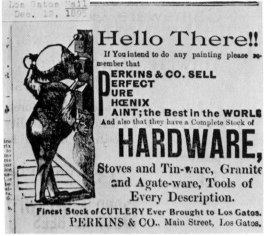

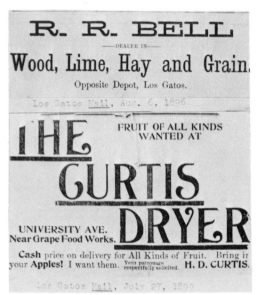

Advertisements of early Los Gatos businesses from original newspapers. *(Courtesy Leland Walker family)*

25

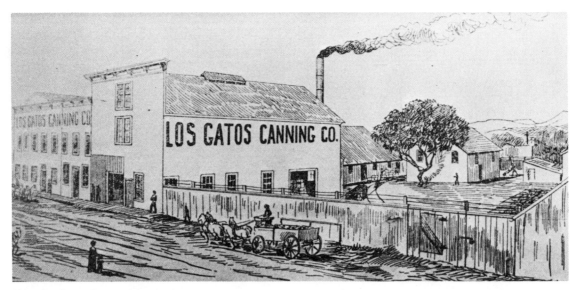

Sketch of Los Gatos Canning Co. plant located at 57 North Santa Cruz Avenue. Erected in 1882 it ran back a block to Lyndon Avenue where it had a 137 foot frontage. Bought by George Hooke in 1894, he added a new warehouse in 1900. Plant moved to Santa Cruz Avenue and Saratoga Avenue in 1907 after Hunt Brothers purchased it. *(Library Collection)*

Curtis Company was the heaviest packer of dried fruits in Los Gatos. This plant was located at the north end of town and had a private spur from the railroad to accommodate the business. Curtis Company fruit was shipped to France, Belgium, England and Germany where it was sold in direct competition with French fruit. It was known by the brand name of "Curtis' Los Gatos Foothill Brand" and sold over one and one-half million pounds in one season. W. J. Allen, of New South Wales, visited the Curtis Drying yard and he told of his experiences in the *Bulletin* of the Intelligence Department of New South Wales. After telling how the prunes were dipped and put on trays to dry he said, "I saw several drying grounds where they were handling from 500 to 1000 tons of fruit. There were 300 tons of prunes lying on the trays drying at the time of my visit. During this season he (Curtis) cured 100 tons of prunes, 700 tons of apricots, and 200 tons of pears."[9]

The huge storage shed on the corner of Cypress and University Avenues burned to the ground in 1901. The sheds had been well stocked with more than 200 tons of dried peaches, pears, prunes and other fruits and the destruction of that stock meant a loss to the Curtis Dried Fruit Company of over $70,000. The company never recovered from this loss.

Los Gatos Canning Company

Besides drying yards and the shipment of prunes Los Gatos saw related industries develop from that of fruit growing. The easiest way to get fruit to market was to process it and put it into cans. Canneries sprang up all over the valley and Los Gatos was determined not to be left out of this growing industry. On October 26, 1881 a group of prominent citizens met in the office of the Los Gatos *News* to discuss the matter of a cannery for Los Gatos. Samuel Templeton was chairman and W. S. Walker, the publisher of the *News* was secretary. Messrs. Shannon, Johnson, Hall, Allen and others spoke in favor of a cannery. Some recommended a winery connected with the cannery "to attract more capital." W. S. Walker opposed this. He wanted a cannery as an outlet for the fruit and to give jobs to the people. He felt that those who wanted a winery should build one, but not tie it in with a cannery.

As a result of the meeting, the Los Gatos Fruit Company was organized in 1882 with 14 stockholders. Samuel Templeton was President, James Gordon was Secretary and J. W. Lyndon was Treasurer. Others on the Board of Directors included Robert Walker and Michael Miller. The plant was managed by George Hooke, and was located behind Santa Cruz Avenue between Lyndon Avenue and the present Corner Drug Store. The building was 60 by 80 feet and could handle 5,000 cases a season. Although the cannery prospered for a while, hard times forced it out of business in 1886.

The cannery was purchased by D. L. Beck and Son of San Francisco with George Hooke remaining as manager. In 1894 Hooke purchased the plant from the San Francisco owners and operated it alone. It had a 137 foot frontage on Lyndon Avenue near the Catholic Church and 100 feet on Santa Cruz Avenue. A spur track curved to the plant from Main Street.

The cannery now saw better days. It packed an

average of 50,000 cases of fruit a year and employed between 250 and 300 people during the season. Among the fruits canned were peaches, apricots, apples, cherries, pears, plums and nectarines, much of which was shipped abroad, especially to England. In 1887 a new steamer and more cooking vats were added to the equipment, doubling the output. It was a much-needed expansion since their agent in Liverpool, England informed them that he could dispose of four times as much fruit as they had canned the year before.

Since cannery work was seasonal, the cannery often had difficulty finding enough workers, especially toward the beginning of the school year. On August 15, 1890 the Los Gatos *News* pleaded for people to help out in the cannery and for those working there to stay on the job and not "go on a pleasure jaunt."

The local press reported on the fruit canning and shipping activities quite regularly. For example, on October 20, 1890 it reported that during the canning season between June 4 and October 21, the cannery paid out $21,000 in wages, "mostly to women and persons under 21 years of age." During the same season the cannery paid out $60,000 for fruit and canned 2,359,000 pounds of fruit in one million cans. In August 1891 it shipped 2000 cans to Liverpool and in September it sent 3000 cans to London. During the week of October 27, 1894 the Los Gatos Cannery shipped five carloads of canned fruit to New York and several carloads destined for England.

The following table of goods shipped out of Los Gatos tells the story of the increase in canning and other fruit activities in Los Gatos between 1894 and 1895.

	1894	1895
Canned goods	32,170 tons	61,426 tons
Peaches	54,900 pounds	90,815 pounds
Dried prunes	None	128,660 pounds
Wine	255,685 pounds	312,160 pounds

One important development came soon after Hooke took over the plant. Heretofore only the narrow gauge railroad came into Los Gatos. This made it necessary for fruit shipped from Los Gatos to be unloaded and re-loaded on the broad-gauged railroad cars in San Jose for shipment east. In September 1902 the first shipment of canned goods was loaded on a broad-gauged railroad car in Los Gatos and shipped directly to the markets without the necessity of re-loading in San Jose. The broad-gauge railroad was a boon, not only to the canning industry but to Los Gatos as a whole.

Hunt Brothers in Los Gatos

In 1906 Hunt Brothers of Hayward purchased the Los Gatos Cannery from George Hooke. After selling the Los Gatos plant Hooke established the Sunnyvale Cannery which was purchased by Schuckel & Company who operated it for many years. Mr. Hooke had built a home on Glenridge Avenue next to the Turner house. This was purchased by A. E. Falch, the former owner of the Los Gatos *Mail-News.* Both the Turner home and the Falch home are still standing on Glenridge Avenue.

Early in 1907, Hunt Brothers moved the cannery from the old Lyndon Avenue location to the corner of Santa Cruz Avenue and Saratoga Avenue. The cannery remained one of the leading employment sources for Los Gatos for a long period, and with its warehouses and workers' cabins beside the railroad tracks remained a landmark for years.

The new owners improved the canning facilities, more than doubling the capacity of the plant and bringing the equipment up-to-date. The local press was, perhaps, a bit worried lest the new owners produce an inferior grade of canned goods, for it commented, shortly after the company took possession of the plant: "Los Gatos has an enviable reputation in the fruit world for its celebrated foothill fruits." The paper expressed the hope that

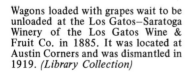

Wagons loaded with grapes wait to be unloaded at the Los Gatos–Saratoga Winery of the Los Gatos Wine & Fruit Co. in 1885. It was located at Austin Corners and was dismantled in 1919. *(Library Collection)*

The California Grape Food (Sanitas) Company plant. It was built in 1893 at the north end of University Avenue. Building was demolished in 1912. *(Library Collection)*

the newly enacted Pure Food Laws would protect the words "Packed in Los Gatos" to the advantage of both the town and the new canning firm.

During the early years of its operation Hunt Brothers Cannery turned out 3 million quarts of canned fruit a season and employed more than 400, and often as many as 800 persons. It produced 40,000 cases of apricots and another 40,000 cases of peaches, as well as other fruits each year.

But as the town grew and as canneries were combined for "greater efficiency" the local plant lost its importance and was abandoned in 1955. The cannery and related buildings were torn down to make room for the Little Village Shops and offices. With the closing of the cannery another era in the history of Los Gatos passed.

Sanitas Grape Food Company

Another industry related to canning sprang up in the 1890's and had a brief existence in Los Gatos. A company called the California Sanitas Grape Food Company (or the California Condensed Juice Co.) was started in 1890. It was "the only product of its kind in the world" and was the brain-child of E. R. Shaw of Los Gatos. In 1892 Mr. Shaw conceived the idea of making a table syrup from grape juice. A machine was constructed and work was begun. The company was incorporated in January 1893 with a capitalization of $50,000. The stock was divided into 1000 shares at $50 a share. E. R. Shaw, of Los Gatos, subscribed $10,000, his brother S. W. Shaw of San Francisco, $250, H. C. Swain of San Francisco another $250, H. A. Merriam of Los Gatos, $10,000 and George Lander $250. The rest was subscribed by lesser stockholders.

In 1893 the company built a plant at the north end of University Avenue consisting of a production room and a labeling room. The product was described as a "syrupy product containing all the original flavors of the fruit." At first it was distributed to physicians throughout the country and was recommended as a valuable medicine for all kinds of ailments. Requests for it came from all over and in the fall of 1893 the Sanitas Grape Food—its trade name—was manufactured on a large scale. It produced many gallons a day and required several tons of grapes to produce a gallon of syrup.[10] The product was sold in bottles with "Los Gatos" stamped on the glass.

Sanitas expanded its plant to meet requests for the product. On October 18, 1893 the Los Gatos *Chronicle,* the maverick newspaper, announced that the Grape Food Company "will commence next week to erect an addition to their factory to be used for bottling their Grape Food. The addition will double the size of the plant." In the

Wagons hauling grapes to the Los Gatos Co-operative Winery 1889. Located on Villa Avenue against the hill below Cleland Avenue behind the present Civic Center. After the winery was removed in 1913, it became the site of the Town Pageant Grounds. *(Library Collection)*

same issue it was reported that the company had "more orders than they can supply this year."[11]

The demand soon dwindled and the company went out of business in 1896. The building was demolished in 1912. Perhaps if refrigeration had been as available in those days as it is today, Sanitas would have become the first concentrated fruit juice in the country.

Los Gatos Co-Operative Winery

Because vineyards were so extensive in the valley it was necessary to find a local market for the grapes. The Grape Food Company consumed only a small part of the crop produced. Furthermore, it was more profitable to sell the grapes to wineries, which were springing up in the valley, the largest being the Co-Operative Winery of Los Gatos. It was initiated by John Cilker who owned 174 acres of vineyards and orchard lands along the Los Gatos-San Jose Road (now Bascom Ave.). A leader among the fruit and vine growers in the county, Cilker persuaded a group to join in founding the Co-Operative Winery in 1886. Cilker became President, and W. B. Rankin Secretary and General Manager. The Winery was located on Villa Avenue against the hill below Clelland Avenue. It produced between 400 and 600 thousand gallons a year, including port, sherry, claret, and white wines. In 1899 Mr. Delpech took over the winery and enlarged it. The winery was removed in 1913 when

John Bean, inventor of the Bean Spray Pump. *(Courtesy F.M.C.)*

the town bought the land for municipal purposes. The Pageant grounds occupied the land until the new civic center was built on part of the land formerly occupied by the winery.

Bean Spray Pump Company

Los Gatos is the birthplace of one of the largest industrial establishments in the nation. One of the problems faced by the orchardists was the destructive tree scale which attacked fruit trees of the valley. The only implement available for spraying the trees was a small low-pressure pump that was

John Bean holds his spray pump at the right, and below gives an early demonstration of its pressure and effectiveness. *(Both courtesy F.M.C.)*

John D. Crummey, the founder of the giant FMC Corporation and Honorary Chairman of its Board of Directors. *(Courtesy J. D. Crummey family)*

Residence of John Bean and Dr. R. P. Gober, corner of Bean and Santa Cruz Avenues. Dr. Gober was a prominent physician in the early days. Building torn down in Nov. 1938. *(Courtesy Geo. Place and Los Gatos Museum)*

puny and ineffective. John Bean came to the rescue of the orchardists. Originally from Michigan, he had come to California from Springfield, Ohio, in 1883. Bean purchased an orchard near Los Gatos which, like those of others in the valley and in the entire state, was plagued by scale. Finding the only pump available completely useless, he went to work on a new pump. He had invented a continuous flow turbine pump for windmills which had been adopted all over the middle west, and is still used throughout the world.

Working on the same principle of continuous flow, he developed a high pressure spray pump. It was exhibited at State Fairs all over the country and proved to be very popular. Crude at first, it

was improved continually until the Bean Spray "Magic" Pump was patented in August 9, 1904.

At the turn of the century John Bean sold his share in the company to his son-in-law, D. C. Crummey. Mr. Crummey had worked for an agricultural implement company in Springfield, Ohio and when he came to Los Gatos in 1888, he was familiar with the pump business. He organized the Mountain Spring Water Company and became its President. His father-in-law formed the pump company and asked D. C. Crummey to be Vice-President. When Mr. Bean retired, Crummey took over the business in Los Gatos. Originally the plant was in an old two-story house on Wilder Avenue behind the Bean residence on the corner of Santa Cruz and Bean Avenues. Later it moved to West Main Street behind what is today the Corner Drug Store. In 1902 Mr. Crummey moved the plant to 171 Santa Clara Street in San Jose, the site having been owned by J. W. Lyndon of Los Gatos. In 1910 John D. Crummey, the son of D. C. Crummey, purchased a site on Julian Street and built a new plant there. It was on this site that the huge FMC developed. Today the FMC is a vast complex which sprawls across vast acres on Coleman Avenue in San Jose and Santa Clara.

D. C. Crummey wanted to expand the company and it was his son John D. Crummey who suggested that a corporation be formed. Money was needed for this and young John was determined to get it. He had saved $500 from his $65 a month job in a Sacramento bicycle shop, and offered to

D. C. Crummey, President of the Mountain Spring Water Co. in the late 1880's and later Vice—President of the Bean Spray Pump Co. which was the forerunner of the giant FMC Corporation. *(Courtesy J. D. Crummey family)*

30

put this into the corporation. Young Crummey went to A. E. Wilder, at the Los Gatos Bank and asked for a $2000 loan. When the banker asked what security he had, J. D. Crummey showed him the savings book with a $500 balance. When banker Wilder found that this sum had been saved out of a $65 a month pittance, he was amazed and agreed to the loan. A well-known citizen of Los Gatos, Mr. D. P. Simons, advanced another $2,500. To this $5000 was added the equity the elder Crummey had in the Bean Spray Pump Co., which brought the total capital up to $15,000. The Bean Spray "Magic" Pump Company was incorporated in May 1904. D. P. Simons became Vice-President of the Corporation.

D. C. Crummey's son John D. Crummey was the sparkplug for the new corporation. His spirit, enthusiasm and hard work made the corporation prosper. It absorbed several other orchard machinery companies, including the Anderson-Barngrover Co., and developed into the huge Food Machinery Corporation---FMC---of today. Today FMC produces, in addition to food machinery, heavy equipment for military purposes.[1][2]

Macabee Gopher Trap Company

Gophers and squirrels were traditional enemies of the orchardists. W. L. B. Cushing was the first to counter-attack. He invented a gopher and squirrel trap in 1885, and from his little shop he and his helpers produced over 200 traps a day. Between

The first gopher trap made by Z. A. Macabee in 1900. Today's trap is still the same. *(Photo by the author)*

January and May 1889 he sold more than 3000 of his traps. Indeed, there was a great demand for a mechanism that could cope with the orchard pests. However, the Cushing trap, while helpful, was not as successful as that later developed by Zepf Macabee. The second son of a family of 8 children, Zepf came to Los Gatos when he was 7 years old. His father lived on a ranch in the Union District for a while and then came to Los Gatos to operate the Coleman Hotel, later the El Monte Hotel. Young Zepf worked in the hotel as clerk, handyman, and bus boy. Tiring of this he took a job as barber, later acquiring his own shop which became known as the Royal Shaving Parlor. It was located in the Arlington Hotel building on the north side of West Main Street next to the bridge. After 10 years of this his health broke and his doctor advised him to get out-of-door employment.

A cousin had an orchard just outside of Los Gatos and the gophers were ruining his trees. The cousin pleaded with Zepf, who was known to be handy with tools, to do something about those

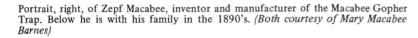

Portrait, right, of Zepf Macabee, inventor and manufacturer of the Macabee Gopher Trap. Below he is with his family in the 1890's. *(Both courtesy of Mary Macabee Barnes)*

bothersome gophers before they ruined his entire orchard. Zepf "jammed away at the jigger" and, using a pair of pliers and some wire and a piece of metal, produced a trap. It was an instant success. He obtained a patent on October 22, 1900 and began the manufacture of the famous Macabee Gopher Trap in a house at 110 Loma Alta Avenue.[13]

Made of steel wire and a piece of sheet iron, the trap was simple, cheap, and easy to handle---and very effective. It outsold its two nearest competitors. At its height in the 1920's the enterprise employed six people with a payroll of $10,521 a year. It had an output of 1000 traps daily. The enterprise is still going strong at the same house on Loma Alta Avenue where it started over 70 years ago. It employs 8 workers and the output is still over 600 traps a day which are sold all over the West Coast and as far away as Texas and New Mexico. Ron Fink has been the local manager since R. Z. Macabee, the son of Zepf, retired in 1959.[14]

Perfume Factory

This chapter cannot be closed without mentioning an unusual industry which flourished for a while and then died. Dr. Alexander P. Whittel was a wealthy eye specialist in San Francisco who, with his wife and daughter, traveled a great deal in Europe. Dr. Whittel had always been fascinated with the perfume industry and it was his dream some day to make a fine perfume. He came to Los Gatos in 1896 and decided that this was the place to make his dream come true. He purchased 15 acres at the top of the hill on Saratoga Avenue near Rose Avenue and here he planted seven acres of roses. He was not interested in just any rose. He imported the famous Castilian rose from Spain which was famous for its fragrance. Dr. Whittel and

Original Hubbell Squab Farm, 1905, then located off of Santa Cruz Ave. near Royce Street — where Rao's Market and *Times-Observer* are today. In the picture are Dr. G. M. Hubbell, Mrs. Hubbell and two of their sons, Carl and Willys. *(Courtesy Carl Hubbell)*

his wife planned to make rosewater from the petals. They also distilled geranium oil from the three acres of geraniums he had planted.

He operated two distilleries with a total capacity of 125 gallons. Children were hired to pick the tender petals during the harvest season, a job which had to be done carefully by hand. The Whittels soon discovered that it cost more to produce the perfume than they received for their efforts and their investment. They persevered for ten years, then gave up the project.[15] That's as close as Los Gatos came to becoming the perfume center of California.

Macabee Gopher Trap Co., 110 Loma Alta Avenue. In continuous operation for more than 70 years. *(Courtesy Ron Fink, Plant Manager 1970)*

FOOTNOTES

1. Library *Collection*, Book 34.
2. Charles M. Shortridge, *Sunshine, Fruit and Flowers.* San Jose *Mercury* Souvenir, p. 88ff. Also Los Gatos *News* November 9, 1890.
3. Los Gatos *Mail News,* April 15, 1910.
4. *Ibid.* April 10, 1891. Shortridge, *op. cit.,* p. 90.
5. Library *Collection,* Book 34.
6. Alley, Bowen & Co., *History of Santa Clara County,* p. 24.
7. Sawyer, *op. cit.,* p. 138. White King Pamphlet, p. 3.
8. Foote, H. S. ed. *Pen Pictures, Garden of the World Santa Clara County, California.* pp. 172ff.
9. Quoted in the Los Gatos *Mail,* May 10, 1907.
10. Shortridge, *op. cit.,* p. 70.
11. Library *Collection,* Book 34.
12. Most of the information here was given by Mr. John D. Crummey to the writer in a personal interview.
13. Sawyer, *op. cit.,* p. 1289.
14. Information obtained from R. Z. Macabee, the only son of Zepf, and manager of the business for many years. Ron Fink, the present manager, was also very helpful.
15. Lutheria Cunningham, Los Gatos *Mail News,* January 29, 1931.

CHAPTER IV

Mountain Roads and Railroads

ROADS

ROADS WERE first built for, and used by, the lumbering industry in the canyons of the Santa Cruz Mountains. At first there were no roads across the mountains to the coast, only an ancient trail, originally made by the wild game as it migrated from the valley into the mountains near Umunhum and Loma Prieta. Later the Ohlone Indians used this treacherous trail on their travels from the Santa Clara Valley across the mountains to the Pacific.[1]

The white man could not follow the steep climb and the sudden drops of the Indian trails. But interestingly enough it was a white *woman* who first made the trip across the Santa Cruz Mountains. Mrs. Farnham, a woman of inordinate courage, drove a sulky alone to the summit at Mountain Charley McKeirnan's ranch and down the other side. It is regrettable that we have no further information on this intrepid pioneer woman or the reason for her ride.

The first mountain road builder was Isaac "Buffalo" Jones, an early settler who came into the canyon in 1850 and claimed all the land he could as a squatter. In addition he covered the surrounding country with school warrants and claimed the redwoods in the entire vicinity. As a further financial venture he built a turnpike road which the lumber trucks had to use to get to their destination, grading the rise so steeply that only half a load could go over it at a time. Furthermore, he charged extortionate rates. The people became so angry at Jones that they petitioned the county Board of Supervisors in 1853 to create a public road. The Board requested an exploring expedition to investigate the feasibility, and to estimate the cost of a public road from Los Gatos to the summit. In 1854 Sheriff James Murphy, a great horseman and daring man, accepted the assignment. He followed the Jones Turnpike and then went up to Mountain Charley's place where he learned that Mrs. Farnham had made the trip across in a sulky. He named the Santa Cruz Gap after this daring lady and called it Farnham Pass.

Murphy and his party returned to report to the Supervisors that it would cost at least $10,000 to build a road from Jones' road to the county line.

They also advised the Board to buy the Jones Road.[2]

Jones had too good a business going and was not about to give up his road. He tried to prevent its surrender by taking his case to court. After months of litigation Jones conceded, selling his mountain land holdings to Stillman Thomas and J. P. Hennings. Hennings built a sawmill and a town which he called Lexington, after his home town, Lexington, Kentucky.

The Santa Cruz Turnpike Joint Stock Company was next in the toll road business. This company was organized on March 13, 1858 and incorporated on June 14, 1859. It had as its purpose the construction of a road from Forbes Mill on the Los Gatos Creek through the Santa Cruz Gap "thence southeasterly until it strikes the county line dividing Santa Clara and Santa Cruz Counties."[3] Incorporation signers included John Roork, Rufus F. Herrick, James Howe, D. D. Briggs, E. Wilcox, John S. Fabor and others. Stephen I. Easley was President, James Howe was Secretary and Alexander Logan was Treasurer. The rates were posted as follows:

Single Team	.50
Two-horse Team	.70
Four-horse Team	.90
Six-horse Team	1.00

In 1867 James Kennedy was put in charge of the tollgate which was on the south end of town. The old Tollgate house which Kennedy built that year is still standing on south Santa Cruz Avenue and Wood Road. Teamsters did not relish paying the toll, and a conflict between them and the toll road operators resulted. On November 15, 1877 John Shepherd and several other irate toll-payers tore down the tollgate and dragged it to the Main Street bridge and dumped it into the creek. The gate was put up again, but on November 17 it was torn down a second time. The Turnpike Company obtained a court order enjoining the men from further use of the road without paying toll. Furthermore, they were ordered to pay for using the road while the gate was down. They were also fined $25.00 for each infraction.

Original tollhouse of Turnpike Company, above, built by James Kennedy in 1867 and below the building today after many remodelings. It stands at Wood Road and Santa Cruz Avenue. *(Library Collection and by the author)*

The gate was erected again in January 1878 by D. B. Moody, the Secretary of the company, and James Kennedy, the gate-keeper. But this did not settle the matter. The first team that went through the gate hooked on to it and dragged it to the edge of the creek and dumped it over. Mrs. Flora Riggs, an old-timer, recalled this incident when she said, "Right there, under that oak, my grandfather Herman Jarisch, with his lumber team white Mollie and mouse-colored Fanny, pulled the last gate from its hinges, an historic occasion."[4]

The county Board of Supervisors declared the road a public road the latter part of 1878. The company took the matter to court, where the county argued that the Charter had expired and the road should be a public thoroughfare. The court agreed and stage coach lines began to travel the dusty road to Santa Cruz. The George Colgrove Stage Company charged $2.50 per person for the bumpy one-way trip over the mountains. Stages

were always endangered, not only by rough roads, steep inclines, and sharp curves, but by highwaymen who had no trouble hiding in the mountains.

Several roads branched into the mountains from Los Gatos. Among these were the Old Franciscan Trail, the Johnson Avenue Stage Route, and the Old Stage Coach Road. The Johnson Avenue Stage had a tollgate in the gulch beyond the end of Johnson Avenue, probably the end of the present Spring Street. All of these "east side roads" led up Jones Hill, then passed near the present site of the Novitiate, then down into Lime Kiln Gulch over to the Lexington area.[5]

The valley roads to and from Los Gatos followed the county roads and consisted mainly of the San Jose-Los Gatos Road via Dry Creek Road into San Jose, the Saratoga Road and the Santa Cruz Avenue-Winchester Road. All were narrow, dusty in dry weather and veritable quagmires in wet. In 1888 H. C. Houghton wrote a letter to the Town Board complaining of the poison oak on Saratoga Avenue. He said this bush was so thick and the road so narrow that it was dangerous for people to walk the street or to drive it. He, Mr. Brunshull, and Mr. Massol offered to give 10 feet of their land to the town if they would widen the road. The humane offer was accepted.

Like all roads and streets, Saratoga Avenue remained dusty and muddy. Citizens complained to the Town Board about the dust, so the water sprinkler wagon made regular rounds of the streets to settle the dust. In 1914 Saratoga Avenue was finally widened and paved. Other streets paved that same year included Main Street and San Jose Avenue. Glenridge and streets on the West side were paved some time later.[6]

Narrow Gauge Railroad

Lumber from the Santa Cruz Mountains had to be hauled out in heavy wagons, a slow, dangerous process. A railroad could connect the lumber industry with the populous area of the San Francisco Bay and the Valley. Furthermore, Santa Cruz, with its tanneries, powder works and fishing industry, was a profitable prize for a railroad system.

One of those who hoped to reap a profit from such an enterprise was James G. Fair. In combination with J. W. Mackay and two saloonkeepers, James C. Flood and William S. O'Brien, Fair had acquired valuable holdings in the Comstock Mines. In the spring of 1873 this group struck one of the richest ore bodies of the lode. The fifty-foot-wide vein was estimated to yield at least one-half billion dollars in silver.[7]

Fair became a multi-millionaire from his silver

Chas. H. Cook and his helpers who were the road crew that maintained the old Santa Cruz road to the summit in the early 1900's. *(Courtesy Mrs. W. O. Craddock)*

mining activities. However, in 1875 his health gave out and the doctor ordered him to retire to the San Francisco Bay area. But he could not retire. While attending the Centennial Exposition in Philadelphia in 1876 he became interested in the Denver and Rio Grande Railroad, which was operating hundreds of miles of narrow gauge lines in the east. The D. & R.G. planned eventually to put a line through the mountains to connect to the Pacific. Fair's talks with railroad officials convinced him that a narrow gauge railroad over the Santa Cruz Mountains was possible.

He organized the South Pacific Coast Railroad in 1876, and the company was incorporated on March 25 of that year. The capital stock was one million dollars and was owned almost exclusively by Alfred Davis, who was President of the company. The immediate objective of the company was Santa Cruz, but it hoped to go on to the Salinas Valley and across the Coast Range to an ultimate connection with the Denver and Rio Grande, which was building a narrow gauge westward.[8]

Most of the work in building the line from Los Gatos to Santa Cruz was done by Chinese laborers, who, at one time numbered several thousand, working in the hills above Los Gatos. A Chinese syndicate contracted gangs of coolies, not only to work on the railroad but to cut wood and clear the brush and stumps from the hillsides. The Chinese were also used to clear the chaparral and poison oak from Glenridge and Hernandez Avenues.

The Chinese lived in dilapidated shanties on the edge of the creek near the bridge and up near the railroad track. Fred Berryman, an old timer in Los Gatos, estimated that during the 1880's some five

hundred Chinese lived in Los Gatos.[9] On July 10, 1886 the local press was gratified that the old Chinese shanties east of the depot, on what is now Montebello Way, were torn down and "respectable structures" put up instead.

The Chinese also created problems for the town. After the railroads were completed, many of these Orientals became merchants "peddling their wares in bamboo baskets balanced on their shoulders by long shoulder sticks." They also operated laundries

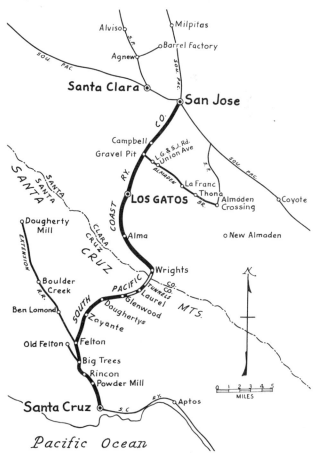

Route of the narrow-gauge railroad through Los Gatos to Santa Cruz. *(Map by Crawford C. Anderson)*

At the Los Gatos Depot, 1886, Geo. Fletcher is in the Wells Fargo wagon and Geo. Wilson the agent stands behind the wagon. *(Library Collection)*

in the town. Sing Lee and Quong Kee operated a laundry at 23 Montebello Way. The laborers for the laundry were contract laborers, working and sleeping in the laundry building. The problem was that their only pastime was gambling, which often ended in a brawl.[10]

The South Pacific Coast Railroad completed its line from Alameda to Los Gatos before the middle of 1878, with the first narrow gauge train arriving in Los Gatos from that East Bay City on June 2, 1878. It was a big day for Los Gatos! The special train rolled in during the afternoon and the people of the town served a lunch at the little depot. Los Gatos was the terminal for the railroad line for almost two years until the line was completed to Santa Cruz in 1880. Until that time, passengers wishing to go to Santa Cruz had to depend upon Colgrove's Stages.[11]

In order to build the line into Los Gatos and have a place for a depot, the railroad company needed the land on which the Los Gatos Hotel stood. J. W. Lyndon agreed to give the land for a token payment if the company would move the hotel across the street to the west side of Santa Cruz Avenue. This the company readily agreed to do.

To get the railroad through the mountains to Santa Cruz required extensive tunnelling. By May, 1880, two tunnels had been completed, each over a mile in length. One was between Wrights and Soquel Creek and the other between Laurel and Glenwood. Six tunnels in all were cut through the mountains. Three smaller tunnels were required to complete the line to the coast.

The Wrights tunnel presented problems. On the night of February 12, 1877 there was an explosion in the tunnel killing M. C. Highland, the foreman on the job, and more than 20 Chinese workers. Gas

had been accumulating, and it was the practice to light a torch and approach the entrance cautiously to burn the usually small amount of accumulated gas. On this night Mr. Highland and his Chinese crew walked into the tunnel to light a piece of waste on a big pole. As Highland struck a match a terrific explosion resulted, killing the entire crew and the foreman.[12]

The tunnel between Laurel and Glenwood was also the scene of tragedy. On February 23, 1879, as a result of oil seepage from the walls of the tunnel, an explosion occurred, injuring 15 men. Again on November 16, 1879 an explosion in tunnel #3 resulted in 30 deaths, mostly Chinese. Tunnel #3 was the scene of another explosion on Sunday, February 1, 1880. The Chinese working in the tunnels now had had enough of explosions and refused to go back to work. More than 60 of them

Narrow gauge train in the Los Gatos Canyon about 1890. *(Courtesy Nancy Gober Schmidt and Los Gatos Museum)*

36

Wright's Station which became a popular resort spot for Bay Area vacationers after the railroad was built. Picture of 1904. *(Courtesy Mrs. May Snyder and Mrs. Stanley Sanders)*

left the job, and the railroad company had to enlist a crew of Cornishmen from the Almaden Mines to take their places.[13]

The Wrights Tunnel was important, for it made Wrights a shipping point for lumber and fruit. A side track was built for picnic trains that later came to Wrights every weekend and on special holidays. The Reverend James Wright, a Presbyterian minister from Michigan, had homesteaded a large acreage in the mountains in 1869. In 1873 he opened a summer resort for visitors and tourists. When the railroad came in 1879 Wrights Station was named after the minister. In that year the railroad entered into a contract with A. J. Rich, the owner of the land at Wrights station, giving the railroad the right-of-way in return for a guarantee that the railroad would maintain a station, an express office and a telegraph office at that mountain village. If the station were ever abandoned the

right-of-way was to revert to the owners of the tract. In 1932 the Southern Pacific was given permission to close Wrights Station, and in 1936 the San Jose Water Works acquired the land to protect its watershed. Wrights no longer exists, having been buried in history.

As for the tunnel at Wrights, it had been plagued by cave-ins, especially during the rainy winter of 1892 and 1893. A concrete wall was built in 1893 and this lasted until World War II, when the military blew it up in a demolition practice in 1942.

During the construction of the line, Los Gatos was a center of activity. Construction material and engine fuel were kept on the property on Montebello Way. Besides a freight shed and later a passenger depot, Los Gatos had a small engine terminal and roundhouse on the corner of Elm Street and Boon Lane.

By 1880 the narrow gauge line was completed, at a cost of more than 12 million dollars. It was a paying proposition from the start. Not only passenger traffic but freight traffic was heavy enough to require six or seven local freight trains and two passenger trains a day from the Bay Area to Santa Cruz. In April 1887 the Los Gatos *News* reported that eight trains a day were leaving Los Gatos. On May 10, 1895 the same newspaper reported the largest excursion in several years passed through Los Gatos. More than "2,500 persons, carried by 41 cars made up of three sections."

Los Gatos Canyon in 1901 showing portion of the railroad. *(Library Collection)*

37

A ride through the canyons and tunnels was described in words attributed to General John C. Fremont, who had camped near Los Gatos on February 12, 1846. He returned in 1888 and with Mrs. Fremont rode the train through the mountains to Santa Cruz. Fremont is quoted as having said of this trip, "It was an honor to ride one of those aristocratic pioneer coaches of the new narrow gauge railroad, a joy to view the beautiful landscape while watching the wildlife jump or fly to safety; a thrill to be thrown about---up, down, right, left---over the crude uneven ballast of the slender rails and around the frequent rough mountain curves where 20 miles an hour was a reckless speed."[14]

The coming of the narrow gauge railroad had its effect on Los Gatos. In 1887 a writer noted that the scene changed from a peaceful hamlet to a busy village. "The mountains looked down on a bustling little village at their feet, and the people following the greatest resource-developer of the 19th century, the railroad, soon increased the village to a town. They divided up the mountainsides, grubbed up the chaparral, planted trees and vines and built homes."[15] Los Gatos was on its way!

The railroad also brought the commuter to live in Los Gatos. As early as May 1885 the Los Gatos *News* predicted that "many persons who do business in San Francisco reside in the vicinity of Los Gatos, and as time advances many more will avail themselves of this advantage to make a pleasant home."

That is exactly what happened. Commuter trains from Los Gatos through all the Peninsular cities to San Francisco were a part of the life of the town for many years. The Commuter system and the Southern Pacific were almost synonymous. The great Southern Pacific had purchased the South Pacific Coast Railroad on July 1, 1887, allowing the Southern Pacific more than 100 miles of main branch line narrow gauge rails from Oakland and Alameda to Santa Cruz.[16]

The railroad also brought new life to the mountain towns such as Alma, Aldercroft, Glenwood, and Wrights. Not only freight business but holiday passengers pushed the railroad to capacity. The mountain picnic areas such as Sunset Park at Wrights, Glenwood Magnetic Springs, and Skyline Park were crowded on weekends and holidays. Three, four and even five sections of picnic trains, each running to ten cars, followed each other up the hill from Los Gatos.

The "picnic trains" as the Sunday and Holiday specials were called, took crowds to the mountain resorts and the beaches, returning the frazzled merrimakers in the evenings. Some of the celebrants were thrown off the train along the way if they became too obstreperous as a result of too much "celebration." Gerton Keyston, in a letter to Dora Rankin, recalled the excursions. The Sunday picnic trains, "loaded in the morning with lively happy, singing picnic crowds, and returning in the evenings with tired, and dirty persons, grabbing faded wild flowers, many of them slightly intoxicated."[17]

Standard Gauge Railroad

The narrow gauge road served well, but as business increased and as standard gauge main lines became more common, it became apparent that a change to standard gauge was necessary. The narrow gauge equipment was wearing out and was costly to replace or maintain. Los Gatos merchants

Locomotive No. 1370 was the first to come to Los Gatos on broad gauge track. Right is a section of broad and narrow gauge track toward Campbell in 1897. *(Library collection, and courtesy Nancy Gober Schmidt and Los Gatos Museum)*

complained because their shipments had to be unloaded from the narrow gauge and transferred to the standard gauge line in San Jose. Early in 1891 the village of Campbell was prodding the Southern Pacific to bring the standard gauge line into that town. Los Gatos felt that such a line was as important---if not of greater importance---to it as it was to any other town along the line. The Town Trustees called a meeting of interested citizens on April 27, 1891 to consider the best means of getting a local broad gauge railroad to Los Gatos. The San Jose *Mercury* was even concerned over this, for in its issue of April 24, 1891 it stated, "The growing trade and shipment to the west side demands it."

On July 20, 1892 the Los Gatos *Mail* urged the people of Los Gatos to "present every argument possible to the Southern Pacific Company to get a third rail into the Gem City in time to handle the grape crop." But it was to be several grape crops later that work on the standard gauge into Los Gatos was begun. The construction began in June 1894 and the line was completed to Los Gatos in September 1895.

The first standard gauge train arrived in town on September 7, 1895. It was a great day for the townspeople, who greeted its arrival with a big celebration. Of this the Los Gatos Weekly *Mail* wrote, "Early in the morning, buggies, wagons, and conveyances of all kinds loaded with people from the surrounding country began to arrive, and by 11 o'clock the streets were crowded."

The depot and area around it were packed with people. As the first train came to the station a great cheer went up from the crowd. The train, carrying more than 500 passengers, was in charge of Col. Menton, the Excursion Agent for the Southern Pacific. Santa Clara's 15-piece band was first off the train, and immediately commenced a program of martial music for the occasion. The crowd followed the band to Shore's Grove to enjoy more music and speeches.

The President of the Los Gatos Board of Trade, Mr. Skinkle, gave a flowery speech which ended with the following advice to the visitors: "When you grow tired of the fogs and the raw chilling winds or burning suns of other less favored places, let your minds revert to this scene and the beautiful city amongst the foothills, and come and make your home with us and I assure you that both man and nature will conspire to see that you never regret it."[18]

The regular standard gauge passenger service between Los Gatos and the Bay Area did not start until April 15, 1900. Definite passenger and freight schedules were instituted and Los Gatos now had direct access to the markets of the Bay Area and the East. It was a hope fulfilled for the Gem City of the Foothills.

Los Gatans welcomed the first scheduled passenger service to the Bay Area on the new broad gauge tracks on April 15, 1900. People came from San Francisco and Oakland to help celebrate. A picnic and exercises, below, at Bunker Hill Park — later Memorial Park — marked the completion of service on the new standard gauge railroad. *(Library Collection)*

While it was a comparatively simple task to convert the narrow gauged line to a standard gauged railroad in the flat lowlands of the valley, it was quite another matter when it came to the mountains. Bringing the wider tracks over the mountains was a difficult and expensive job. Some tunnels had to be widened. Curves had to be straightened and a great deal of the track had to be reinforced. The job was undertaken, however, and by 1903 the third rail extended to Wrights.

The earthquake of 1906 delayed further extension of the standard rail through to the coast. That upheaval twisted rails, collapsed tunnels and ripped tracks from the roadbed. It took almost three years to complete the job of repairing and rebuilding. Not until May 1909 was the rail to Santa Cruz reopened, and regular traffic on the line resumed.

Los Gatos returned to the status of a terminal point during the time the line across the mountains was being repaired. When it was opened again in May, 1909 Los Gatos and the mountain communities celebrated with gusto and finesse. All day, along the line from Mayfield to Los Gatos, to Wrights and Santa Cruz, huge celebrations took place. At Alma, the "Anvil Chorus" greeted the trains. At Wrights, people from the entire mountain area came to town to see the trains that came from as far away as Sacramento. Torpedoes were placed on the tracks along the way. The venerable conductor, Sam Davis, had been requested by friends to be given the honor of taking the first train through from San Francisco to Santa Cruz. Sam had been running this road on the narrow gauge from its beginning in 1880. So great was the celebration in Los Gatos that the Los Gatos *Mail* reported on June 3, 1909, that "Los Gatos has not

Southern Pacific Tower and gateman on south side of West Main Street crossing. Erected in 1910 it stood until 1928. Before the tower, a flagman guarded the crossing. *(Library Collection)*

Incidentally, the coming of the regular trains to Los Gatos presented a problem to the town and the police. It seems that the young boys would pry open fruit boxes in the depot and also practice "jumping the cars." The Town Trustees passed an ordinance forbidding anyone to board a moving car or jump from such a car. But the ordinance was hard to enforce. On September 26, 1895 the Southern Pacific Agent sent a letter to the Town Trustees to complain that numerous boys were violating the ordinance against boarding or alighting from trains while in motion. The Town Marshall explained that he had made all possible effort to keep the boys away from the depot but to no avail. It seems that boys were typical adventurers and daredevils even as boys have ever been.

Santa Cruz Gap through which the railroad traveled to Santa Cruz. The early 1920's. *(Museum Collection)*

yet recovered from its ecstasy over the opening of the mountain route to Santa Cruz. It will take a week or two to get settled down to every day routine business again."

Los Gatos had the railroad but it needed a "good depot." On September 10, 1890 the *News* announced that the "railroad company have about completed the work on the track across Main Street. But it would now be in order to put up a comfortable depot." Again, on December 2, 1892 the paper asked for a new passenger depot for Los Gatos. "The present building was amply sufficient ten years ago, but the growth of the town and the increase in railroad traffic warrants a new depot. The present depot is not in keeping with the prosperity of the town." The "present depot" had been built in 1878 when the railroad first came into Los Gatos. In August 1901 Mr. E. L. Ford, the depot agent, said he had received word that Los Gatos would get a new depot "in the near future." The "near future" lasted until 1924 when the Southern Pacific finally remodeled the old depot.

The question of warning gates across the track on Main Street was discussed for some time. Finally in May 1905 the railroad put a tower and drop gates across Main Street. The tower stood on the east end of the depot about in the vicinity of the Town Plaza. A watchman was assigned to the tower and the gates.

Except for several accidents in the mountains during the early period of the railroad there were no serious train wrecks. The only wreck on the Los Gatos-San Jose run occurred on December 24, 1906. Mrs. Jessie Cruickshank, who was present when the last train made its special run ending the Los Gatos Commuter train in 1959, was in that wreck and told about it. She was at the time Mrs. Edward Stoldt and was on her way, with her

Original S. P. Depot on Front Street (Montebello Way) looking south in 1900. *(Library Collection)*

And, in 1922. Picture is from opposite side but little else is changed.

But, in 1924, a remodeled depot — not a new one. *(All Library Collection)*

41

husband and 3-year-old son, from San Jose to Wrights to spend the Christmas holidays.

Heavy rains had softened the roadbed, and when the train neared Vasona Junction where the tracks ran beside the Los Gatos Creek, the train left the rails and jumped along on the ties for a short distance. The engine and baggage car remained on the track, but the smoker and passenger coach left the track and slid down the riverbank and turned over. None of the dozen or so passengers was seriously hurt. "The only thing that saved us," said Mrs. Cruickshank in 1959, recalling the incident, "was that it was a steel coach, and they were rare in those days."

The engineer and fireman rushed to the wreckage, smashed the windows of the car and helped the dazed passengers out. They took them on to Los Gatos, sounding the whistle all down the line. The passengers were taken to the lobby of the Lyndon Hotel where local people had already gathered with blankets and cots. Mrs. Cruickshank's husband and a Mr. A. Bashford of San Francisco were the only ones hospitalized.[19]

The railroad was an important part of the life of Los Gatos for more than 80 years. Fruit shipments, commodities and passengers were all a part of the railroad business. Commuting became popular. Every morning lines of automobiles gathered at the depot, dropping off the Bay Area commuters, and each evening, shortly after seven o'clock, wives returned to pick up their commuter husbands. It was a friendly crowd on the trains. A Los Gatos Commuters Club was organized in March 1912, composed of Los Gatans working or doing business in San Francisco or peninsula cities. The purpose of the club was to look after the train service, correct schedules, etc. The officers at the time of organization were: President, Richard Spreckles; Secretary, H. B. Hambly; Trustees, Messrs. Cameron, Henkle, Cottle, Fuller and Walker. The club planned social activities also, especially the annual Christmas parties on the train.

But business slackened during the 30's and 40's. The State Railway Commission granted a franchise in October 1924 to the Los Gatos-San Jose Stage Line, permitting the company to operate between Los Gatos, Campbell and Santa Clara. This was the beginning of stage lines that gradually extended to San Francisco and Oakland. Improved roads brought trucks that freighted goods to the market. The railroads were losing traffic in both passengers and freight. It was only a question of time before railroads through Los Gatos and on to Santa Cruz would cease to operate.

Rumors were rife in December 1931 that the Southern Pacific would soon petition the Interstate

Standard gauge train in gap above Los Gatos in the 1920's. The run to Santa Cruz was abandoned in 1940. *(Museum Collection)*

Santa Cruz highway and S. P. Railroad tracks in 1926. The highway was completed in 1920. *(Library Collection)*

Los Gatos Canyon, showing part of the original road to Santa Cruz, about 1916. *(Library Collection)*

Interurban electric train on corner of Santa Cruz Avenue and Main Street, early 1900's. *(Library Collection)*

A larger and faster interurban at the same intersection in the 1920's. *(Museum Collection)*

Commerce Commission for permission to abandon the line between Los Gatos and the Olympia Station on the Santa Cruz County line. Heavy storms in the winter of 1939 and 1940 did such extensive damage to tracks and tunnels in the Los Gatos canyon that the railroad was given permission, on September 20, 1940, to abandon the poorly patronized line between Los Gatos and Santa Cruz.

From then on it was only a matter of time before the commuter trains would be abandoned also. Rumors of the impending move were denied by the Southern Pacific officials in San Francisco. On February 3, 1954 they stated that there was no truth to the rumors, despite the fact that the Los Gatos Town Council had already made overtures to the company to turn the area of the tracks into a parking area.

On Friday, January 23, 1959, the commuter train made its last run into Los Gatos. It made a Commemorative run on Sunday afternoon, January 25, 1959 from Los Gatos to San Jose. Appropriate spike-pulling ceremonies were held at the conclusion of the ride. Almost 1200 people were present for that last train. They crowded in

the aisles and were crammed seven to a seat. But no one complained and everyone had a wonderful time, including the writer.

At the conclusion of the ceremony, the spike was presented to the town officials. Vasona became the end of the line in 1959, and in 1962 even this was abandoned. Thus, after 85 years of service, the railroad was torn up. Progress had again overtaken one of the characteristic features of this West Valley community.

Interurban Railroad

Shortly after Thomas A. Edison had invented the storage battery at the beginning of the century, he predicted that in a few years "horses will have disappeared from the streets as beasts of burden and automobiles become so cheap as to be within the reach of all." Of course, Edison thought that automobiles would be run by electric power from his batteries.

Even before this prediction that electric power would replace horses, some citizens of Los Gatos dreamed of an electric transportation system for our town. As early as October 3, 1887 a group of businessmen petitioned the Town Trustees to tran-

43

chise a street railway. The power for this was to come from one of three sources---horse, electricity, or cable. The line was to run from the east end of Main Street to the end of town on Santa Cruz Avenue. The Directors of the proposed road were to be Magnus Tait, H. C. Houghton, A. Berryman, N. E. Beckwith and J. H. Lyndon.[20]

Again on October 14, 1891 a petition for a franchise for an electric railroad within the town limits was presented to the Town Trustees. This petition was made in behalf of Felix Chapellette *et al.* On October 19, 1891 by Ordinance Number 43 the franchise for an electric railroad within the corporate limits of the town was granted. It was to run on San Jose Avenue, through Main Street to Santa Cruz Avenue and up to Saratoga Avenue and the corporate limits. Construction was to begin within a year.[21]

However, neither group went ahead with the project, probably because the interurban railroad people were making application to the county for an electric rail line from San Jose to Los Gatos, where it would run the length of the town.

Los Gatos had wanted an interurban line for some time. In 1899 the Los Gatos newspaper reported strong community sentiment in favor of such a transportation system. On December 1, 1902 the *Mail* reported that the *pros* and *cons* of an electric interurban line were still being discussed. It was argued that an electric line to San Jose would increase the population and also increase the trade of the merchants. It would also induce many San Jose businessmen to make their homes in Los Gatos.

On the very day this article appeared, on December 1, 1902, the County Supervisors passed an Ordinance granting a franchise to L. A. Sage and others, giving them a right to construct and operate an electric railroad from San Jose to Congress Springs and from Saratoga to Los Gatos.

In the meantime James W. Rea, an ex-Railroad Commissioner, and F. S. Granger headed a syndicate of local citizens in the fall of 1902 to provide for an 18-mile electric railway. The line was to be known as the San Jose, Saratoga and Los Gatos Interurban Railroad Company. They contemplated a standard gauge 600 volt overhead trolley line from San Jose via San Carlos Street, and Stevens Creek Road to Meridian Corners, Saratoga and Los Gatos. The company was incorporated on October 17, 1902 with a capital stock of 2 million dollars. It also obtained the necessary county franchise so that construction was begun in January 1903.[22]

Despite the fact that Rea and Granger chose county roads to avoid costs of private rights-of-way, they had to halt construction after a month

INTERURBAN APPLIES FOR FRANCHISE ON MAIN AND SAN JOSE

ELECTRIC ROAD WILL PAY HALF ON A $12,000 STONE ARCH BRIDGE.

B. F. Williams Appointed Trustee to Fill Vacancy Caused by D. C. Crummey's Resignation.

A large budget of business was trans-acted by the Town Board of Trustees at its meeting last Monday evenir ~~~i-
~~~ of the greatest im~~
~ nro~

News item in Los Gatos *Mail*, Oct. 23, 1903.

because of lack of funds. It seems that the public's enthusiasm for the project did not extend to its pocketbook, and the hoped-for investment money was not forthcoming. The company was re-incorporated in May 1903 as the San Jose-Los Gatos Interurban Railway Company. Mr. Rea remained as President and Mr. Granger continued as Vice-President. In June James Rea was successful in getting the Germania Trust Company of St. Louis to accept $500,000 worth of bonds and construction was resumed on June 13. This was another occasion for a big celebration in Los Gatos and the driving of a silver spike.[23]

But a rival San Jose Railroad Company tried to stop the construction by the Rea and Granger group. Failing this they planned a shorter route to Los Gatos through Campbell. But Rea announced that his own line was taking the shorter route, and indeed, it had already spent several thousand dollars on the project. Rea's backers promised him 2 million dollars to stop the San Jose group's plans. Unable to fight that kind of money the San Jose Railroad Company gave up and let Rea have the cut-off in November 1903.

The San Jose-Los Gatos Interurban Company's line was completed early in 1904, and the first interurban train came into Los Gatos on Saturday morning, March 17, 1904. Another celebration was in order for Los Gatos, featuring a banquet in the Lyndon Hotel. The town was indeed happy to have an electric line to San Jose and intermediate points.

Hourly trips were instituted between Los Gatos and San Jose. On August 18, 1904 the shorter line to Los Gatos was completed. This came by way of Bird Avenue to Coe, to Lincoln, to Willow Street, then to Meridian Road to Hamilton. From here it took the San Jose-Los Gatos Road into Campbell

Old wooden Main Street bridge 1900. This was replaced in 1906 by a new stone bridge which stood until the freeway came. *(Library Collection)*

and back to the San Jose-Los Gatos Road into Los Gatos.

The line changed hands in April 1904 when O. A. Hale took it over. Rea resigned and so did Granger. After the resignation of these men, Hale became President, and F. E. Chapin of San Francisco was chosen General Manager.

When electric railroads proved profitable other lines were started by other companies. Three interurban lines in the valley were finally combined in 1909 under the name of Peninsular Railroad Company. Eventually, control passed to the Southern Pacific System.

Only one serious mishap occurred on the interurban in the many years it served the area. On Monday, June 4, 1906 an accident occurred at the junction of Saratoga and Santa Cruz Avenues. One man, John Davey of San Jose was killed and 4 others were injured. This record was especially remarkable since, in the early stage of the service, young boys would jump on the cars and try to shake them off the tracks.

The Interurban Line was a part of the economic life of Los Gatos for over a quarter of a century. In the 1920's and early 1930's many students from the Willow Glen area came to Los Gatos Union High School on the interurban cars. It was a convenient means of getting to San Jose and back for the people in Los Gatos, especially during the years when the electric cars came and went every hour.

With the improvement of county roads and the resultant increase in automobile traffic, and the chartering of the Peerless Stages for their run between San Jose and Los Gatos, the electric train lost business. The interurban railroad was abandoned in 1933, the last electric train leaving Los Gatos for Saratoga and San Jose in March of that year. A planned farewell had to be cancelled because of rain.[24]

It is interesting to note that when the line was abandoned the Los Gatos Kiwanis Club cheered.

They had denounced the electric railway as an obsolete means of transportation and an obstruction to trade in the main streets of Los Gatos. What a contrast to the cheers and loud acclaim by the people when the electric interurban made its first trip to Los Gatos! One wonders, with the smog and the heavy traffic and the hodge-podge of freeways and expressways that deface the present landscape, whether the Kiwanis Club wouldn't have second thoughts about an electric interurban railway today.

The Main Street Bridge

Much of the history of Los Gatos concerns the bridge that spanned Los Gatos Creek on Main Street. Evidence points to the use of a small wooden foot bridge by the early Indians and the people from the Santa Clara Mission. This had to be rebuilt each year. In the 1840's the first wooden bridge was built of redwood logs with split logs covering the redwood logs. But this structure was too low to withstand the floods of the creek in winter. In 1882 a new wooden bridge was built high enough for a team to drive across. To cross the creek from East Main Street to the West side, one had to go down a sharp incline to the bridge and up another sharp incline on the other side.

The Town Board called a special meeting on May 9, 1888 to consider repairs on the bridge. County Supervisor Samuel Ayres was present, and he told the Board that the county would pay $300 toward repair of the bridge. He pointed out that the bridge would need to be raised 5 feet and that the California Hotel would need to be raised to correspond with the grade of the street.[25]

In 1890 the Town Board again considered repairing the old bridge. It suggested covering the bridge with "cloth and asphalt for 13½ cents per square foot." This would mean $635.04, which the Board considered prohibitive. Add to this the sidewalk coverage and it would mean a total expenditure of almost $1000, and that was more than the Board was willing to spend.

On July 1, 1895 the Town Board called a mass meeting for July 6 to consider the matter of a bond election for a new bridge. Henry Hatch thought that a wooden bridge was better than a steel bridge, which the Board was suggesting, because a wooden bridge "gives warning before collapsing," hence is safer. He optimistically believed that the old bridge could be repaired for a few hundred dollars and "it will stand for another 15 years." Furthermore, the California Bridge Company said that with reasonable repairs, it would stand another 50 years.[26]

On October 19, 1903 Mr. Granger of the Interurban Railroad appeared before the Town Board on the matter of the Main Street bridge. He had estimates for a stone arch bridge, full-width of the street, that would cost about $12,000, of which his company was willing to pay half. On August 14, 1904 Mr. J. B. Leonard, a Civil Engineer of San Francisco, presented two plans for a bridge. One was for a solid stone single arch bridge at an estimated cost of $32,000. The other was an armored concrete bridge at a cost of $25,000. Both spans would be 120 feet. On September 6 Leonard reported that the cost would be $19,000, but on the 19th he stated that there had been a misunderstanding and that the cost would be $22,050 instead of $19,000. The Town Board understandably took no action.[27]

On October 3, 1904 the Board set its specifications for the proposed bridge. It was to be "a bridge built of concrete and rubble stone, reinforced with steel." Town Engineer J. G. Williams estimated the cost at $20,000. The engineer also proposed a sewer septic tank system for the people on the West side of the bridge, which would cost another $4,000. The Board accepted the recommendations. However, since the cost was greater than the town income could stand, the Board proposed a bond issue. Ordinance 125, October 17, 1904, called for a special election to be held on Monday, December 5, 1904 to vote on a $20,000 bond issue for the bridge and $4,000 for the sewer.

The bridge bond issue passed by a margin of 333 to 7, and the sewer bond by a vote of 324 to 14. On January 19, 1905 the Board passed Ordinance 126 incurring a bonded indebtedness of $24,000.[28]

When the Town Board opened the bids for the bridge on March 6, 1905 the lowest bid was $7,000 above the estimated cost. New bids were called for, and again the lowest was $3,000 above estimates. But on March 21, 1905 the Board accepted the bid of John Doyle Company for $23,327 for the bridge and allowed 150 days for its completion.

The Doyle Company could not complete the job in the time-limit set and was granted a 60-day extension. The bridge was completed on November 3, 1905 and accepted on March 5, 1906. A celebration for its dedication was to be held on May 1, 1906, a joint town barbecue and May-Day observance. But the earthquake of April 18, 1906 forced a change of plans. The remarkable thing about the new bridge was that it sustained absolutely no damage as a result of the earthquake.

This substantial bridge carried traffic from East Los Gatos to the Santa Cruz Avenue area for many years. When the Los Gatos Creek was diverted and Highway 17 came through in 1955, the 1906 bridge was torn down and a new crossing was erected. The Creek is no longer visible, being diverted into huge pipes, and the new bridge serves only as an over-crossing for the freeway.

FOOTNOTES

1. The Burrell *Letters*. Footnote p. 55.
2. Mrs. Fremont Older in Hamsher Collection, Bk 34.
3. Library *Collection, Historical Notes*. Records of the Department of State, Sacramento.
4. Addicott, *op. cit.,* p. 41.
5. *Ibid.* p. 51.
6. Library *Collection*, Book 34.
7. Cleland, Robert F. *From Wilderness to Empire,* A History of California 1542 to 1900. A Knopf, 1944, p. 331.
8. Bruce MacGregor, *South Pacific Coast.* Howell North Books, Berkeley, 1968, p. 25. This is the best study of this subject in print.
9. *Times-Observer,* August 10, 1962.
10. Addicott, *op. cit.,* p. 55.
11. Bruce MacGregor, *op. cit.,* p. 97.
12. *Ibid.* Also Wm. H. Wulf, Historian of the Central California Railroad Club, in Los Gatos *Times-Observer,* January 22, 1959.
13. Library *Collection, Historical Notes.*
14. Addicott, *op. cit.,* p. 22.
15. Mrs. Carrie Stevens Walker, *Central California,* Santa Clara County, San Jose, 1887, p. 107.
16. The Public Relations Department, Southern Pacific Transportation Company, in a letter to the writer dated October 2, 1970.
17. Dora Rankin, "As It Was" *Times-Observer,* November 8, 1965.
18. Los Gatos *Mail* September 12, 1895.
19. Library *Collection,* Bk 37.
20. *Minutes* of Town Trustees, October 3, 1887. Office of Town Clerk. Also Hamsher Collection Bk. 37.
21. *Ibid.,* October 19, 1891. Also Los Gatos *News* October 23, 1891.
22. Charles S. McCaleb, *San Jose Railroads,* Centennial 1868 to 1968. Foothill Junior College District, p. 44ff. This is an excellent study of the entire railway system of Santa Clara County.
23. *Ibid.*
24. Los Gatos *Mail-News,* March 16, 1933.
25. Town Board *Minutes,* May 9, 1888, Bk. I, p. 78.
26. Los Gatos Weekly *News,* July 12, 1895.
27. Town Board *Minutes,* Book IV, p. 46.
28. *Ibid.,* p. 99; also December 7, 1904, p. 121.

CHAPTER V

Newspapers in Los Gatos

W. S. Walker and his Competitors

EVEN before the town was incorporated, Los Gatos had a weekly newspaper. William S. Walker, a printer and journalist, founded the Los Gatos Weekly *News* in July 1881. Walker's career took in farming in Missouri, printing and newspaper publishing in Illinois, Missouri, Nebraska and California. The Cloverdale *Reveille* and the Santa Rosa *Republican* were only two of his previous California newspaper ventures.

After three trips back and forth between California and the middlewest, he decided that the mild climate in California was better than the cold winters of the middlewest. Looking about for a place to locate, Walker was advised by friends to go to the picturesque town of Saratoga in the Santa Clara Valley. While on his way there he stopped off in Los Gatos and was so pleased with the town that he decided to settle here instead.

The initial issue of the Los Gatos Weekly *News* made its appearance on July 2, 1881. Its compositors included C. C. Suydam, Walter L. McWhorten and Miss Lily Goldsworthy. The first subscriber was a Mr. Lundy. Originally published in a house on Alpine Avenue, it soon moved to an old wooden building at 128 East Main Street on the south side of the street—probably where Sorenson Plumbing Shop is today. Mrs. W. S. Walker recalled, in 1928, that the building belonged "to the Tobin girls." One of these girls was employed by Walker in his newspaper office. Later the paper moved to a building near the present site of the Town Hall. Its third home was a building on the ground that is now the high school lawn, then owned by James and John Lyndon. Finally, it settled in its own building on East Main Street south of the bridge where Green's Pharmacy was located and is now occupied by the Dental Laboratory.

William S. Walker was a veteran of the Civil War and a "Radical Republican" of the day. He was a fearless editor. The motto of the *News* came from a famous poet's words:

"To the cause that lacks assistance;
For the wrongs that need resistance;
For the future in the distance

And the good that we can do.
Independent of all things and at all times."[1]

The few Democrats in Los Gatos were displeased with Walker's Republican partisanship and decided that Los Gatos should have Democratic views expressed also. In 1884 H. H. Main, Chairman of the County Board of Supervisors, editor of the San Jose *Herald,* and a leading county Democrat began to counter-attack. He formed a stock company which purchased printing equipment and launched the Los Gatos *Mail* as a rival to the *News* in 1883. It was a seven-column folio edited by J. D. Mason, an able and dedicated scholar, who tried to make a success of the paper. After two years the *Mail* was sold to William P. "Billy" Hughes, who had become its editor a short while before.

Always restless, Walker retired from the *News* in 1885 and moved to Santa Cruz. After his retirement the paper passed through several ownerships. First, Trantham, Webster, and Suydam. Then Trantham and Webster, then Trantham and Dodge, next Trantham and Jenks, and finally, in January 1905, Trantham took over sole ownership of the *News.*

W. H. B. Trantham had been a former school teacher, principal, and newspaper publisher in Missouri who had come to Los Gatos for his health in 1884. He was six feet tall and had an imposing appearance. He was an able journalist, conservative in his politics and a man with a variety of civic interests, serving as a member of the Los Gatos School Board for 20 years.

Between 1881 and 1905 a number of other newspapers were born, lived a while, and died in Los Gatos. The *Enterprise* was founded by C. C. Suydam, who had been on the staff of the *News.* Walker carried no grudge against Suydam for his action. When the new paper appeared, Walker wished it well and called attention to "its neat appearance" in his columns on March 21, 1885. He expressed the hope that advertisers would support the new paper. The *Enterprise* was devoted entirely to local news and social activities. Local advertising could hardly support several papers so the *Enterprise* folded less than a year after it made its first

W. S. Walker, founder and editor, Los Gatos Weekly *News*, the first newspaper in Los Gatos. *(Photo courtesy Mrs. Leland Walker)*

Titles of newspapers published at various times by W. S. Walker. *(From originals supplied by the Leland Walker family)*

appearance. In 1886 L. B. Woodruff started the *Los Gatan* and it lasted a little over two years.

The maverick newspaper of the town was the Daily *Chronicle*, started in August 1893 by P. H. Jordan. Interested mostly in real estate, Jordan knew very little about journalism. He hired a "fire-eating" editor named Clancy. He was a fire-eating editor, indeed!! He made the fur fly, roasting everyone and everything. Going through its files one gets the idea that no one in town was good, honest or respectable except the editor. After a year Clancy ran out of people and things to roast, and money enough to keep going, and the Los Gatos *Chronicle* passed into history. It's doubtful that anyone in town regretted its passing. With the *Chronicle* and all the others gone, the Los Gatos *Mail* and the *News* were left to fight it out.

W. S. Walker returned to Los Gatos in 1892 and became the publisher of his former rival newspaper, the *Mail*. Trantham and Dodge were the publishers of the *News* and the hot rivalry between these two made exciting reading for the people of Los Gatos for several years. It seems that Walker, in order to attract subscribers, cut the price of his paper from $1.50 a year to 75 cents a year. The publishers of the *News* cut their price to 50 cents a year, and urged people to subscribe to their paper. "It is difficult to determine," it said in its columns on September 8, 1892, "how long opportunity will remain open; the price may drop to 25 cents or go back to $1.50 within a week. It all depends on our competitor, the *Mail*. That sheet inaugurated the cut-rate, and the *News* will stay with Mr. Walker as long as he lasts." Trantham said that they would keep cutting the price to half what the *Mail* cost "as long as that superannuated relic of typography continues his practical mode of warfare, and when he gives away his alms-soliciting publication we expect to go him one better by throwing in a chromo." The *News* said it would go back to

regular price of $1.50 only after the *Mail* returned to sanity and went back to legitimate business.

On August 15, 1894 the *News* made a personal attack on W. S. Walker of the *Mail*. It seems that Walker, who had used the services of the American Press Association, had dropped this service. The reason, reported the *News*, was that the press association had carried an article to the effect that the Los Gatos editor "got gloriously drunk because a school bond election didn't go his way."

Again on September 14, 1893 the *News* said that Walker's assertion that the *Mail* "is the only live paper" in the county was the assertion of a man seeking popularity through his own conceit. "A man of sound sense would hesitate a long time before proclaiming such a *non compos mentis* sheet as the *Mail* superior to all others."

On August 3, 1893, after Walker had petitioned the Town Trustees for a fair share of the town printing, the *News* reported that "after the docu-

Mr. C. C. Suydam, publisher of *The Enterprise*, and a leading business man in the 1890's and early 1900's. *(Courtesy of Mr. C. R. Suydam)*

Front page of *The Los Gatos Enterprise* for Nov. 29, 1894. *(Courtesy C. H. Suydam)*

---

ment had been read by the Town Clerk, a painful silence ensued, which was at last broken by an audible whisper from someone in the audience inquiring where that paper was published." The Trustees laid that petition on the table.

In August 1893 Walker complained that some people were circulating a paper to the effect that the *Mail* was strongly in favor of closing out the liquor bars then existing in Los Gatos. The *Mail* felt that "unfriendly persons" were behind this to "injure the business relations with some of our old patrons."

While the *Mail* was not rabidly prohibitionist it advocated leaving things alone. The town had outlawed saloons and that was that. "This is a model temperance town, there being only three places here where liquors are sold, two hotels and one saloon."[2]

Walker sold the *Mail* on September 14, 1894 to D. D. Bowman, of the Mountain View *Register* and the Saratoga *Sentinel*. The *News,* in announcing this said, "Wherever Mr. Walker's lot may be cast the *News* wishes him much success."

But the *News* had not yet heard the last of Mr. Walker. In his retirement, and before he moved to Santa Cruz, Walker often wrote articles for the *Mail*. One of the articles which brought on a clash with the *News* dealt with the Town Ordinance banning the beating of drums or making other loud noises on the streets of Los Gatos.[3] This was specifically aimed at the Salvation Army and its brass instruments and drums. Walker contended that the ordinance was not only discriminating against the Salvation Army but a silly non-enforceable law. "The ordinance," said Walker, "places a check on every individual who chances to use a drum, a horn or a whistle, etc. in connection with his business or recreation on the streets of Los Gatos. I regard the ordinance in question as un-Christian, uncharitable and un-American!"

Walker pointed out that such an ordinance, if carried to its logical conclusion, would exclude Fourth of July firecrackers, railroad train whistles or any other noise by a business establishment or society in the town. He said he was not defending the Salvation Army drummer or "any other noise maker in frightening horses or disturbing sick people. All this is wrong if done wantonly."

The *News* took issue with Walker, accusing him of harassing the Town Trustees. An article, sup-posedly written by "An Old Citizen" appeared on June 6, 1895 which roasted Walker for his stand. Never afraid of a journalistic exchange, Walker replied in an article in the *Mail* entitled, "And You Too Brutus." Among the barbs in his reply were: "Why did he not sign his individual name to his gatling gun. I know not, perhaps he reasons (and wisely too) that some individuals look better while their heads are covered up and concluded to put his light under the bushel."

Continuing his facetious reply, Walker said "Old Citizen shake! I respect old age---always did---and if there is one thing in this world of good things that I love better than another, it is 'An Old Citizen'---the older the better I love him."

He reminded his readers that it is a sad day when one sees his pet schemes and cherished objects of life's ambitious aims slip from one's grasp one by one. But all these trials and disappointments do not seem half so sad as the "rebuke" by "An Old Citizen". And then he poeticizes:

"Old Citizen" shake---I'm half amused;
I've laughed till I am sore---
You rebuke me (I'm some better now),
Please don't rebuke some more.

"Old Citizen" you're a crusher,
And when you put up your 'dukes',
I'll know just what to look for---
One of those sad rebukes.

The whale, it swallowed Jonah,
Then it went on shore and puked;
That was sad, but not so bad
As it is to be rebuked.

Ending his "refutation" Walker got in one more dig when he said:

"P.S.---As I intend to go to Santa Cruz County in a few days to be gone an indefinite period, I have made arrangements with a 'kid' from the fourth grade in the public schools to look after 'Old Citizen' during my absence.

---W. S. Walker"

Later Newspapers

Los Gatos enjoyed the luxury of two newspapers until 1916. In February 1915 W. H. B. Trantham and Edgar Williams obtained control of the *Mail*. Andrew Falch became the editor and manager, and on July 1, 1916 Falch became the owner of the combined newspapers. The Los Gatos *Mail-News* was the only Los Gatos paper for many years. Falch changed the date of publication from Friday to Thursday and made the paper a prosperous enterprise.

In 1925 Llewellyn Peck of Saratoga was publishing the Saratoga *Star*. Hoping to branch out, Mr. Peck entered the Los Gatos field by starting the Los Gatos *Star*. It soon consolidated with the *Mail-News*.

In the fall of 1927 Hiland Baggerly gave up the San Jose *News* which he had been publishing, and purchased the *Mail-News* from Falch. Charles Saylor was the editor. Baggerly was an excellent journalist. His "Man on The Street" column was read throughout the county. On October 27, 1927 Hiland Baggerly told his readers what the policy of the paper would be.

"Under the new administration," he said, "the *Mail-News* will carry no party flag. The time has come, we believe, when parties mean much less than they once did. People are now voting for men, not for parties---at least the thoughtful people are. We voted for Theo. Roosevelt and we were equally proud to vote for Woodrow Wilson. So the *Mail-News* will stand for independence in political action, but whatever it stands for it will always be ready to give the other fellow a hearing in its columns."

In February 1928 the *Mail-News* took over the Mountain *Realty* which had been started by J. J. Bamber at Skyline in 1903. This gave increased circulation to the Los Gatos paper. On October 1, 1929 Baggerly also purchased the Saratoga *Star* and the Los Gatos *Star* from L. B. Peck. Mr. Peck became the editor of the *Mail-News* in 1931 after Chas. Saylor moved to Nevada, and retained this position for 11 years. With the entire West Valley to draw from Mr. Baggerly's paper grew in circulation, popularity and influence.

Mr. Baggerly made good his promise of "honest and fearless reporting." It resulted in a famous court case, testing the issue of freedom of the press. In July, 1929, a San Francisco socialite, Josephine Grant, was arrested in San Jose for drunken driving and possession of intoxicating liquor. She was also accused of driving recklessly, striking another car and failing to stop and give her name to the other car owner. The case came before Judge Percy O'Connor, of San Jose, who gave Josephine Grant a mild reprimand and set her free.

This was too much for the Los Gatos *Mail-News.* On July 25, 1929 the paper severely criticized Judge O'Connor for his leniency toward Miss Grant. A common person, said the article, "would have been given a $250 fine and a jail sentence." Could it be that Josephine Grant's wealth and social position influenced the judge's decision? "That Judge O'Connor would have dealt with the ordinary defendant as he dealt with Josephine Grant, is beyond belief. His past record as judge shows too clearly that of her he made a brilliant exception, that it will stand out as a bright light in his career, pointing to the power and influence of money." Although this was signed "A San Jose

W. H. B. Trantham, part owner of the Los Gatos Weekly *News* 1895, and after 1905, the sole editor and publisher, competing with the *Mail*. *(Courtesy of Carl Lipscomb)*

Andrew E. Falch, editor and publisher of the Los Gatos *Mail–News* 1916–1927. *(Courtesy Mrs. Harold Eichelberger and Mrs. Ross Dwyer)*

Front page of the short-lived *Chronicle* for Sept. 28, 1894. Founded by P. H. Jordan in 1893 it lasted about a year. *(From the original, courtesy of the Leland Walker family)*

Subscriber" Baggerly, as befits a good editor, assumed full responsibility for its contents.

Judge O'Connor sued the *Mail-News* and Hi Baggerly for criminal libel. It was the issue of Freedom of the Press. Baggerly's attorneys were George W. Patterson, Nils Writman and Senator Herbert C. Jones of Los Gatos. The trial aroused the interest of people beyond Santa Clara County and even beyond the State of California. Dare a newspaper print the truth, even when it reflects on the integrity of a judge?

On August 5, 1929 the court rendered its decision in favor of Baggerly. The Los Gatos publisher did not consider it a personal triumph. He wrote, "In no sense do we regard it as a personal victory, but rather a triumph for freedom of the press which is being assailed in other parts of America today."

The *Mail-News* and Hi Baggerly's "Man on The Street" column continued in popularity. The paper outgrew its old quarters in the Rex Hotel Building, and in January 1930, moved into its beautiful new building on Bean Avenue, just off Santa Cruz Avenue.

Another newspaper made its appearance in Los Gatos on November 1, 1937, when the Los Gatos *Times* was published by L. B. Garrett. It was located on Main Street and Lundy Lane. In July 1939, Mr. Lloyd E. Smith purchased the *Times* from Mr. Garrett, but continued at the same location, although taking additional space. Lloyd E. Smith had been publisher of the Gilroy Evening *Dispatch* and the Gilroy Weekly *Advocate*. He also wrote a regular column, "It Happens to Me" for the San Jose Evening *News,* which was widely read.

Lloyd E. Smith with the Speaker of the U. S. House of Representatives, the Hon. Joe Martin. Smith (on the left) was editor and publisher of the Los Gatos *Times* from 1939 to 1952. *(Courtesy Los Gatos* Times–Observer*)*

Hiland Baggerly, Editor and Publisher, Los Gatos *Mail–News* 1927 to 1944. *(Courtesy John Baggerly) (Original photo in San Jose* Evening News*)*

In a long editorial on August 4, 1939 Lloyd E. Smith explained the policy of the paper and gave some of his own philosophy.

> "We believe that the simple things are the real things in life. We should like to see a return to the old-fashioned religious worship, where whole families go to church, stand up and sing hymns, bow their heads reverently in prayer, and, in general, strive to live the Golden Rule. We believe that our civilization needs some such revival."

To this we might all add "Amen".

Hiland Baggerly died in 1944 and his son John published the *Mail-News* for a while. Charles Saylor, who had been the original editor under Mr. Hiland Baggerly from 1927 to 1931, came back to Los Gatos in 1942 to edit his old paper. On December 2, 1949 the *Mail-News* was sold to Lloyd E. Smith and his *Times.* The *Times* had gone daily in August of that year, but Smith kept the *Mail-News* as a weekly along with his *Daily Times.* On February 20, 1953 the *Mail-News* was finally discontinued and Los Gatos once again had only one newspaper.

Lloyd Smith expanded the *Daily Times* and secured the confidence of the people of Los Gatos through his fearless editorial policy. One of the great accomplishments of Lloyd E. Smith's *Daily Times* was the successful campaign to assure the safety of the Lexington Dam. There was consider-

able question concerning its safety in the early stages of construction. Editorials in the *Daily Times* between July 15 and September 15, 1952 challenged the safety of the dam as originally planned. His editorials were largely responsible for the request by the Water District for an additional $3,500,000 bond issue to cover the additional cost over the original estimates. Because of the *Daily Times* editorials the State Engineer demanded deeper foundations and a wider base.

Editor Smith gained the admiration and respect of journalists throughout the country. Hans Christian Adamson, editor of *The Log,* official publication of the Circumnavigator's Club of New York, wrote of the Los Gatos *Daily Times* in the Fall 1952 issue, Smith's paper "has no syndicated columnists to pollute its contents. When the Los Gatos *Daily Times* has an editorial it planks it on its front page. When it comes to news it treats news for what it is worth." Editor Adamson goes on to say that if newspapers were, like the Los Gatos *Daily Times,* more concerned about the neglected responsibility of the Press, instead of the grossly abused Freedom of the Press, we would have a more competent press devoted to maintaining the rights of a free people.[4]

Another innovation by Lloyd Smith was the "Special Editions." His "Progress Editions" and his "Extras" on the night of local elections were especially valuable to the community. During World War II he issued special editions listing the local men in the service of their country. In

John S. Baggerly who published the *Mail–News* for a time after Hiland Baggerly's death in 1944. He is now associated with the Los Gatos *Times–Observer*. *(Photo by Peggy Hitchcock of the* Times–Observer*)*

George R. Kane, Editor and Publisher, Los Gatos *Times–Observer* since 1958. *(*Times–Observer *photo)*

September 1948 the *Times* moved into its new building at 114 Royce Street.

In November 1952 Lloyd E. Smith retired from the newspaper business because of his health. His papers were sold to Joseph Houghteling and Patrick Peabody. John Baggerly, who had retained his interest in the *Mail-News* after the death of his father, was also a member of the publishing company.

The Times-Observer

Joseph Houghteling edited the *Times* until May 1956. At that time Mr. George Kane, editor and publisher of the Gilroy *Evening Dispatch* became the editor. Kane and Peabody also published the Sunnyvale *Standard,* and in 1947 they started the Saratoga *Observer.* The Los Gatos Publishing

Company was the owner of the paper. Joseph Houghteling was President and Patrick Peabody was Associate publisher. Peabody resigned his office of Associate publisher on April 1, 1958 and George Kane succeeded him as Vice-President of the local publishing company and the Gilroy Publishing Company.

Under Mr. Kane the *Times-Observer* became a well-established newspaper. It has been given a number of awards in recent years. In May 1965 a nine-section New Look Edition was published which won a top award at the California Newspaper Publishers' Association Convention in Palm Springs. The citation was given for "superior continuity, organization, and effectiveness of coverage of all aspects of community living." The award was in the category of 10,000 or less circulation. Another honor came to the Los Gatos paper in February 1967, when the same organization awarded the *Times-Observer* first place in

Business advertisements in the Weekly *News* and the Los Gatos *Mail*. From original files. *(Courtesy Mrs. Leland Walker)*

C. V. Gopher Trap!

DIRECTIONS FOR SETTING:

Scoop out the Gopher Hole; set the trap as represented by cut, then shove the trap well into the gopher hole, covering up the points thoroughly. Set lightly, so that the dirt, when shoved out by the gopher, will spring the trap.

This trap has been on the market a long time and it gives entire satisfaction.

FOR SALE BY ALL DEALERS.

Cushing Gopher Trap which was made earlier than the Macabee trap. Los Gatos Weekly News Jan. 8, 1886

LOS GATOS Kindergarten

Pupils taken from Four to seven years of age.

Tuition: $2.50 per Month

——LOCATION——
Mrs. Gray's Cottage Opposite Keeley Institute.

Miss Lulu Stonehouse,
TEACHER

Private Kindergarten seeks pupils. Los Gatos Mail Aug. 6, 1896

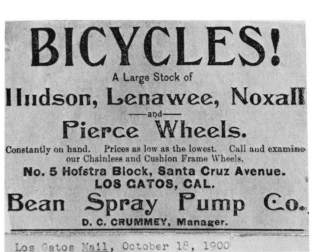

BICYCLES!

A Large Stock of

Hudson, Lenawee, Noxall
—and—
Pierce Wheels.

Constantly on hand.   Prices as low as the lowest.   Call and examine our Chainless and Cushion Frame Wheels.

No. 5 Hofstra Block, Santa Cruz Avenue.
LOS GATOS, CAL.

Bean Spray Pump Co.

D. C. CRUMMEY, Manager.

Los Gatos Mail, October 18, 1900

53

the "Youth Interest" classification. This was in competition with daily newspapers in the state with a circulation up to 15,000. Publisher George Kane received the plaque from Governor Ronald Reagan at the San Francisco meeting of the Newspaper Publishers' Association.

The Los Gatos *Times-Observer* dropped its daily status on March 1, 1969, and appeared twice weekly. From February 2, 1970 to April 14, 1970 it was published three times a week. Since then it has been issued two times a week—Tuesdays and Thursdays. The newest newspaper in Los Gatos is the Los Gatos *Weekly*. Started by Dan Pulcrano in March 1982, it now appears every Wednesday. It carries on the high standards set by all the previous newspapers in Los Gatos.

As can be seen from all that has been recorded in this chapter, Los Gatos has been singularly fortunate in its newspapers. The editors have all been men of high caliber and the newspapers have been courageous in fighting for what they thought was right.

FOOTNOTES

1. Los Gatos Weekly *News,* May 1882.
2. Los Gatos *Mail,* August 31, 1893.
3. Town Board *Minutes,* Bk II, p. 230. This ordinance was passed May 6, 1895.
4. *The Log* of the Circumnavigators Club, Vol. 40, No. 2, (Fall 1952) p. 9.

Town election results as reported in the Los Gatos *Mail* April 12, 1884.

Municipal Ticket

The following is the result of the town election, held on Monda giving the names of the candidates and the number of votes they r ceived:

Trustees.

1	THOS. J. DAVIS.	REPUBLICAN.	325
2	L. S. EDWARDS.	INDEPENDENT.	41
3	J. P. LANGFORD.	INDEPENDENT.	48
4	GEO. R. LEWIS.	INDEPENDENT.	108
5	FEN MASSOL.	REPUBLICAN.	245
6	H. SCHOMBERG.	REPUBLICAN.	238
7	PETER SIMON.	INDEPENDENT.	79
8			
9			
10			

Trustee, Unexpired Term.

11.	E. N. DAVIS.	REPUBLICAN.	298
12.	D. J. FARLEY.	INDEPENDENT.	66
13.			

Clerk and Ex-Officio Assessor.

14.	J. D. BEGGS.	INDEPENDENT.	161
15.	GEO. A. BUTLER.	REPUBLICAN.	217
16.			

Marshal and Ex-Officio Tax and License Collector.

17.	M. F. BLANK.	REPUBLICAN.	218
18.	W. G. McMILLAN.	INDEPENDENT.	154
19.			

Treasurer.

20.	J. J. STANFIELD.	REPUBLICAN.	247
21.	L. C. TRAILER.	INDEPENDENT.	133
22.			

CHAPTER VI

Early Town Government and Politics

From Temporary to Permanent Headquarters

FOR A short time after incorporation in 1887 the town was quiet and the 1645 people of Los Gatos were content with the five Trustees — Palmer Perkins, Herman Sund, D. D. Holland, J. W. Lyndon and George Seanor. Having no town hall in which to meet, they met in the office of Justice A. E. Wilder. On September 13, 1889, the owners of the Commercial Bank Building on the corner of Main and Oak Streets, near the railroad — now Main and Montebello Way — offered to rent a room in the basement for town offices. "The hall is large and well-ventilated. The vault is fire-proof and is provided with a combination lock thus making it secure for the safe-keeping of the town papers." The town leased the basement for $15.00 a month.[1]

In March 1895 the Town Board asked Herman Sund to lease the Keeley Institute building as a town hall for one year at a rental of $12.50 a month. The edifice had been built by Sund for the Institute, which will be discussed in a later chapter.

The Town Board had appointed a committee to investigate possible sites for a town hall and jail. A site on the corner of College and Wilcox Avenues was suggested. But the owner would not sell just a part of the land. He wanted $2000 for the entire parcel, a price too high for the Town Board. Other possible sites were Seanor's lot on East Main Street, about where the Masonic Temple now stands, and the McMurtry lot. The former could be had for $1600, and the McMurtry lot could not be had unless all of the land, plus the barn, were purchased.

In the meantime, on September 25, 1891 the Board had authorized the town attorney to draw up an ordinance to submit to a vote of the people a bond issue to build a jail, a town hall and complete the sewer lines. On April 28, 1893 the Los Gatos *News* argued for the bond issue. "The Town Hall," said the *News,* "is small, damp and poorly lighted. The fire department is meager and the jail is a disgrace to any civilized community." It urged immediate action to bring about improvements in all these areas — the jail, fire department, sewer and city hall.

A breakdown of the bond requests was as follows:

For sewer	$12,000
Town Hall	10,000
Electric light plant	10,000
Town Hall site	2,500
Fire Alarm system	2,500
Purchase of Park	2,500

The Town Trustees asked people to come to the town hall on March 31 from 1 to 8 P. M. to cast an "informal" vote on these issues. In the "informal" vote, all bonds received a majority "yes" vote.

Building on left foreground served as the Town Hall from 1895 to 1913. It was originally erected for the Keeley Cure Institute in 1891. It was located where the Methodist and Recreation Department parking lot is today. *(Library Collection)*

However, when the true election was held on July 22, 1901 only the sewer bonds passed. Less than half of the voters bothered to come to the polls. This probably should teach a lesson of some kind: "If at first you succeed, don't try again."

The town still needed a town hall and other civic improvements. Although it had purchased six acres from Alexander English for the town dump, and property on Lundy Lane in October 1906 for a corporation yard from Mary L. Miller for $200, no great progress had been made on other civic projects, including a site for a town hall.

It was not until 1912 that concrete plans were made for civic improvements. The Town Trustees viewed various sites for the town hall and studied means of financing civic improvement projects. On August 12, 1912 Trustee R. P. Doolan made a motion in the Town Board that a bond issue for $10,000 for a Town Hall be submitted to the people.

On September 4, Trustee W. C. Short introduced Ordinance #153 calling for a bond election for town improvements, the cost of which were too great for ordinary revenue. This ordinance was passed on September 10. The election date was set for September 30, 1912. The following bond issues were presented.

$10,000 for Town Hall

$ 6,000 for park acquisition and conditioning

$30,000 for sewer

$35,000 to pay 48% of the cost of acquisition, construction, and completion of curbs, gutters, grading and paving of streets — Main Street on to Bay View, Santa Cruz from Broadway to Saratoga Avenue.

Erickson's Blacksmith Shop, corner east Main and Jackson Ave. 1900. Served as Ferini's garage for many years. A creek ran underneath the building. *(Library Collection)*

Although these bonds passed by large majorities, opposition voices were loud. Attorney H. A. Hardinge sent out flyers claiming the Town Board had no jurisdiction to call a bond election for improvement of certain streets since the owners of the property had already improved the streets — particularly West Main Street. He further stated that the ordinance had not been published as required by law; that the 10th of September meeting of the Board was not a regular meeting day; that the ordinance did not state where the park was to be located, nor where the Town Hall was to be erected. He also objected to the sewer dump on ground that it was too small and too expensive.[2]

Attorney Hardinge was a "thorn in the side" of the Town Board on numerous occasions. As early as May 1, 1911 he sent a letter to the Board saying that as an elector he objected to the payment of any claim connected with the alleged election to be held or attempted to be held on April 17. He objected to paying any claim against the town amounting to more than $100 unless contracts were let out to lowest bidder. "I also object to the wholesale allowance of clames (sic) against said town, and insist that each and every claim against said town be acted upon separately."[3]

The feeling against Mr. Hardinge was reflected in a poem by Wells McGrady, published in the *Mail* February 25, 1909.

Lawyer Hardinge

Lawyer Hardinge, Lawyer Hardinge
Once a person of renown,
You've abandoned your profession
to besmirch this foothill town.

Native Sons of the Golden West Parade Sept. 9, 1892. *(Library Collection)*

The winning float in the May Day parade, May 1, 1901. Judge and Mrs. J. R. Welch owned the much-decorated auto and are seated in the front seat. Two cups were presented for this float: One was for the best decorated auto, presented by the Santa Clara Auto Club; the other for the best decorated car driven by a lady, presented by Mrs. William Randolph Hearst Sr. Those in the second row are Camellia M. Metzger and Judge F. B. Brown and Ione Welch. In the rear seat are Mrs. F. B. Brown, Judge and Mrs. J. E. Richards on her left. Cars in the background are the electric interurban trains that ran between San Jose and Los Gatos. *(Courtesy Ione Welch and Los Gatos Museum)*

Lawyer Hardinge, Lawyer Hardinge,
   How we tremble at your frown!
Can it be you're so relentless
   As to crush our growing town?

We have read your late effusion
   In the print at Santa Cruz.
Was your great mind so affected
   By absorbing too much booze?

All the stories you have printed,
   Can in no wise harm this town.
Lawyer Hardinge go you way back,
   Shut your mouth and sit right down.

But Lawyer Hardinge would not shut up. Believing that in a democracy criticism is necessary he watched every opportunity to disagree with the city Fathers.

After passage of the much-needed bonds the Town Board passed a Resolution of thanks on October 7, 1912. It addressed it to the people "for their expression of civic pride in voting the $81,000 bonds and showing thereby that they had confidence in the Town Board." The Resolution gave special thanks to the Chamber of Commerce, the Civic League and the women of the History Club for "helping to bring about this result which means so much to the future prosperity and welfare of Los Gatos."[4]

The town hall site, which is part of the present location of the Civic Center, was purchased from Mrs. Schofield for $3,500. In March 1921 Senator and Mrs. Sanborn Young donated the lot adjoining the Town Hall to the town. Miss Donna Winning, the Town Clerk, upon order from the Town Board, wrote a letter of appreciation for the generous gift. "The spirit of good-will and co-operation manifest in such action on your part is a source of real satisfaction to the Board."

Bids were called for the Town Hall and the P. F. Speidel Company of San Francisco was awarded the contract on June 30, 1913. The Town Hall cost $8,959 and was completed in December, the first Trustees' meeting being held there on December 22, 1913. Los Gatos now had a town hall of which it was very proud.

Early Town Board Actions

After organizing itself, setting the time and place of meeting, and assigning the salaries and bonds of certain officers, the Town Board was ready for business. The first appointment by the Board was the Poundmaster, whose office was created by Ordinance #6 on October 12, 1887. Ordinance #11 forbade playing ball on the streets of the town.

Like many other California towns, Los Gatos collected a poll tax which was opposed by most people. This small tax could be paid either by cash or by working for the town. Because of the strong

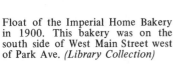

Float of the Imperial Home Bakery in 1900. This bakery was on the south side of West Main Street west of Park Ave. *(Library Collection)*

The John Bean and Dr. Robert Gober residence on Bean and Santa Cruz Avenues. The Crummey and Bean families and children are on the porch and in the yard. The house was built in 1889 and demolished in the 1930's to make room for business establishments. *(Courtesy Nancy Gober Schmidt and the Los Gatos Museum)*

opposition to the tax the Town Board passed Ordinance #99 on June 6, 1898 abolishing it.

The office of Town Attorney was created by Ordinance #101 on October 3, 1898. R. F. Robertson was appointed to this post, acting as legal advisor to the town and prosecuting all violations of local ordinances. His fee was $15 for each misdemeanor prosecuted. He was paid out of fines collected plus such other compensation as the Board might grant.

Since the Town Marshal operated only in the day time and since his duties also included collection of town taxes, there was need for further protection. The businessmen asked the Town Board for a night watchman to be paid by contributions from the business houses of town. However, it was better to have him Deputised, and that required Board approval. At a special meeting of the Town Board on April 30, 1888 Claude Shannon was approved as Deputy Marshal after bondsmen passed his appointment. He was not paid from the town treasury but from contributions by business people.

The trouble with this arrangement was that some businessmen felt that the watchman was protecting those who contributed most toward his pay and forgetting the the small contributor. The result was that the Town Board agreed, on November 4, 1889 to hire the night watchman at a salary of $50 a month.

Town ordinances reflected the mode of life of the times. Some examples of ordinances passed during the early years of town government illustrate this. Ordinance #48 limited the speed of vehicles across the Main Street bridge. "No person shall ride or drive on, over, or across the bridge on Main Street faster than a walk." It also forbade the herding of more than 500 sheep or 25 cattle across the bridge at one time. Ordinance #20 made it illegal to leave horses on the street without being tied to a post. An ordinance of 1890 made it unlawful to lead horses and cattle along the sidewalks of the town. Fines up to $50 or ten days in jail or both were to be meted out to violators of these ordinances.

Another ordinance dealing with speed was #110, which limited the speed of horses, bicycles and automobiles to 12 miles an hour on the streets of Los Gatos. This followed the County Ordinance which set the speed at 12 miles an hour on valley

A page from the Los Gatos Directory 1902. *(Courtesy Charles Torrey)*

LOS GATOS CITY
1902

CITY GOVERNMENT.

BOARD OF TRUSTEES.

J. H. Lyndon, President.
R. R. Bell.
D. C. Crummey,
Jas. H. Pearce.
B. P. Shuler.

CITY OFFICIALS.

City Attorney—R. F. Robertson.
City Clerk and Ex-Officio Assessor—J. F. Henderson.
City Marshal and Ex-Officio Tax Collector—E. E. Springer.
City Treasurer—F. F. Watkins.
City Engineer—C. H. Pieper.
Town Recorder—E. C. Farley.
Chief of the Fire Department, Jos. A. Freshour.

STANDING COMMITTEES.

Finance—J. H. Lyndon, R. R. Bell, D. C. Crummey.
Sewerage—J. H. Pearce, B. P. Shuler, J. H. Lyndon.
Claims—D. C. Crummey, J. H. Pearce, B. P. Shuler.
Fire and Water—R. R. Bell, D. C. Crummey, J. H. Pearce.
Streets—B. P. Shuler, J. H. Pearce, J. H. Lyndon.
Library—R. R. Bell, D. C. Crummey, B. P. Shuler.

BOARD OF SCHOOL TRUSTEES.

R. R. Bell, W. H. B. Trantham, C. H. Wheeler.

BOARD OF HEALTH.

President, Dr. S. G. Moore,
Secretary, Dr. F. W. Knowles.
Dr. R. P. Gober, Dr. R. A. Urquhart.

Thomas Cleland, son of William Cleland, after whom Cleland Avenue was named. *(Courtesy Los Gatos Museum)*

George S. McMurtry, about 1884. Son of Dr. W. S. McMurtry, George was Town Treasurer for more than 40 years. *(Los Gatos Museum)*

Two prominent early physicians, Dr. Robert Gober and Dr. Frank Knowles, 1885. *(Museum Collection)*

roads and forbade automobiles on the Mount Hamilton Road and the Santa Cruz Road.

Ordinance #32 of February 1890 provided for the appointment of a City Engineer and a Superintendent of Streets. Mr. N. E. Beckwith was appointed City Engineer, and Mr. E. W. Keifer was made Street Superintendent. The latter's salary was set at $30 a month, raised to $45 in January 1907. Ordinance #133 dated March 2, 1908 made it unlawful to ride or operate any vehicle at a speed greater than one mile in six minutes. Violators were fined $100 or 30 days in jail or both. Obviously they believed in stringent punishment for violations of the law.

Health was of concern to the Town Board. People complained of wandering animals and filth in the streets and alleys. Ordinance #75 of September 1895, provided for the burial of dead animals and "the arrest of chickens, geese, ducks, pigs, hogs, sheep, goats, calves, cows, and horses if found upon the public streets" or upon private property without the consent of the owner or occupant. All dead animals were to be buried at least 4 feet underground, "by people upon whose premises they are found." Persons who failed to report the death were subject to arrest.

As a further health precaution the Board created a Board of Health in April 1908. The first Board of Health consisted of Dr. E. S. Yelland and W. S. Short, who were to serve for two years, and Dr. Frank Knowles, Dr. Urquart and S. D. Balch to serve for four years.[5] This Board reported numerous unhealthy conditions which no doubt led to Ordinance #136 in September 1908. This provided that horses, cows, pigs, chickens, etc. should be kept in clean quarters. Manure was to be removed every two weeks between April 1 and October 1, and at least every 4 weeks from October 1 to April 1. Furthermore, not more than **two pigs per house-** hold were to be kept in the city limits, and these had to be more than 300 feet from a house. All hotels, restaurants etc. were to have recepticles for "slop, garbage and waste materials" and remove such at least every three days.

Examples of the small but numerous problems dealt with by the Town Board are many. One such example is a request by Henry Mineo on October 6, 1902 for $38.75 damages to himself and his bicycle. Mr. Mineo claimed that there had been no warning at the bridge while it was under repair and he ran into it. He asked for $20.00 for loss of time, $10.00 for doctor bills, and $8.75 for repair of his bicycle. On November 2, 1902 the Board ordered this amount paid.[6]

In June 1903 Mrs. A. K. Smith sent a communication to the Board saying that she was being annoyed by boys and stray chickens and stock running on her premises. She insisted the Marshal was not enforcing the ordinances and she was annoyed that he had sent her a notice in regard to cleaning the grass from the sidewalk in front of her premises.

Mr. Bell, of the Board, advised Mrs. Smith that the Marshal could not take up the stock or chickens unless he found them on her premises and that the notice regarding grass on her sidewalk had been sent to all who had not cleaned their walks.

But that was not the last of Mrs. Smith. On July 17, 1905 Mrs. Smith filed another complaint on exactly the same subjects. On August 7, 1905 Mr. J. P. Mogenson, the proprietor of the Lyndon Hotel, complained that the Interurban Railroad was loading and unloading freight in front of the hotel. He also complained that the Southern Pacific was loading and unloading freight cars on the track opposite the hotel, both companies leaving debris for the town to clean up. He asked that both be requested to cease such activities.[7]

Gober family on porch of their home. Left to right are Dr. Gober, Mrs. Nellie Bean Gober, daughters Nancy and Helen Gober and Grandma Bean (Mrs. John Bean) about 1900. *(Courtesy Nancy Gober Schmidt and Los Gatos Museum)*

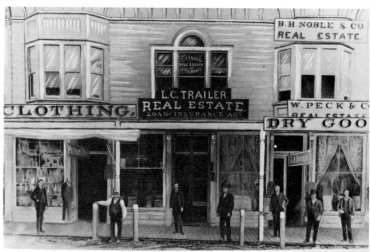

The Parr Block before 1895 at 140 West Main Street on the north side. Destroyed by the fire of October 13, 1901. Ford's Opera House, later Crider's Dept. Store and now the Opera House Antiques have since been located on the property. *(Library Collection)*

A business license was established by Ordinance #141 in December 1906. It provided for a regular schedule of payments. An establishment or an individual who did $5000 worth of business a month paid $2.00 a month for license.

$2,500 to $5,000 paid $1.50 a month
1,500 to 2,500 paid 1.00 a month
500 to 1,500 paid 75 cents a month
300 to 500 paid 50 cents a month
less than $300 paid 25 cents a month

This was a lengthy ordinance, dealing with everything from merry-go-rounds, cigar stores, organ grinders to peddlers and delivery wagons. This detailed law probably resulted from complaints that some persons were selling milk without a permit. The complaint was made by Zeigler, Woodward and Mullen, milk dealers who wanted protection for their business.

An interesting request came to the Board in March 1890. It seems that a "book agent" who claimed to be a reformed criminal, wanted to "make an honest living." He asked to be excused from paying the $10 a month license fee required at that time. He made it clear that if the Board did not grant him special favors, he would be obliged to go back to his old trades of thieving and gambling for a living. He even threatened to burn up the town unless his request was granted. The Board refused to be blackmailed and refused his request.

Ordinance #138 forbade awnings of other materials than cloth or canvas to be permitted to hang or project across from any building, post or pole, over or across the sidewalk, streets or alleys in town. Awnings had to be securely fastened to buildings and no awning was to hang less than 7 feet from the sidewalk, nor could it project beyond the width of the sidewalk. A fine of not less than $10 nor more than $50 or 25 days in jail, was to be given violators.

By Ordinance #139, August 16, 1909, Taylor Street was changed to Glenridge Avenue. Homes in this area were selling fast. Several years before this, when it was still known as Glenridge Park, lots were selling for $200 to $300 each.

The Cemetery Problem

One of the first major problems facing the town was the matter of the old cemetery. This doleful spot was located on the land occupied later by Hunt Brothers Cannery, and now the Little Village stores on the corner of Saratoga and Santa Cruz Avenues. The land had originally been given as a cemetery site by a Los Gatos family on the unusual condition that the land would revert to the family in case it was no longer used as a cemetery. Miss Dora Rankin, writing in her "As It Was" column in the *Times-Observer* on February 16, 1965, recalled that "It was truly a spooky place, all overrun with shrubbery and a mass of oak trees." At the very corner "was a little grave with the inscription 'Willie has gone to God'." Miss Rankin, along with others, has wondered all these years who was "little Willie."

As early as 1889 it was evident that a new cemetery was needed as no ground was left for new burials. Furthermore, the growth of the town had resulted in the complete encirclement of the old graveyard. Augustine Nicholson offered a 17½ acre tract of land to the town for a new cemetery, a tract encompassing the area on Wheeler Avenue and Whitney. The town Fathers accepted this offer with gratitude. After all, it was both free and located some distance out of town! However, B. L. Bartlett presented a petition to the Trustees on February 4, 1889 signed by 210 tax payers, objecting to the use of this land as a cemetery. People had bought land in that area with the intention of building homes. A burial ground would inhibit the growth of the town in that direction. "No section of the town," said the petitioners, "should have any nuisance thrust upon them or anything else that so hinders the advance in the price of real estate." On February 8, 1889 the Town Board deeded the land back to Mr. Nicholson, with a Resolution commending him for his generosity.

During 1889 some members of the Odd Fellows Lodge studied the cemetery problem. On December 9, this group, as individuals, not as members of the lodge, organized the Los Gatos Cemetery Association. It was incorporated with J. H. Lyndon, President, E. E. Dow, Vice-President, R. F. Robertson, Secretary and Charles F. Wilson, Treasurer. The other Directors included E. C. Yocco, Daniel Walker and L. E. Hamilton. The proposed new cemetery was located on the Almaden Road about 3½ miles from town, and originally consisted of 13½ acres of ground.

The Town Board passed an ordinance on July 1, 1890 prohibiting further interments in the old cemetery and E. E. Place began to remove bodies from the graves. An interesting incident occurred in connection with this. The city had prohibited further burials since they did not want to remove newly-interred bodies. However, an old man insisted that his wife be buried in the family plot instead of the new cemetery. To prevent the city from serving him with an injunction, he and his friends buried the body at midnight on Saturday when the city offices would be closed the next day and no injunction could be served until after the body was buried.[9]

Angelia Castro Lucero, known by all as "Old Tamale." She lived in one of the little houses on Fiesta Way. She made tamales and delivered them around town in a little red wagon. She kept them warm by wrapping newspapers around them and covering the wagon with a blanket. Mr. Edw. C. Yocco supplied her with the meat used in the tamales. After Mr. Yocco's death she made a quilt for Mrs. E. C. Yocco, patched from pieces of materials used in her skirts and aprons. Mrs. Mary Yocco Rugh still has this quilt. Mrs. Lucero died February 14, 1902 and is buried in the Los Gatos Cemetery. *(Picture and story from Mrs. Mary Yocco Rugh)*

Cleared of most of the bodies the land was used for commercial and industrial purposes. Hunt Brothers Cannery occupied the land until it left Los Gatos. Then the Effie Walton Realty office developed the area for shops. No one would ever think that the Little Village Shops are located on land once a "spooky cemetery" where "Little Willie" lies buried.

The new Los Gatos Cemetery operated at first on a virtual "shoestring." Director E. C. Yocco acquired majority control of the stock and upon his death, his wife managed the cemetery. She bought more shares of the corporation and managed it, with the aid of her son, Edward S. Yocco, until 1940. In that year, Edward took over the management and expanded the holdings. In 1962 the Yocco family---Edward S. and his sister, Mrs. Mary Rugh---sold their majority stock in the corporation. The new Los Gatos Cemetery Corporation now operates the Almaden Road interment grounds.

Edw. C. Yocco, owner of Los Gatos Meat Market and member of School Trustees. Picture taken about 1900. *(Courtesy Yocco family and Los Gatos Museum)*

DIED, LOS GATOS, JULY 1ST., '06.
Cause of Death PROHIBITION.
THIS PROPERTY FOR SALE AT
D—, Dead, Dull, Dry Town Prices.
APPLY AT ROOM 10 KNOX BLOCK SAN JOSE CAL.

Posters in the Prohibition election of April 1906. *(Courtesy Los Gatos Museum. Photos by Don Wiley, Los Gatos High School Photography class)*

On April 11TH What Shall The Harvest Be?
TEMPERANCE OR PROHIBITION
WHICH PRODUCES WHICH PRODUCES
SOBRIETY AND DRUNKENESS AND
ADVANCEMENT STAGNATION

Saloons an Issue in Los Gatos

Like most towns in California the Los Gatos Town Board had the privilege of issuing licenses for saloons. As dispensors of alcoholic drinks the saloons became so numerous that the people began to demand some limitations on the "dens of iniquity." As early as June 14, 1888 Trustee W. J. Parr gave notice of intention to "move an ordinance closing saloons on Sunday." Action on this was not surprisingly deferred. On May 12, 1889 Mr. Gibson, a member of the Town Board, said that the $5.00 a month license on saloons was a disgrace, and moved that all should be closed. Herman Sund seconded the motion, not because he wanted to get rid of saloons, but because he did not want a higher license fee required of them. A higher license, he said, would "cause the saloons to poison the whole town by selling poor whiskey." J.

W. Lyndon thought the Board had no power to do this without a vote of the people. Gibson then moved that the license be raised to $25.00 a quarter. The motion was adopted. Sund, who had voted against the motion, facetiously asked that all licenses for business be doubled.[10]

The fight was now on the issue of high license vs. prohibition. A special meeting of the Town Board was called for May 28 to consider adoption of an ordinance prohibiting the sale of distilled liquors. Long before the meeting time, the hall was filled with men and women. The women had dropped in to see "the final consummation of the act by which Los Gatos is to be freed from saloons." Trustee Lyndon still insisted that to outlaw saloons would mean the loss of much revenue to the town.

The local option ordinance was adopted unanimously on June 3, 1889. Los Gatos was now, supposedly, without saloons.

62

Ordinance #24 stated that it was unlawful for any person or persons "either as owner, principal, agent, servant or employer, to establish, open, keep, maintain, carry on, or assist in carrying on, within the corporate limits of the Town of Los Gatos, any tippling house, dram shop, cellar, saloon, bar, bar-room, sample room, or other place where spiritous, vinous, malt or mixed liquors are sold, or given away." It also forbade gambling rooms or other places of "indecent or immoral character." The sale of liquor for medicinal purposes was permitted if sold by a regularly licensed druggist upon the prescription by a physician entitled to practice medicine in the State."[11]

But all this did not settle the issue. On July 15, 1889 a petition signed by 176 citizens was presented to the Town Board asking for repeal of the Ordinance against saloons. Still another petition, signed by 210 people opposing repeal, was presented to the Board. The Board argued the matter at great length. Some favored a high license fee and others favored prohibition. The petition favoring repeal was signed by some important people of the town and could not be ignored. Dr. Robert Gober, Dr. Frank Knowles, Zepf Macabee, A. Berryman, James Stanfield, Ed. Yocco and Charles Wilcox were only a few of the names on the petition asking for repeal. The petition sternly argued that prohibition had resulted in stagnation of business, secret drinking and fraud. The spokesman for the anti-prohibitionists was Trustee C. F. Wilcox. According to him the town was losing business. Even closing saloons on Sunday was not good, for it took business away from the town. He propounded the remedy for intemperance was an enlightened public opinion.

After a heated debate, mostly between Trustees Gibson and Wilcox, Ordinance #27 was adopted on August 5, 1889. This was known as the High License Ordinance, requiring a license fee of $25.00 a quarter of all saloons.

But the issue still would not die. In November 1905 D. P. Simons introduced an ordinance to regulate the saloons. A petition had been presented, signed by 190 persons asking for strict regulation. They wanted an ordinance that would limit a saloon license to one year and force closing on Sundays and holidays. Saloons were also to be closed from 11 P.M. to 5 A.M. week-days. The Board decided to put the matter to a vote of the people.

Three petitions were presented to the Town Board on March 5, 1906 signed by 34 voters asking that the question of saloons be put on the ballot in April 1906. The resolution read: "There will be submitted to the electors of said town, at said election, the question whether or not the Board of Trustees shall license the sale of intoxicating liquor."

Feeling ran high and vocal before the election. The "wets," as usual, contended that prohibition would cut off a needed source of revenue. The "drys" put forth appeals to emotion. "Prohibition is bound to come. This generation may not be worthy of it. We as a town may go back to the wilderness for a year or two. But let it not be so; let us go forward." Another appeal was more dramatic: "Think of what is expected of us by our wives and children---think what we ought to be as patriots and Christians. Think of the husbands and brothers and sons sinking down into drunkards' graves every year."

Signs appeared on houses pleading their particular viewpoint. One such sign read:

"Wanted 1500 Suckers---to buy the vacant property in this Rank, Rotten, Rusty, Dull, Dead, dry town before we lose it for taxes. U may apply here. Died. Los Gatos, July 1, 1901. Cause of Death, PROHIBITION."

Mass meetings were held Sunday evenings. Reverend Robert Whitaker, pastor of the Baptist Church, was the leader of the "drys." Reverend Henry Wintler of the Presbyterian Church and former Councilman George Lews were among the other leaders of the prohibition group. On Sunday evening April 3, 1906 Dr. David Starr Jordan, President of Stanford University, spoke to an

Anti-prohibition signs, 1909. This empty house located where the high school campus is today, was often posted with political signs. Local option was a big political issue from the 1880's until 1909. *(Library Collection)*

Main Street bridge over Los Gatos Creek completed in 1906. Removed in 1953 to make way for the Freeway overpass. *(Library Collection)*

overflow crowd at the Ford Opera House (now the Opera House Antique store). It was a hard-fought campaign. In the election the vote was 169 for, to 199 against granting licenses to saloons. Los Gatos was the second town in California, after Palo Alto, to go dry under local option.

As a result of the election the Town Board passed Ordinance #130 entitled "An Ordinance relative to the alcoholic liquor traffic in the town of Los Gatos." Its provisions were almost exactly the same as those of Ordinance #24. It specifically repealed Ordinance #115 regulating liquor licenses which had been passed in June 1902. The new ordinance of July 1, 1906 made violations subject to heavy fines.

Although Los Gatos was now legally dry, barrooms continued to exist. However, because of continued harassment by law officers, the last bar closed on August 29, 1907. But it seems that three licenses were granted by the Board at a fee of $1000 a year each. On March 9, 1908 an effort was made to get the Board to submit to a vote of the people the question whether the Board could grant three liquor licenses at a cost of $1000 a year. The Board refused.

The liquor interests continued their fight. According to the local press at the time, they began a campaign "of unfair and libelous statements about Los Gatos, calling it a 'dead' town with business going downhill and a great tax loss due to no saloons." Then the paper pointed out that business had actually increased and Los Gatos had a boom after it went dry. "Over 26 business firms reported a resoundingly prosperous business climate."[12]

Still the "wets" got the question of saloons put to a vote of the people again in the election of April 13, 1908. Although one "wet" candidate was elected to the Town Board, the vote was 238 to 189 in favor of prohibition. The Los Gatos *Mail* reported on April 16, 1908 that "the result of Monday's election is clearly an indication that the people of Los Gatos do not want saloons in any form again fastened upon them. They have tasted the sweets of prosperous business activity by day and peaceful quiet at night, and we do not believe any amount of argument now could persuade them to return to the reign of saloons."

In September 1909 the Town Board received complaints that the Hotel Lyndon was selling liquor in violation of the law. The Board offered a reward of $150 for evidence leading to the conviction of the guilty. Two or three Japanese places on Front Street, or Railroad Avenue (Montebello Way) were also said to be violating the anti-liquor law.

Ordinance #144 of June 6, 1910 gave the Town Board the right, by majority vote, to grant permission to any person, firm or corporation to sell liquor with bona fide meals in hotels and restaurants. Written application had to be made and applicant had to be an elector of the town, or at least one of the party had to be an elector, before permission could be granted. Permits were revocable at any time. "However, nothing in this Ordinance shall be construed to authorize or

Dr. R. P. Gober, long-time Los Gatos physician and leader in civic affairs. Started practicing in 1883 and passed away on March 24, 1943 after 60 years of service to the people of Los Gatos. *(Museum Collection)*

Town Hall built in 1913 and the subject of a dispute over its destruction in 1965 to make room for the new civic center. *(Museum Collection)*

permit, the establishment, maintenance, or conducting of any bar, saloon, or tippling place."[13] This went into effect December 1910.

Other Protective Measures. Many townspeople complained about loose handbills that were distributed in the residential area and the many "free samples" of medicines, cosmetics and what-have-you that were left at their doors by peddlers. Ordinance #152 was passed on July 1, 1912, prohibiting "delivery, or depositing of drugs, medicines, anticeptics, disinfectants and cosmetics, either for internal or external use, upon the doorsteps or premises of another, or the distribution or circulation of handbills, etc. upon any street or sidewalk within the town of Los Gatos."[14]

The Town Board held its first meeting in the New Town Hall the latter part of December 1913. The first Ordinance passed by the Board at its new headquarters was Ordinance #162 against dogs running loose in town. And on January 7, 1916 the *Mail News* reported that Mayor Balch asked the City Attorney to draw up an ordinance outlawing BB guns because birds had been killed and windows broken by boys with these guns. An ordinance had been passed against hypnotism and palm reading, but the Town Clerk, Miss Donna Winning, declared this illegal since it had not been published, nor did it state when the ordinance would go into effect.[15]

The Election Dispute of 1910

One of the bitterest local elections in the history of Los Gatos was that of April 1910. A San Francisco capitalist, R. P. Doolan, moved to Los Gatos and made a "big splurge in the town." After a year or two he put on a gala May Day festival. It was so widely publicized that 10,000 to 15,000 people poured into town. J. D. Farwell recalled that Los Gatos was really given attention by this event. "Newspapers sent out so much publicity that Western Union had to put on an extra operator to handle the copy." All this also gave Doolan notoriety.

Doolan wanted to be President of the Board of Trade but the rules forbade a Director to be a candidate for that office. Doolan felt that this was simply a plot against him and to get revenge he ran for Town Councilman in 1908. T. E. Johns ran against him and won by two votes. Doolan demanded a recount and the fight was so bitter that it broke up the Board of Trade, "which slept until the Chamber of Commerce was organized."[16]

The inexhaustible Doolan was a candidate again in 1910. The election was a contest between "old timers" and "new comers." Doolan's opponent in the April 11 election was F. M. Derrickson. D. P. Simon and George Turner were the other candidates, the former an "administration" candidate, and the latter an "anti-administration" candidate. Both Turner and Simon were elected, but Doolan and Derrickson ended up with a tie vote. Emotions were aroused. The official canvas of election results was not completed until after 9 P.M. the next evening, while a milling crowd remained in the vicinity of the town hall. Marshal J. D. Shore had special watchmen on hand in case of trouble, as both sides were nervous about the safekeeping of the ballots.

Mr. Eli A. Winning, the Town Clerk, hoping to take the ballots to a safer place, made the big mistake of taking the ballots out of the hall and starting home with them. The Marshal saw him and immediately took the Town Clerk into custody. Actually, in matters of this kind, the Clerk was the custodian of the returns, but the law required that they be kept in the place provided, which was in the safe at the Town Hall. In removing the ballots Mr. Winning "made a great mistake."

The ballots were returned to the Town Hall and Argyle Tolley and Fred Thackery were sworn in as deputies to guard the safe where the ballots were kept.

Doolan claimed that there was fraud in the election and took the matter to court. Deputy Chief District Attorney Coolidge, sitting as Superior Judge, found in favor of Doolan. He was given five more votes than Derrickson and was declared elected. Doolan attended his first meeting of the Board on May 31, 1910.

Doolan and Turned teamed up to be the "Peck's bad boys" of the Town Council. They opposed the rest of the Board often, and many times kept that body from carrying on the business of government.

In August 1911 Mr. Doolan and his family moved back to San Francisco, although he continued to maintain residence in Los Gatos and held on to his seat on the Town Board. But he failed to attend Board meetings regularly. His presence was essential, for no quorum could be had without him since Mr. D. P. Simons had died and the vacancy had not been filled. The rest of the Board wanted an election held and on March 20, 1911 set the date for such election for April 17, 1911. Doolan was absent when this date was set. When he returned he moved for repeal of the election resolution on the ground that it was illegal since the law provided for 30 days notice for an election. Sporleder refused to second the motion for repeal. Turner then asked Sporleder to take the chair temporarily and Turner seconded the motion. But it did not receive the required 3 votes to pass--- Wheeler was absent, there was one vacancy, and Sporleder voted against the motion.

When the minutes of this meeting were read later, a parliamentary bickering followed between Turner and Doolan on one side and Sporleder on the other. From April 17 on both Turner and Doolan refused to attend Board meetings. There could be no quorum so town business was at a standstill and bills were left unpaid.

The case went to court again and the Superior Court ordered an election to be held. In that election R. R. Bell was elected, but Turner and Doolan refused to join in canvassing the votes. The result was that there was still no government. The Los Gatos News on August 25, 1911 lamented the continued neglect of town affairs by the absence of Doolan and Turner. "How long," said the paper, "will Los Gatos be hampered by the unbridled audacity of two town trustees? They have absented themselves from both regular meetings this month

and bills go unpaid." In fact, one of them was in town but failed to attend the meetings. "It is time," continued the News, "a public indignation meeting were called and some action taken in this matter."

For this, Doolan tried to get even with the News. On July 11, 1912 he introduced a resolution to the effect that since both Los Gatos papers refused to submit to the general laws of the State of California, the Town of Los Gatos should give all official notices to the San Jose Morning Times as the official organ of the Town of Los Gatos.[17]

Because of Mr. Doolan's "neglect of his duties" it was suggested that he resign. Finally, on March 3, 1913 the Board decided to take action. In a Resolution of that date it said that Doolan "ought and is hereby requested to resign his position as Town Trustee in order that some one may be chosen for the place who can and will attend to the duties of the office." The Resolution recited the fact that Mr. Doolan had moved in August 1911 with his family to San Francisco where he now resided. He had not attended Board meetings for six months---months that were important to the town in point of moneys to be spent. "The said R. P. Doolan has absented himself 16 out of 20 of the meetings held by the Board, thus depriving the Board and the town of the wisdom, judgment and knowledge of the law at the very times when they were most needed."[18]

Mr. Doolan appeared on March 17 to protest the Resolution. From then on, however, he appeared off and on at the meetings of the Board until the expiration of his term. Never has Los Gatos had a more exciting political hassel than that created by the doughty Mr. Doolan.

FOOTNOTES

1. Library Collection, *Town Board*, p. 14.
2. *Times Observer*, October 16, 1958 Special Historical Edition.
3. Town Board *Minutes*, Book V, p. 248 ff.
4. *Ibid.*, Book IV, p. 398.
5. *Ibid.*, Book III, p. 271.
6. *Ibid.*, p. 377 ff.
7. *Ibid.*, Book IV, p. 197.
8. *Ibid.*, Book V, p. 53.
9. *Times Observer*, January 16, 1958.
10. Town Board *Minutes*, Book I, p. 79.
11. *Ibid.*, Ordinance #24, June 7, 1889.
12. Library Collection, *Town Board*, Book II, p. 75.
13. Town Board *Minutes*, Book V, p. 216.
14. *Ibid.*, July 1, 1912.
15. *Ibid.*, January 7, 1916.
16. Library Collection, Book I, p. 177.
17. Town Board *Minutes*, Book V, p. 336.
18. *Ibid.*, Book IV, p. 446.

CHAPTER VII

Utilities in Los Gatos

Water

IN THE early years of Los Gatos there was no central water system. Different areas of the town received their water from the private supply of an individual or group. Judge B. J. Rankin, for instance, owned property near the bridge across the Los Gatos Creek. He set up a water-supply system for his family and for his neighbors, sinking a well on the west side of the creek and another on the north side of Main Street. He operated this until the San Jose Water Company bought him out. Other groups supplying water included the Los Gatos Water Company, the Mountain Spring Water Company and the Cold Spring Water Company.

The Los Gatos Water Company was the first to supply water to a major portion of the town. In September 1886 this company was taken over by the Los Gatos Manufacturing Company.

On April 14, 1888 an Ordinance was passed granting the right to A. Richardson, his heirs and assigns, to furnish fresh water to the residents of Los Gatos. Such right was to last 50 years. It gave Richardson the right to lay pipes in the streets and alleys. However, the Town Board reserved the right to fix the rates Richardson could charge. He was given 12 months to show reasonable progress or forfeit his $1000 bond.[1]

Richardson evidently did not take advantage of his franchise. He probably feared competition from other companies, especially the San Jose Water Company, for on June 14, 1888 he asked the Los Gatos Town Trustees to enjoin the San Jose Water Company from taking more water in the flume than it had carried in the past. The Board took no action.[2] On May 18, 1889 the Mountain Spring Water Company had been given the same rights that had been granted to Richardson, and thus another possible competitor faced Richardson.

The Mountain Spring Water Company was the largest supplier of water to Los Gatos before the coming of the San Jose Water Company. This company was owned by local people headed by Dr. R. B. Gober, who was President, and John Bean and D. C. Crummey, the principal stockholders. The company operated very successfully until taken over by the San Jose Water Company. It built a reservoir at the end of Bean Avenue, another on Overlook property, and one on the Conroy tract east of Los Gatos. On April 1, 1892 the *News* reported that the work was being rushed on the large reservoir on the McCullagh property. When completed the dam would be 30 feet high. A ten-inch main was to carry the water. "The company is expending much money," said the *News* "to give Los Gatos good water under high pressure." The reservoir would hold nearly 3 million gallons of water, supplying water for the fire hydrants of the town at a cost of $5.00 per hydrant plus 20 cents per 1000 gallons of water a year.

During the years of its operation the Mountain Spring Water Company did much to extend water service in Los Gatos. It extended main lines on University Avenue and on Main Street. It also built branch lines to connect with the main lines. But the Town Board was penny-wise in granting rate increases to the company. On February 19, 1894 the company requested the town to fix rates comparable to the rates charged by water companies in San Jose, Eureka, Stockton and other towns.

The company had been supplying the town with water for fire protection and other services. But on January 15, 1894 the Town Board instructed the Town Clerk to notify the Mountain Spring Water Company that "from and after February 15, 1894 the Town of Los Gatos will not be bound by the terms of the contract existing between the Water Company and the Town of Los Gatos for the furnishing of water for fire purposes," and that after February 15, 1894 the contract was to end.[3]

The town was careful to protect the people against impure water. On September 4, 1893, the Town Clerk was instructed to send a bottle of water from the Mountain Spring Water Company to the State University at Berkeley for analysis.[4]

In 1890 another company made a bid for water rights in Los Gatos. On November 14, 1890 W. H. Murphy, representing the United States Water Pipe and Construction Company, was granted a franchise to erect a water plant called the Los Gatos

In 1869 the San Jose Water Works constructed a flume from the tail race of Forbes Mill for supply to its Los Gatos customers. *(San Jose Water Works photo)*

Cold Spring Water Company.[4] The company secured the O. G. Sherwood Estate and some of the Mason property to lay a line for the distribution of water. The main supply was to run from Blue Mountain Creek, a tributary of Guadalupe, and a tunnel of 1200 feet through Mount Baldy, two and a half miles from Los Gatos.

When Mr. Murphy made his request to the Town Board for the franchise there were objections. Some people in town believed that there was no need for such a water system. Others were suspicious of the plan---it was just too big! The editor of the *News,* in the issue of August 28, 1891 expressed his disgust with these people. "There are too many critics in town and not enough boosters," he said. He called these critics "old fossils," prefacing the editorial with the jingle:

"A man may chin, and a man may grind,
    From early break of day,
But he can't build up a town by running it down
    Because it isn't built that way."

The franchise was to last 25 years and citizens could buy stock in the company. Furthermore, the town could buy the plant at fair evaluation any time. Work on laying the pipes began in December 1890 and the work was to be completed in seven months' time. Storage capacity was to be 2 million gallons and the pressure 90 pounds to the inch. The town was to pay $5.00 per hydrant per month, plus 20 cents per 1000 gallons of water to the city for fire protection for two years.[5]

Many people still doubted the ability of the company to fulfill its contract. When the seven months passed without completion of the project, they complained bitterly. The Los Gatos Weekly *News* reported, on December 1, 1891, that "there is a good deal of righteous indignation expressed in regard to the action of the Town Board on Monday evening, in granting 90 days more time to Cold Spring Water Company to complete its project. This makes the fourth extension of time." The project was finally completed and operation began in May 1892.

The next company to come to Los Gatos was the San Jose Water Company, later known as the San Jose Water Works. This group had, for a time, furnished water to the Cleland Avenue area but had given that up in 1893. At that time the town had asked them to take over the water supply for the town, but they refused. Cleland Avenue area was supplied by the Mountain Spring Water Company, after the San Jose Company left.

The San Jose Water Company was organized on November 26, 1866 by Donald Mackenzie and John Bonner of San Jose and R. Chabot of Oakland. Peter Carter was also a member of the first Board of Directors. The capitalization of the company was $100,000, and both San Jose and Santa Clara granted the company exclusive privileges for a period of 25 years.[6]

D. C. Crummey, organizer in 1889 and President of the Mountain Spring Water Company, and later Vice-President of the John Bean Spray Pump Co., the forerunner of the giant FMC Corporation. *(Photo courtesy FMC)*

Donald McKenzie, founder of the San Jose Water Works and President of the company from 1866 to 1869. *(Courtesy San Jose Water Works)*

Mr. Ralph Elsman, President, San Jose Water Works, 1937 to 1969, during period of its great growth. *(Courtesy San Jose Water Works)*

The San Jose Water Company decided to come to Los Gatos the latter part of 1899 to serve the water needs of this foothill community. On November 23, 1899 it purchased the Mountain Spring Water Company for $20,000 cash and $24,000 stock in the San Jose company. In March 1900 the Mountain Spring Water Company deeded to that company its lands on Laurel Avenue, part of Glenridge Park and other rights of way.

The San Jose Water Company early realized that artesian wells could not supply enough water for the needs of the people in the valley. It therefore sought to obtain rights to get water from the Los Gatos Creek by authorizing, in 1869, the construction of a flume line from the Los Gatos Creek

from the tail race of Forbes Mill to a proposed Seven Mile Reservoir on what is now Bascom Avenue. It had purchased such rights on the Los Gatos Creek north of town from the Los Gatos Manufacturing Company. The Seven Mile and the Three Mile Reservoirs were built during 1870 and 1871 at a cost of more than $96,000.

In 1874 the company entered upon a 20-year growth period. Some 7000 acres of watershed land were acquired in the Santa Cruz Mountains, and impounding reservoirs were built to collect and store the run-off from streams. Of the numerous reservoirs and lakes built, the largest was Lake Elsman, built in 1951 at a cost of $1,600,000. This is located on the confluence of Austrian Creek and the Los Gatos Creek in the heart of the Santa Cruz Mountains.

With the numerous reservoirs and lakes in the

Los Gatos Creek before automobiles and freeways. Highway 17 now runs where once this stretch of creek flowed through the town. *(Library Collection)*

69

Gas light, typical of street lighting in the 1890's. This is in front of the Wheeler house, later the Yocco residence on Church Street. *(Courtesy Mary Yocco Rugh)*

West Main Street about 1900 with street light over center of street near Christian Church on left. *(Museum Collection)*

mountains and valley, its aggressive leadership under Ralph Elsman, and its constant alertness for the needs of its patrons, the San Jose Water Company has been able to supply the fast-growing population of San Jose and the West Valley. Since Mr. Elsman's death, the new leadership is no less responsive to the needs of the people. New and larger mains are constantly being installed, so that by 1970 there were more than 1600 miles of main lines serving 120 square miles of the Santa Clara Valley.

Electric Lights

Los Gatos had no street lights until after 1888. The streets were dark and the sidewalks uneven and dangerous at night. In 1888 the town ordered 10 gas lights installed at a cost of $3.00 each for a period of 2 years. The Los Gatos Gas Company supplied the artificial gas for the lights. The company had been organized in 1885 and had its plant and office about where the Beatrice Foods buildings are now located on Santa Cruz and Elm Streets.

The lights were designated for the following places: "Near P. Johnson's house, James Pearce's store, near Whitings or Gray's corner, Junction of East Main and Church Street, Call's or Yocco's corner, West end of the bridge, the railway crossing of Main Street, corner of Broadway and Santa Cruz Avenues, corner near Edward's store or Los Gatos Hotel, and near the Catholic Church."[7]

When electricity proved to be more satisfactory than gas, the town fathers gave consideration to the matter of electric lights for Los Gatos. This drew ecstatic praise from the San Jose Evening *News* on March 14, 1890 when it said: "The beautiful town of Los Gatos, the queen of the foothills, the diamond setting in the bright zone that enriches the Santa Clara Valley, is steadily advancing on the highway of material prosperity. She is about to add to her many other attractions, a system of electric lighting."[8]

The first electric lights were put in operation January 31, 1891. The electricity was furnished by the Los Gatos Manufacturing Company.

In 1892 W. D. Tisdale, President of the Los Gatos Ice and Power Plant, promised a light plant for Los Gatos "with the very best dynamo and incandescent lights, besides sufficient number of arc lights to light the whole town." The company ran a few wires up to the lumber yard on the corner where the Park View Building (formerly Bank of America) now stands. This line was used only for the downtown area and a few stores and residences. The first street light was at the corner of Main and Santa Cruz Avenues.

But these lights and the gas lights were not very satisfactory. On January 28, 1896 the Los Gatos Weekly *News* lamented the lack of street lights at night. "In the daytime Los Gatos is a thing of beauty and a joy to every beholder," said the paper. "At night, we are sorry to say, everything is changed, and the town outside of the business center looks like a village of 50 years ago, and all because our streets are gloomy and forbidding, being lighted only by an insufficient number of gas lamps."

On February 24 of that year the Town Trustees called for bids for better street lighting. The Hume Company of Glen Una was in the best position to give lights to the town. This company, managed by J. D. Farwell, had combined with the Los Gatos Ice and Power Company in 1896, and in 1898 it had also acquired the Los Gatos Gas Company.

From then on the Hume Company had a monopoly on the gas and electric power for Los Gatos. On July 6, 1896 the Town Board asked the Hume Company to place 21 electric lights into operation in the town. After public notice on April 15, 1897 for bids, the Hume Company was the only bidder. They agreed to furnish lights at $9.75 per light per month. Each time the town asked for bids for lights, the Hume Company was the only one to respond. On March 7, 1898 the company agreed to furnish the town with 24 arc lights of 2000 candle power for $10.50 per light per month.

Again on March 21, 1898 the Town Board called for sealed bids for a franchise to "construct, lay down, operate and maintain an electric light plant and system with all the necessary appliances in the public streets of Los Gatos for a period of 2 years." The Hume Company's was again the only bid received, and its bid was accepted on March 26, 1898.[9]

On March 5, 1900 J. D. Farwell of the Hume Company appeared before the Town Board and stated that if he were given a three-year contract,he would give a cheaper price. But the town Attorney said it would be illegal to give such a contract without public notice of bids. Again the Hume Company was the only bidder, but it was given only a one-year contract. The price was $8.75 per light per month for one year. When the year was about up, Mr. Farwell appeared before the Board, on June 17, 1901, and generously offered to supply lights until August 1, 1901 free of charge "in view of the fact that the town was in need of finances." The offer was accepted with thanks.[10]

In November 1902 the Town Board asked for 27 street lights at $8.00 each a month, with the privilege of cutting down the number when the Board saw fit. In December 1903 the Los Gatos *News* reported that Los Gatos had both a gas works and an electric light plant, both being under

the management of J. D. Farwell. The electric company "has facilities for furnishing both light and power. It is equipped with both incandescent and arc machinery, using the latter in lighting streets and stores, and the former in stores and residences." The company also was able to manufacture fuel oil for the town.

An interesting incident connected with the electric lights of the town happened in October 1900. Los Gatos has traditionally been Republican in its politics. As early as October 6, 1864 the San Jose *Herald* told of a "meeting of the enemies of government" at the Mansion House to organize a Democratic Club. It described those who attended as "a rough-looking lot of men."

On October 15, 1900 the Bryan and Stevenson Club---a Democratic group---reported to the Town Board that on two different occasions while the club was meeting the lights of the town were turned off. Trustee Sullivan declared that this was done deliberately. He had affidavits to show that when he asked J. T. McClellan, the electrician for the company, about the shut-off of the lights, McClellan said that "the Democrats would show off to better advantage without the lights." He also told Mr. Sullivan that he would see to it that the lights were turned off at any time the Democrats tried to meet.

Sullivan, a member of the Town Trustees, introduced a resolution charging the Hume Company with "wilful and unlawful violation of contract," specifying that the turning off of the lights was "premeditated and deliberate" on the part of the Hume Company or agents. The Resolution instructed the city Attorney to bring suit for $5,000 damages. It is indicative of the political leanings of the Board that no second was given to the motion for some time. Sullivan left the meeting in anger. George Lewis, to get the matter before the floor for discussion, finally seconded the motion. The

Howard Tyson, Manager, Los Gatos office of the P. G. & E. from 1923 to 1930. Secretary-Manager of the Los Gatos Telephone Co. from 1930 until his death in 1941. *(Courtesy Mrs. Howard Tyson)*

Paul Straub, manager of the Los Gatos P. G. & E. office from 1930 to 1968. Well known for his many civic activities, which included playing Santa Claus to the children of our town. *(Courtesy the Straub family)*

Board voted the resolution down without debate.[11]

The Republicanism of the government and voters of Los Gatos was further demonstrated by a short sarcastic notice in the Los Gatos *News* in 1908 which reported that "Lee Darneal is doing honors of the six Democratic voters of Los Gatos at the Fresno Convention." (Little did this paper realize that the time would come when Lee Darneal would for many years be the Postmaster of Los Gatos.)

The Los Gatos Ice, Gas and Electric Company (The Hume Company) furnished the gas and electricity for Los Gatos until 1913. As early as July 26, 1912 the Pacific Gas and Electric Company had asked the State Railway Commission for permission to buy, and the Los Gatos company had asked permission to sell, the Los Gatos Gas and Electric Company. The price named for the sale was $187,762.21.[12]

On September 4, 1912 John D. Kirster, the San Jose District Manager of the P.G. & E., appeared before the Los Gatos Town Board to outline the plans of his company to enter Los Gatos. The Board laid down certain requirements that had to be met. On November 18, 1912 Mr. Kirster again appeared before the Board to say that his company was ready to accept the terms suggested by the Town Board. He was instructed to draw up a three-year contract for $6.00 a month per arc light and $1.00 per month for each incandescent light. The town reserved the right to ask for an increase or reduction in the number of lights at any time.

Ever since 1913 the P.G. & E. has given service to the town and citizens of Los Gatos. Howard Tyson was the manager of the Los Gatos office for seven years before becoming Secretary-Manager of the local telephone company in April 1930. Paul Straub, who had been with the P.G. & E. in San Jose, then became manager of the Los Gatos Office. He served until his retirement on March 1, 1968 after 38 years with the company. During his tenure the service of the company was greatly expanded, both in the electricity field and the gas field.

For many years the Los Gatos office was on Main Street, where the "Family Affair" Beauty Shop is now located. Miss Elsie Calef, now Mrs. A. L. Cilker, came from the San Jose office of P.G. & E. to the Los Gatos office, where she was a familiar face to many "old timers." The new offices of the P.G. & E. are now located on Saratoga Avenue, where an efficient staff serves the customers of the area.

Santa Cruz Avenue and Main Street with interurban electric tracks in foreground, 1927. *(Library Collection)*

Telephone Service

The first telephone service in Los Gatos was established by the Sunset Telephone and Telegraph Company in the middle 1880's. The exchange was in a building located where the Rex Hotel stands today. It was destroyed by the fire of July 1891. The exchange was then opened in a drug store owned by F. F. Watkins on Santa Cruz Avenue. A public telephone was installed in the drug store on January 7, 1893 where messages "can be received from, or sent to, all points reached by telephone." Mr. Watkins operated the little telephone office behind his drug store on a commission basis. When the La Canada building on the corner of Main Street and Santa Cruz Avenue was completed, the phone company moved into the little office behind the building. The monthly rate for telephone service at that time was $1.00 for a single-party line and 75 cents for a two-party line.

The Sunset Telephone and Telegraph Company changed its name in 1891 to the Pacific Telephone and Telegraph Company. Its exchange remained in the small office behind the drug store until 1909 when it moved to the building now occupied by Crall's Book Store.[13]

In 1908 many telephone customers in Los Gatos petitioned the company for a free switching to San Jose. A number of Los Gatos businessmen transacted a great deal of business in San Jose by telephone. They were required to pay a switch fee to connect with San Jose. "Since Santa Clara, Campbell and many other towns have free switching to the county seat" Los Gatans wondered why they could not have it also.[14]

To get wires connected to the main business district, the Sunset Telephone and Telegraph Company had put up a "Liberty Pole" on the corner of Santa Cruz Avenue and Main Street. This pole was blown down on the morning of October 9, 1903. Fortunately only a few people were on the street at seven o'clock in the morning when that happened. Business people were relieved when it fell, because they had, for some time, feared it would fall and bring injury to people.

In 1910 a newly organized local company purchased the local plant of the Pacific Telephone and Telegraph Company. The Los Gatos Telephone Company was incorporated with a capitalization of $25,000 and received its charter from the State on November 10, 1910. The original Directors included F. F. Watkins, George W. Turner, J. D. Farwell, De Laney Lewis, D. C. Crummey, A. E. Wilder and F. H. Crosby. A. E. Wilder was President, J. D. Farwell, Vice-President, De Laney Lewis was Secretary and J. A. Case was Treasurer. The company served 326 subscribers.

George Smith acted as manager for the exchange which was at first located in the little building behind the La Canada building, on West Main Street. Later it moved to the Crall location. Smith turned over the management to J. O. Jensen in 1912. In April 1913 the Los Gatos company issued stock in the amount of $15,000, the proceeds to be used for new equipment and erection of a building. In September the company installed a new and modern switchboard, enabling an inexperienced operator to handle 550 calls per hour compared to 350 an hour an experienced operator handled before.

When J. O. Jensen went into the Army in July 1917, F. F. Watkins became the Secretary-Manager of the Company. He held this position until January 1, 1931 when he was succeeded by Howard Tyson, who had been local manager for the P. G. & E. for seven years. During that year the exchange was moved to 37 West Main Street.

In the ten years from 1911 to 1921 the local telephone company gained 501 new subscribers. By 1923 there were more than 1100 telephone connections in Los Gatos. The number service was started in 1927 and two prominent Los Gatos physicians got the low numbers. Dr. Frank Knowles' number was 2 and Dr. Robert Gober's was 3. In 1925 the telephone directory listed 1200 telephone users.

In September 1934 the telephone poles were removed from the business district and in August 1938 they were removed on East Main Street to Loma Alta Avenue. Underground cables replaced the poles and above-ground wires.

Lyndon Farwell, son of one of the founders of the company, became Secretary-Manager in 1941. The company grew steadily so that by 1946 it was serving 2,449 subscribers in Los Gatos. With the rapid growth of the area after World War II the company expanded to meet the new demands. In 1947 it purchased the Santa Cruz Mountain Telephone Association, adding 80 new subscribers. It also purchased exchanges in Morgan Hill and other communities.

A great step forward was taken by the Los Gatos Telephone Company in September 1950 when it changed from the manual to the dial system. In 1956 the name of the company was changed to Western California Telephone Company, reflecting its greatly expanding operations. This expanded operation was also evidenced by the more than 1268 telephones connected in 1955.

Lyndon Farwell became President of the company in 1955, and Harold Davis succeeded him as Secretary-Manager. Another expansion program was undertaken, providing for 1000 new connections at a cost of $100,000. In 1958 the new Blossom Hill dial equipment office on San Jose-Los

J. D. Farwell, originally the manager of the Hume Company of Glen Una which supplied electricity to Los Gatos. He was manager of the Los Gatos Gas and Electric Co. until it was purchased by the P. G. & E. in 1912. In 1910 he helped organize the Los Gatos Telephone Co. and became President of this local corporation. *(Courtesy Mrs. Lyndon Farwell)*

Lyndon Farwell, business and civic leader. Served as General Manager of the Los Gatos Telephone Co. and was President of the Western California Telephone Co. at the time of his death in October 1959. *(Courtesy Mrs. Lyndon Farwell)*

Gatos Road was erected. This gave the company an ultimate capacity of 10,000 telephone connections.

In August 1963 the Western Telephone Company became a subsidiary of the General Telephone and Electronics Corporation, but retained its local name. Most of the local personnel and management were continued. Under the new arrangement the company has continued to grow and by the end of 1970 there were more than 24,244 telephone connections in Los Gatos. The company now has three central offices and subscribers have nation-wide direct distance dialing.

The Sewer System

The sewer system in Los Gatos was built in sporadic fashion as the need arose. For example, the Los Gatos Hotel had a private sewer line, as did the Co-operative Winery. The Miles Sewer served Edlen Avenue. These piecemeal sewers gave temporary relief but they were not "conducive to the pleasure, health, or neighborly feeling at the terminal end of the line."

A bond issue of $25,000 for a town sewer system and a town hall was submitted to the voters on December 1, 1891. It was defeated by a vote of 143 to 46. The Los Gatos Weekly *News* blamed poor publicity and poor planning for the defeat of these bonds.[15] The Board of Trustees received many complaints about the unhealthy conditions at the sewer outlets. The town sewage dump, consisting of 6 acres, had been purchased from Alexander English but it was located only a third of a mile north of the bridge.

In July 1892 the local press was greatly disturbed over the unhealthy conditions. "There are localities in Los Gatos absolutely reeking with filth and the poisonous gases are stifling passersby." And then becoming specific it said, "The Alley back of Richardson's Hardware store and the vicinity north of the creek bridge are among the many which might be mentioned. Considerable sickness has resulted already and there is good reason to fear that the worst has not been realized. What is everybody's business is nobody's business, and consequently nothing is done."[16]

On December 3, 1892 the Town Clerk was instructed to advertise for sealed bids for "construction of the certified stone pipe sewer according to specification on file with the Clerk." Bids were opened on December 19 and C. D. Vincent was awarded the contract for $1380. The line was to run from a point on Main Street to "a point north of the gravel bed."[17]

Piecemeal sewer connections and outlets continued, as did the unhealthy conditions. Ordinance

Looking East on Main Street, showing lines of steam and electric railroads, in the early 1900's, and three cars on the street at one time. *(Library Collection)*

#64 passed by the Board on November 26, 1894 created a Board of Health. The first members were Dr. F. W. Knowles, S. G. Moore, Dr. R. G. Gober, Chas. H. Peiper and N. F. Blank. The Board of Health reported continued violations of Ordinance #52 concerning sewer outlets. It recommended an immediate inspection of all premises fronting streets or lanes where public or private sewers were laid and that the rules be strictly enforced. Owners should be compelled to "disinfect and fill with earth the cesspools and privy vaults maintained upon their premises."[18]

Even in those early days people were prone to abuse public property. On March 6, 1899 the Street Superintendent reported to the Town Board that persons were burying dead horses and hauling their "old rubbish on the town sewer dump." He was ordered to put a stop to that immediately.

It was very evident that a town-wide sewer system was needed. On May 20, 1901 the Town Trustees planned a bond issue for town projects including a town hall building, a lot for the town hall, a park, a fire alarm system, a new dumping ground for the sewer, an electric light plant and a library.[19] On September 23, 1892 the Los Gatos *News* praised the Town Board for its intention to provide an adequate sewer system for the town. This was a good move, not only from a sanitary standpoint but it "will attract capital and a good class of citizens; in short, it will create a demand for real estate at advanced figures and largely add to the material prosperity of the Town."

The bond election was held on September 22, 1904. The issue was to be for $20,000 and was to include the sewer, a new bridge across the creek on

Main Street and a sewage disposal tank. The bond was passed by a vote of 160 to 5 for the bridge, 153 to 6 for the sewer. But opposition to the bond issue was strong. Before the election, a circular was sent to the residents of the proposed sewer district telling them a "yes" vote would mean mortgaging their homes for 20 years. "With plumbers getting $6.00 a day, the expense will be terrible." In attacking the bridge bond it said, "Are you voters of Los Gatos willing to mortgage your homes for the next 20 years to benefit the rich, powerful, and grasping corporation of the Southern Pacific Railroad Company by giving it a bridge? Why not let the S.P. Co. build its own bridge. It must do it or repair the old one sufficient for its use, and if the company repairs it sufficient for its own use, it will be sufficient for all purposes."

These arguments did not affect the outcome of the election. The bond issue was widely carried and a town sewer system was now begun. A main line was put in and connections from secondary lines were made as applications were approved. The Town Septic Tank received the sewage and discharged it into the Los Gatos Creek. Hunt Brothers Cannery was one of the first to connect when it received permission on February 25, 1907, to construct a private line from its property on the corner of Santa Cruz Avenue and Cemetery Lane (now Saratoga Avenue) to connect with the public line at the junction on the corner of Santa Cruz and Saratoga Road. Hunt Brothers agreed to pay one dollar a year for the privilege of connecting.[20]

After the passage of the Sewer Bond the Town Board asked for bids for the septic tank at the town dump. The firm of Osen and Floore of Los Angeles said they could build the tanks and not ask for a cent until they were proved in good working order. The company said that they would guarantee that 75% of the material coming into the tank would leave it pure and clear. A tank for 2,500 people would cost $2,500, but it could be constructed for any number of people up to 50,000.

The Town Board asked for bids from Bay Area companies, but all were too high. Finally on June 9, 1905 the bid of $675 by John Doyle was accepted.

Once the main lines and tanks were in the sewer system expanded as need arose. The minutes of the Town Board are filled with requests for permission to connect up with the town-wide system.

In 1948 the County of Santa Clara organized Sanitation Districts and Los Gatos became a part of District #4. Since then all sewer connections must go into the Main Line of the District and to the conversion plant. As new areas are opened up they connect with the Los Gatos sewer lines and these in turn enter the Sanitation District lines. This assures a sanitary disposal of all sewage in the area.

FOOTNOTES

1. Town Board *Minutes*, Book I. Ordinance #19.
2. *Ibid.*, p. 29.
3. *Ibid.*, Book II, p. 147 ff.
4. *Ibid.*, p. 126.
5. *Ibid.*, Book I, p. 208.
6. *Nine Men* and 100 years of Water History. San Jose Water Works, 1967.
7. Town Board *Minutes*, Book I, p. 29.
8. Hamsher Collection, *Town Board*, p. 12.
9. Town Board *Minutes*, Book III, p. 67.
10. *Ibid.*, June 17, 1901.
11. *Ibid.*, p. 93.
12. Hamsher Collection, *Town Board*, Book 2, p. 80.
13. *Ibid.*, Book 34.
14. *Ibid.*, Book 8, Febr. 1908.
15. Los Gatos Weekly *News*, December 4, 1891.
16. Hamsher Collection, *Town Board*, p. 46.
17. Town Board *Minutes*, Book 2, p. 87.
18. *Ibid.*, Nov. 26, 1894.
19. *Ibid.*, Book 2, p. 208.
20. *Ibid.*, Book 4, p. 360.

Main entrance to the Los Gatos Cemetery looking north from Los Gatos-Almaden Road. Picture dates to early 1900's. *(Courtesy Mary Yocco Rugh)*

Hose Company #2 in the early 1890's. Los Gatos had two volunteer fire-fighting companies, one on each side of the bridge. *(Library Collection)*

THE LOS GATOS MURDER.

Father and Son Held for Killing Hepler.

SAN JOSE, March 11.—Early this morning the CHRONICLE correspondent visited the scene of yesterday's tragedy in the Vineland school district, this side of Los Gatos. The marks of the death struggle in front of the Richards' residence are still plainly apparent in the soft earth, together with the blood of the murdered Hepler. The people of the vicinity are still much excited over the affair. At the inquest held at 1 P. M. the following facts were learned: Benjamin Richards owns a strip of land, 60 feet wide by about 450 feet long, running from the county road west to Los Gatos creek. The land is rocky and uncultivated. Adjoining him on the south lived Alpheus Hepler. Both men had families. Hepler's children were small and would stray over on Richards' land and Richards' poultry would stray upon Hepler's land. Richards became much incensed at Hepler and forbade him or his children to put foot on his land. Hepler, in taking a short-cut to neighbors' houses, occasionally disobeyed this injunction, in consequence of which Richards became very vindictive and repeatedly threatened the life of Hepler, and at one time assaulted him, striking him with a shotgun. The gun becoming unbreeched, the attack at that time was abandoned, but Richards subsequently, and as late as last Friday, said the next time he and Hepler met, Hepler would be killed, but he would take care to have the law on his side. Recently Ed Richards is said to have caught one of Hepler's children on his father's place and chastised him severely. This intensified the ill feeling, though there is no evidence as yet that Hepler made any threats.

On Monday Richards and his son were cutting grass for a cow near the county road when Hepler rode by, barebacked, on a horse. Who made the first greeting is not known, but Hepler was seen shaking a switch toward young Richards and apparently addressing him. The witnesses were two or three children, about 100 feet away. They saw old man Richards in the road as he struck Hepler on the head with a pitchfork, knocking him from his horse. Hepler picked up a stone and threw it at Richards, but missed him. Richards struck him twice again over the head with the fork, when they clinched. Richards threw Hepler down and was on top of him beating him with his fists when young Richards fired three shots. The first entered below the left nipple and pierced the heart and left lung; the second passed below the right armpit and clear through the body, piercing the right lung and kidney; the third entered the thigh. Either of the first two was necessarily fatal.

They then pulled the dead man to one side of the road, out of their way, loaded up the sled with hay and went home, young Richards turning for a second and fumbling the dead man's body, presumably for a pistol. It is now believed that Hepler did not attempt to draw a pistol, and that, as a matter of fact, his pistol was not discharged.

The Coroner's jury found that the deceased was a native of Ohio, 45 years old, and that he came to his death from a pistol-shot wound inflicted by Edward Richards, aided and assisted by Ben Richards, and charged both with the willful murder of Alpheus Hepler.

A March 1884 newspaper account of a murder in Los Gatos. 1884 was a year of murders and hangings in our town. *(Courtesy Mrs. Mary Yocco Rugh)*

CHAPTER VIII

Protective Services: Police and Fire

Early Crime in Los Gatos

THE mountains and gulleys behind Los Gatos were perfect hiding places for the lawless elements during the early years of the town. Stages were robbed, gamblers' winnings were stolen, and murder was committed all too often. The 1870's and 1880's saw a rash of major crimes committed in Los Gatos. Indeed, one authority, who was perhaps a bit carried away with statistics, estimated that more than 50 murders were committed in our vicinity up to the late 1880's.[1] Be that as it may, it is possible to document numerous major crimes and a number of murders. George G. Smith had been a school teacher, but he found that robbery paid better. In 1881, he held up eleven stages in three weeks. He was finally caught in a Guadalupe miner's camp, tried, convicted and sentenced to 20 years in prison. On September 19, 1876 Nicholas Boscovich was shot by P. G. Guirevot east of town. On January 13, 1877 Charles M. Parr was "butchered" by Bruno Uyog at the Coleman House---later the El Monte Hotel--- on East Main Street.

Jan Wasielewski was a cattle rustler. He was convicted of stealing cattle, and after his conviction he told his pretty Mexican wife that he would kill her if she obtained a divorce while he was in prison. When he got out of prison he found that she had not only secured a divorce but had married another man. In June 1882 he went to her home, met his wife out of doors, stabbed her to death and fled. He was captured by Sheriff Branham and taken to jail. At his trial he feigned insanity, and even fasted for two weeks, but was nevertheless convicted and hanged.[2] Another ex-convict by the name of Louis Flores came back to Los Gatos and stabbed his wife to death on Main Street.

One of the most famous cases in the criminal history of Los Gatos was that of Vasquez. Garcia and Murival were part of a criminal gang led by Tiburico Vasquez (known as "little Tib") which hid out in the Lexington Hills. They made charcoal from hazelwood and sold it to the Winchester Rifle Company in Connecticut. The gang brought their big supply to Los Gatos on April 17, 1883 on burros from Black Road. With money in their pockets they went to the Los Gatos Hotel to drink and gamble. As often happens, a quarrel developed between members of the gang, and Garcia stabbed Murival in the street in front of the hotel.

Garcia ran into the hills, chased by an angry mob. He was caught behind the old Tollgate House and Sheriff Branham took him to the crude "shanty" called jail, which was near the bridge and locked him in. When the streets were clear, one man got a rope from behind the drug store on North Santa Cruz. A group of men broke into the shabby "jail," tied a rope around Garcia's neck and hung him from a bridge post on Main Street.

One of the most sensational murders ever committed in California occurred in Los Gatos in June 1883. Lloyd Majors had been a lumber dealer, temperance lecturer and saloon keeper in San Jose. He was accused of arson and "came to Los Gatos with a Bible under his arm" and built a saloon next to the Christian Church on West Main Street. He installed a trap door to a cellar into which he threw drunks and robbed them. His dead victims were covered with barrels of lime in the cellar.[3]

Some people became curious about the disappearance of customers at his saloon. The trap door was found and the bodies of the victims discovered. Majors was never convicted for these murders. But in 1884 he was involved in another weird murder for which he was later convicted. In this case Majors tried to get $20,000 he knew had been hidden on the farm of two mountain farmers, Renowden and McIntyre, who lived near the summit. Majors hired a painter by the name of Jewell and another man by the name of Showers to go up to the farm and try to get the $20,000. The hired desperados tortured the two farmers to get them to tell where the money was hid. The farmers refused to tell and the assassins shot both men.

When they came down from the mountain and told Majors that they had not succeeded in getting the money, the saloon keeper gave them $5.00 each, and a shot of whiskey and sent them away. Majors himself went up to the mountain farm to hide the bodies. He stole a horse from the Perkins Stable and rode up, to the farm. He found

Some results of the fire of July 26, 1891. Picture shows the north side of Main Street east of the bridge. The fire wiped out 9 business buildings from Arlington House at 47 E. Main Street west to 23 East Main Street. *(Library Collection)*

McIntyre's body and pulled it into the cabin. Thinking that both bodies were within, he set fire to the cabin. Renowden's body, however, was not in the cabin and was found later. Majors was accused of the crime but had skipped out of town. He was traced to Oakland where he had committed another crime. He was caught and landed in the Alameda County Jail where he tried to escape and was shot by a guard. He was subsequently hung in Oakland. Jewell and Showers were finally caught and tried. The former was hanged and the latter was sentenced to life imprisonment. While in Folsom, Showers was shot by the son of Majors, who was also an inmate of the prison.[4]

Another killing occurred in 1884 when the beautiful wife of Louis Flores was stabbed to death. She had just crossed the street near the Main Street bridge after taking lunch to her husband, who sewed sacks at Forbes' Mill. Her jealous former husband was found guilty of this crime.

In 1887 a house-mover, Charles Goslaw, went to San Jose, leaving H. A. Grant in charge of his tools with instructions not to move them. Goslaw had too much to drink in San Jose, and returning home in a drunken stupor, he found that Grant had moved his tools to another part of town. Angered at this, Goslaw went to Grant's cabin and beat the old man severely. Leaving Grant bruised and helpless on the floor, he went to the Constable and asked to be arrested for assault and battery. A few days later Grant died. People became incensed against these frequent crimes and feeling was running high. Goslaw was brought to trial, found guilty and hanged.[5]

In 1892 Mrs. May Marriott, who lived up the canyon above Los Gatos, came to town to meet

some friends who were to arrive on the train. When they did not come she started walking back up the canyon. Since it was shorter, she walked along the railroad tracks. A man passed her, then turned and followed her to Tunnel Number One. He choked her and dragged her into the tunnel. But her screams had been heard by two men driving a wagon along the road. They ran to the tunnel and found her. They saw a man run away as they approached. They took Mrs. Marriott to the Los Gatos Hotel.

At this time a man by the name of L. M. Landresse was in Los Gatos having a wound dressed. His assailant was a Charles G. Hanson. Hanson was also identified by Mrs. Marriott as her assailant. He was taken to the county jail because of lynching threats. It was found that three years before his attacks on Landresse and Mrs. Marriott, he had shot and wounded a Negro. For this crime he was never brought to trial. It was reported that the Negro was paid $100 to leave town and not appear against him.[6]

Aside from major crimes in Los Gatos there were numerous misdemeanors. At the July 4th

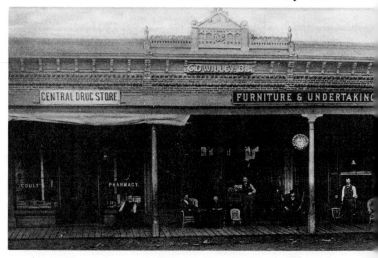

The G. D. Willey Block on north side of East Main Street in 1889. Coulter's Drug Store on left and E. E. Place's Furniture Store and Undertaking Establishment on right. Building destroyed by the great fire of 1891. *(Library Collection)*

Baseball team in 1888. Those in the picture are: *Upper row:* C. W. Holden, John Gaffney, Fred Suydam, Charlie Suydam, Zeph LeFevre, Howard Coult. *Middle row:* George Suydam, Zeph Macabee, Charlie Baker, Dick Shore. *Bottom row:* Lou Nieman, L. A. Wilder, Johnnie Colbert. *(Courtesy Martin LeFevre family and Los Gatos Museum)*

Picnic in 1887 two young boys were found intoxicated. An adult, William C. Dumbruck, was accused of supplying liquor to the boys. He pleaded guilty. On May 23, 1889 Mr. George Wilson, speaking for the railroad, went to the Town Board to ask for regulation to stop the noise and vandalism of boys at the railroad depot. "The boys," said Mr. Wilson, "are annoying, by vulgar and rough conduct in and around the waiting room, in stealing fruit from boxes awaiting shipment and jumping on moving cars."

Complaints were also made that young boys were breaking gas and water pipes and causing other damages. On July 5, 1898 the Town Board instructed the Clerk to offer a reward for the arrest and conviction of the person or persons tampering with sewer pipes in the northeastern part of the town. Previous to that, on August 28, 1893, the Town Board had ordered the Marshal to prosecute the person or persons engaged in the removal of a wooden building from Oak Street to a place on Main Street and erecting it there in violation of the fire ordinance. The owner was instructed to remove the building in three days or it would be removed by the Town Marshal.[7]

Lewis & Son Hardware Store, 23 East Main Street in 1890. This was the Perkins Hardware Store until 1887. The son, George Lewis, is on the right. The store escaped the great fire of 1891 but was burned down in 1943. *(Library Collection)*

On February 8, 1895 the Los Gatos Weekly *News* reported that "Last evening an attempt was made to hold up a lady on Santa Cruz Avenue near the depot." It was not known whether they were tramps or "local talent." In the last few weeks, said the *News,* "a number of very rough citizens have made their way to this town and have given the officers some trouble, to preserve the otherwise good name of the Gem City." The editor urged all citizens to unite in the effort to "capture, convict and send up toughs."

Some of us who are disturbed by vandalism today might take heart from a story in the Los Gatos *Mail* in 1896 which said that "Los Gatos is just now the possessor of as mean a gang of young toughs as can be found anywhere. The gang consists of a number of young boys who go about breaking windows in unoccupied houses, stealing fruit and whatever else may be close at hand and rendering themselves nuisances in a general way."

The situation had not improved much by 1926, for the local press reported "Los Gatos has no jail but one could very well be used to hold the culprit who defaces or destroys public monuments." Then it tells what had happened. "The Pageant canvas sign, purchased at a cost of $25 and stored at the Pageant grounds, has been ripped from end to end by some moron with a pocket knife. Expensive electric light bulbs have been stolen or destroyed and other public property destroyed."

Even speed became a problem. In August 1889 the local press called attention to the serious speed situation. "Horses are raced on the streets of the town. San Jose Avenue is becoming a speeding race track for our young townsmen who own blooded horses."

Los Gatos had no jail, except a little shack that was dark and dingy, and was known as the "Sweat box." The *News* rejoiced when it burned in 1896.

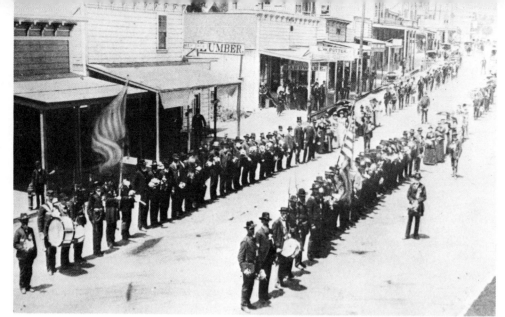

G.A.R. (Civil War Veterans) lineup for the Memorial Day Parade. Organized in July 1885, the last member, James A. Thom, of Culver City, died March 28, 1937. *(Library Collection)*

The G.A.R. in a parade in Los Gatos 1899. View is on Main Street looking west across the bridge from the bend. The Los Gatos *Mail* office on the left across the bridge was located where Sorenson's Plumbing is today. *(Courtesy W. R. Hamsher)*

"The notorious 'Sweat box' reached its final end in smoke last Saturday night. About 11 o'clock Friday night an explosion was heard and flames burst out at the jail, but prompt action by the Fire Department checked the fire without great damage. However, on Saturday the smoldering fire started up again and burned the building to the ground."[8]

The question of a town jail had been discussed for several months. The town needed a place to incarcerate the town drunks. On September 2, 1888 the Town Board asked the Clerk to correspond with the County Supervisors regarding construction of a branch jail in Los Gatos. The Board appointed a committee of three consisting of Johnson, Gibson and Sund to look into possible sites for a jail. On December 3, 1888 the committee reported in favor of the Seanor property on East Main Street---where the Masonic and Methodist Church parking lot is today. Other sites were

G.A.R. members 1917. Shows the thinned ranks of the EOC Ord Post. Portion of the Lyndon Hotel in background. *(Library Collection)*

80

also considered. When the subject was brought up again in the Town Board meeting on December 17, it was "postponed as not practical at present."

A jail was finally built on the Seanor property. It was a two-room affair between Main Street and Church Street. Mrs. Mary Yocco Rugh, in a conversation with the writer, recalled how she and other young people would walk through the passageway between East Main and Church Street and peek in to see who was in the jail.

Town Ordinances reflected the tone of life in the community. In August 1905 the Town Board forbade the operation of slot machines in the town limits. Violations were punishable by a fine of $500 or six weeks in jail or both. It seemed that the only protection against the lawless elements was an alert Town Board. Miss Dora Rankin, in her column "As It Was" in the *Times-Observer* on March 1, 1965, tells of the attempt of a San Francisco Syndicate to move into Los Gatos. At the corner of College Avenue and East Main Street stood a two-story wooden building with a store below and living quarters above. Bill Rankin's Winery, surrounded by a vineyard, was just below the hill from this building. After Rankin died a group of San Franciscans purchased this and built a large house on it. The landscaping was more beautiful than any in all of Los Gatos. This all seemed wonderful, except that the owners hoped to reap a profit from their investment by operating a house of prostitution. The Town Board learned of this and immediately put a stop to such a venture. The San Francisco people sold the house and ground to the Crim family who lived there for many years.

By the way, the building on the other side of College Avenue was the Mariotti Hotel and saloon. Behind it were some winery buildings, later used as a soda works. An interesting brick wall---still standing---surrounded the winery buildings. The building was demolished only recently.

A Modern Police Force

As Los Gatos grew out of its pioneer era, the crime rate decreased and by January 1913 the town Recorder, B. W. Pearce, could report that "During 1912 there were but two fines imposed, both for riding vehicles on the sidewalk." Also a Japanese was arrested and fined $10 on December 16, 1912, "but the nature of the offense was such that I thought it advisable to remit the fine, and also made no charge for filing."[9]

Although Los Gatos had built a new town hall in 1913 it was without a jail, the old Seanor jail having long since disappeared. This disturbed the night watchman and Marshal Barber. In April 1917 the Marshal reported that the night watchman wanted a jail to care for the drunks "coming in on the late cars." It was difficult, because of their condition, to take them to their homes, and "to take them by auto to the county jail is a questionable method of handling them." Judge Bell was asked to comment on this at the Town Board meeting of April 14, 1917 and he suggested a two-compartment jail. He said it shouldn't cost more than $400 or $500.

As a result of complaints from the police and night watchman a jail was constructed behind the new City Hall, but it took until April 1934 to get it completed. Few people knew that it existed, and fewer yet were incarcerated there. But it was available in case of need.

Until 1911 the Town Marshal was elected by the people for a two-year term. J. D. Shore, whose second term expired in 1912, was the last elected Marshal. H. O. Baird, the Town Marshal in the early 1920's, was named the first Chief of Police by the Town Council in 1926. He resigned in August 1928 to open a filling station on the corner of Bachman and Santa Cruz Avenue. Henry C. Noble, who had been Town Building Inspector, was appointed to succeed Baird in November 1928. Lyman Feathers became his deputy in September 1929. The salary of the Chief and his deputy was set at $115 a month, but they had to furnish their own equipment. In 1932 Chief Noble recommended Ralph Phillips to be a deputy police officer and traffic officer.

The Depression years put an extra burden on the police. Many "down-and-out" people came into town. Lyman Feathers, who in 1931 was still a traffic officer, devoted much time to what was known as "Hotel Feathers." This was a place where the unemployed itinerants were given supper, bed and breakfast. It was financed by private donations and the Red Cross. It cost about 12 cents per guest per night.

Ralph Phillips, Chief of Police 1943 to 1970. *(Courtesy Ralph Phillips family)*

West Main Street after the fire of 1901, above, south side of the street, looking west from the bridge. Hotel Lyndon in left background. Right, looking northwest from the Main Street Bridge. All of the buildings on both sides of West Main Street from the bridge west to the railroad were destroyed, as well as some on University Avenue. *(Library Collection)*

Lyman Feathers was the moving spirit behind this project for two years. The extent of this activity is evident from the statistics for one month. In November 1931 it cared for 392 men, served 849 meals and averaged 13 men a day and 28 meals. In February 1932 more than 400 "guests" were served at "Hotel Feathers." Joe Espinosa was the Chef and "house manager" and he and Feathers received many letters of thanks from the men who were helped.

Upon the death of Chief Noble in May 1939, Lyman Feathers was given the temporary appointment as Chief of Police. He was also to serve as temporary tax collector, license collector, health officer, building inspector, electrical and plumbing inspector. His salary was $175 a month plus $12.50 expenses. Bob Harris was appointed temporary police officer.

On June 17, 1940 Chief Feathers asked for an extra man for the police force and named Howard Eaton as his choice. Eaton was to serve until September at a salary of $125 a month.

Lyman Feathers resigned his position on October 23, 1943 to go into the Taxicab business. Ralph Phillips was appointed to succeed him. Chief Phillips took over at a time of great growth for Los Gatos, and the need for an expanded police force. When he became Chief there were only three officers. He had to request more police personnel from time to time. When Chief Phillips retired in 1970 the Los Gatos Police Force was a modern, well-trained force of 20 men. A woman officer was hired to check the parking and there were three girls in the office. The new Civic Center has a complete building devoted to law enforcement. Pamphlets are distributed to educate the people on burglary protection, purse-snatching and car stealing. All in all, Los Gatos now has an efficient police department, one that compares favorably with the best. Mr. Harold A. Johnson, who suc-

The 1915 La France fire engine and the "fire boys." *Top row:* Roy Hunter, Dave Trese, Harry Webley, Walter Peacock, Simeon Erwin, Elton Hatch, and Carl Rodgers. *Second row:* Jesse O'Neil, Clarence Lyndon, John Vodden, Russell Sund, Louis Sporleder and Dick Shore. *Seated:* Zedd Riggs, Jack Sullivan, Hjalman Erickson, Thos. Barbano, Harry Pearce and Lawrence Erickson. *(Photo and identification courtesy C. J. Lyndon)*

ceeded Ralph Phillips as Chief, is continuing the excellent work begun by Ralph Phillips.

Fires and Fire Protection

Before 1890 Los Gatos had only a "bucket brigade" for fire protection. This was handled by a volunteer fire company that was organized in 1886. It organized into a Hose Company in the fall of 1887. A committee from this volunteer group appeared before the Town Board to advise them of their slate of officers and to ask that the hose equipment be given into their hands until such time as the Town Board created a Fire Department.

In April 1889 the volunteer firemen desired a meeting place and a storage place for the Hose Cart. Trustee Suydam reported that his committee had looked into the matter and that they had obtained rooms in the Tower Building of Rankin's Water Works at a rent of $7.50 a month for 3 years. After considerable wrangling the Town Board accepted the report. On April 15 the Hose Company asked the Town Board for a Charter to achieve a legal status. They also asked for a bell to call the members together in case of fire. The Board granted a Charter and appointed a committee to look into the matter of a fire bell. Some townspeople and Board members expressed their opposition to a town fire bell. It was unnecessary "with so many church bells in town."

It took two major fires to bestir the Town Board into action regarding better fire protection. On the night of November 20, 1888 gas escaping from one of the stills of the Co-operative Winery was ignited by a lantern hanging nearby. It sent a blaze into the brandy and burned the hands and face of Herman Rocker, the distiller. The people who arrived at the scene rolled out a few hundred gallons of brandy, but the heat of the fire prevented further rescue efforts. When the firemen arrived they "coupled to the hydrant by the bakery, but got so little force that their work was of little consequence." The brandy continued to burn until 10 o'clock that night. All that could be done was to keep the neighboring buildings wet to prevent the fire from spreading. The building, the engine, two boiler distilleries, pump and other machinery were destroyed, together with nearly 1000 gallons of brandy. The loss was estimated at $3000, and insurance covered only $850 of the loss. The winery was rebuilt immediately.[10]

One of the great fires in Los Gatos started on Sunday night July 27, 1891. Fire broke out in a wooden building in the rear of Place and Fretwell Furniture Store. The night watchman, E. F. Reynolds, discovered the fire and ran for the Presbyterian Church to ring the alarm bell, crying out "Fire! Fire!" all the way. Cartridges exploded in the H. J. Richardson Hardware Store. G. S. McMurtry and Bernard Lee's Los Gatos Store had explosives in the rear which exploded, shaking things for a half mile around, breaking glass in windows and damaging the roof of the Ice Works by Forbes' Mill. It knocked John Baer, a bystander, 20 feet.

The fire spread rapidly. It swept through the block and only the 10-foot width of the alley between Barnes' picture framing store and the George Lewis Hardware Store kept the fire from consuming that block also. The greatest fear was that the fire would reach the bridge and sweep on to the other side with its still more compact wooden buildings. Two houses belonging to Place and Fretwell and the stable in the rear of their building were burned. The Post Office was destroyed, although most of the mail in the delivery

The El Monte Hotel fire of July 3, 1909. This view from the rear and west side of Pleasant Street, southward toward Main Street. *(Library Collection)*

room was saved. The fire destroyed all of the buildings from the east side of the bridge to the present corner of East Main and Church Street.

After these fires the Town Board asked the town Attorney to draw up an ordinance fixing fire limits inside of which all buildings "shall be built of brick or stone and made safe from fire." The Los Gatos *Mail,* in discussing the fire, stated that it proved again "that Los Gatos needs a new water system and a Fire Department."[11]

In August, shortly after the fire, the volunteers of the Hose Company asked for an increase in personnel from 15 to 30. Hydrants were installed at specified places and a Hook and Ladder truck---No. 1---arrived in December.

At a meeting in the El Monte Hotel on the evening of August 5, 1891 the proposal was made to organize a volunteer Hook and Ladder Company. Lynn Austin was chairman and J. D. Mason was secretary. A committee was appointed to ask the Town Board to buy an outfit for the company so that it would not be necessary to approach business people for contributions. On August 24 the Town Board voted to allow the Hook and Ladder Company to form a permanent organization. Mr. A. Berryman offered to erect a building near the bridge to house the equipment.

At this meeting both the Hook and Ladder Company and the Hose Company elected officers. The officers of the former were: Lynn Austin, Foreman; John Zollars, Ass't. Foreman; William Baker, second Ass't.; James Richards, Secretary and R. F. Robertson, Treasurer. The Hose Company chose as their officers M. Dulion, Foreman; E. N. Davis, Ass't. Foreman; Fred Knowles, second Ass't.; C. C. Suydam, Secretary and F. H. Lyndon, Treasurer. The Chief of the department

was J. A. Aram, who was to run with the Hose team. Twenty members signed up at this first meeting. The name "Los Gatos Fire Department" was chosen.[12]

In November 1894 J. W. Lyndon leased to the town the land and a building to house the Hose Company No. 1. A. G. Williams was granted $100 by the Town Board to put the building in repair for the Fire Department. This was a meeting place for firemen. The firemen now had a home in a pleasant quarter opposite the depot. The "house-warming" on April 12, 1895 packed the little room. Because of the rain, the planned-for parade was not held. Dancing was enjoyed in the evening.

But it seems that some of the firemen did other things in the building besides discussing fire protection. On November 3, 1895 a complaint was made to the Town Board that "boys were playing cards and gambling in the Hose House."[13]

On June 15, 1896 the Town Board instructed the Clerk to draw warrants in the amount of $2.00 as salary for each fireman per year. The salary, limited to men between 21 and 60, was to be applied to poll tax for which a receipt was to be given to each fireman.

The Fire Bell

The question of a town fire bell was still to be settled. The editor of the Los Gatos *Chronicle* wondered in its October 18, 1893 edition, what had happened to the Fire Alarm Bell. "It will be remembered," said the editor, "that Mr. Turner, President of the Los Gatos Bank, collected about fifty dollars from the business firms of this town and handed it over to the firemen, which amount was to go towards helping buy a bell." It was

Los Gatos fire bell and tower now in front of a chicken restaurant south of Lodi. *(Photo by author)*

further pointed out that the firemen gave a dance which cleared $100 and which was added to the $50 deposited in the Commercial Bank. "The people are now waiting to see what the Town Trustees are going to do about increasing this sum." The fire bell, with three alarm stations, would cost about $400.

The church bells were used for fire alarms. Every church and school was asked to place keys in boxes available to the firemen in case of need. On September 10, 1898 a petition with more than 200 names was presented to the Town Board asking for a fire alarm system. The Town Board asked for bids and the only bidder was the Hume Company. J. D. Farwell appeared before the Board on April 27, 1899 and agreed to install, within 90 days, a complete fire alarm system for a 5-year period at a rental of $25 per month. The town could have the option of purchasing the same for $2,250 any time within the 5-year period. The system was to consist of six Gamewell Excelsor non-interfering fire alarm boxes with necessary keys and apparatus; a town bell of about 1500 pounds weight, one electric tower-bell striker, a tower 60 feet high, one switchboard, one noon-day alarm clock. These conditions

Alfred L. Lord, the first full-time, paid, resident fireman, in front of the old firehouse on Taite and West Main St. in 1938. *(Museum Collection)*

were accepted on May 3, 1899. However, on that date Mr. Farwell appeared before the Board with a new contract. He proposed a steel tower instead of the wooden one originally planned, and asked the town to lay the foundation and put in place the four piers needed for the tower. The tower was to be located near the Lyndon Hotel on Santa Cruz Avenue.

On August 7, 1899 Mr. Farwell again appeared before the Board saying the 1500-pound bell would be too small and that he recommended a 2500-pound bell. This would add $250 to the contract price. The Board approved this change. The 2500-pound bell was installed on top of the wooden tower. The tower, ironically, burned down during the great fire of 1901 and the bell fell to the ground, sustaining three cracks. Despite this, it was hung on the new steel tower when it was later built, and served well for many years. Actually the cracks were said to have given the bell a deeper tone than before.

The Town Clerk was asked to advertise for bids for a place to erect the steel bell-tower. The only bid received was that of Miss Anna Lee, through her agent Wesley Peck, who offered a lot for $175. This was off University Avenue just east of Main Street. The fire bell was built by Garratt Company of San Francisco and was 12 feet at the circumference of the lip. From the top of the steel tower it served as a fire bell, and a curfew, and sounded the hour of noon daily. For years a jeweler at the

85

corner of Main Street and University Avenue was commissioned to keep the works in order.

When the P.G. & E. bought out the Los Gatos Gas and Electric Company in 1912, it took over the responsibility of keeping the fire bell and system in operation. But the bell soon proved to be inadequate. Seven firemen missed going to a fire on February 4, 1930 because they did not hear the bell alarm. "Whether it is air pockets, buildings, trees, or what," said Fire Chief Sullivan, "something prevented the sound from penetrating to all parts of the city and a more adequate alarm system is needed for the volunteer department."[14]

The town had a siren installed on a one-month trial basis at a cost of $110. In 1951 the famous "bull" horn was installed. It sounded all alarms for fire, giving the location signals for the fire. In 1947 the old tower and bell were removed. Mr. John Whisenant purchased the bell and the tower and finally sold them to a Mr. Pollard who owns a "Chicken Kitchen" restaurant on Highway 99 south of Lodi. The old La France Fire engine rests there, too, beside the tower and the bell. Perhaps all three are wondering what they are doing in front of a chicken kitchen, after such good service calling firemen to their responsibilities for so many years, and sounding the noon hour for all the people in Los Gatos or the curfew every evening to send the young people home.

Progress Toward a Modern Fire Department

The volunteer firemen were a dedicated group of people. When the fire bell sounded they all forgot their business and became "minutemen." A fire isn't a good thing to behold, but to see a group of men forget their own interests for the common good was a moving experience. Then, too, firemen have always been interested in community activities. They decorated trees at Christmas, repaired toys and gave them to the poor; they sponsored community picnics, held May Day celebrations, donated the results of their hunts for a banquet for old timers "just to keep the old spirit burning." They supported a baseball team of their own and sponsored numerous other youth activities. It was only when the local high school had a baseball team that they shifted their loyalty from their own to the high school team.

But fire protection was still the big responsibility of the men. And in 1901 they faced another serious fire. On Sunday morning October 13, 1901 a fire broke out in the livery stable opposite the depot on Front Street—now Montebello Way. All of the buildings on both sides of West Main Street from the bridge west to the railroad track were burned. The fire even went part way up University Avenue.

The meeting place for the firemen was destroyed, as were all of the records. Fire Chief James Fushaw reported to the Town Board in May 1903 that the Fire Company had had no meeting since the fire. He could give no report since all records had been lost in the fire. He also stated that the town should pay the firemen for their services. Since there was no money available, no action was taken. Chief Fushaw was asked to have the equipment cleaned and to make an inventory of all such equipment. The firemen were disgruntled because the Board would not consider paying them. On October 19, 1903 Mr. A. G. Williams appeared before the Board in behalf of the firemen and asked that the town approve 25 firemen to be appointed either by the Fire Chief or by the Town Board, and that they be paid $2.50 or $3.00 each time they were called out to a fire. On November 16 the Board approved the appointments and agreed to set aside $100 a year payable January 1 and July 1.[15]

The three hose carts and hand-drawn hook and ladder wagon were the only fire equipment until

Jack Sullivan, Fire Chief from 1920 to 1955, longer than any other person to hold that position. *(Courtesy Los Gatos Fire Dept.)*

Richard B. Wall Jr., Fire Chief from 1957 to 1970. Became Assist-Fire Chief of the Central Fire District in 1970. *(Courtesy Senior Richard Wall family)*

Fire of July 5, 1943 which destroyed the Lewis & Son business. Ironically, this had escaped the big fire of 1891. Green's Drug Store on the left. *(Courtesy Elton Green)*

1915. As a result of a successful bond election in 1914 the town purchased a La France combination chemical and hose truck in 1915. Another bond issue was passed in 1916 which provided $30,000 for new equipment. A new 750-gallon American La France pumper was purchased. Another bond issue in the amount of $30,000 was passed in June 1926. This made it possible for the town to erect a modern firehouse on the corner of Tait Avenue and West Main Street---the present location of the Los Gatos Museum. It was completed in July 1927.

The Fire Department had seven Fire Chiefs before a permanent, salaried Fire Chief was selected in 1955. The first Chief was Charles Dricoing, a barber. He was followed by Nate Baumgardner. Then came Matt Doolen, who kept a saloon across from Green's Drug Store---the Dental Laboratory today. Lloyd Lyndon, J. D. Shore and Jack Sullivan followed in succession. Sullivan was first selected to that position in 1920 and held it longer than any other man before 1955.

Los Gatos was to experience another great fire in 1943. This was almost a repeat performance of the great fire of October 13, 1901 which destroyed about half the town. The 1943 fire broke out in the John F. Good Second Hand Store at 19 East Main Street. It soon enveloped the entire building and spread eastward, taking in the rear of the Lewis Plumbing Shop and the large garage building next to it with its large stock of goods. Two buildings were completely destroyed and others badly damaged. The red brick Rex Hotel was damaged. The property damage exceeded $50,000 but the priceless loss of personal items was most tragic.

Full-Time Paid Fire Chief

In 1954 the Town Council, upon the recommendation of the Town Manager, began consideration of the matter of a full-time Fire Chief. The volunteer firemen opposed this. In a letter to the Council, J. C. Hooten, Secretary to the Volunteer Firemen, said, "We believe that if there is to be a full-time Chief then you should go all the way and employ full-time fire-fighters and eliminate the volunteer department."

The dispute aroused emotions. Joe Houghteling, the editor of the Los Gatos *Times,* wrote a calm editorial on September 20, 1954 favoring a full-time Fire Chief. He cited the increase in population and the many new buildings in town for which a fire crew was responsible. Some volunteers threatened to resign if the Town Council went ahead with its plans. John D. Smart, President of the Los Gatos Insurance Agents, was asked to bring the firemen and the Town Council together for a meeting. He was successful in bringing the two factions together for a discussion of the issue. Most of the firemen were satisfied and withdrew their threats to resign.

An ordinance was passed on September 30, 1954 creating a full-time Fire Chief. Said Mayor A. E. Merrill, "We have given the issue a lot of thought for a long time, and we believe our decision is right."

In January 1955 the Council appointed Lee M. Schlobohm, Deputy County Fire Marshal and former Central Fire District foreman, as the first full-time paid Fire Chief. He was recommended by the Town Manager, Karl Baldwin, and the firemen agreed to "go along" with the appointment of the Chief on an unspecified probationary period.

In July 1955 a new fire-alarm system was completed, providing for an alarm box within 500 feet of every commercial and industrial building from Roberts Road to North Santa Cruz Avenue and East Main Street.

Lee Schlobohm resigned on February 1, 1957 to become Fire Chief for San Luis Obispo. Pat Mullin became Acting Chief. A Civil Service test was given to 27 applicants for the position in February and Richard Wall Jr., who had been a regular fireman since 1952, was named the second full-time, paid Fire Chief for Los Gatos.

Merger With County Central Fire District

Fire protection service has grown with the town. A new fire station was built on Shannon Road in 1960. In 1962 a bond issue passed which included money for a new Headquarters building for the

The famous brick wall on College Avenue today. Behind this was the old bottling works. The Mariotti Hotel and Saloon stood in front on East Main Street until the late 1960's. *(Photo by the author)*

Central Fire Station on University Avenue. In 1963 the Lark Avenue Fire Station was completed on Winchester Road. Before the merger, the Los Gatos Fire Department had 27 full-time firemen.

During the latter part of 1969 there was a great deal of discussion about the advisability of joining a County Central Fire District which was proposed by the County Board of Supervisors. When the Los Gatos Town Council indicated an interest in the plan, it was strongly opposed by some people. Max Walden, the developer of Old Town, George Tobin, an Attorney, and Sam Yablonsky, manager of the Los Gatos Theatre and sometime candidate for the Town Council, expressed vehement opposition. They feared increased cost and less protection.

Despite the objections, the merger was completed on May 1, 1970. It was estimated that this would save the Los Gatos taxpayers between $80,000 and $100,000 a year. It also did away with the constant objections of having the local fire equipment leave the boundaries of the town to assist in fighting fires. Now the equipment goes to all parts of the Central Fire District.

Fire Chief Richard Wall Jr. became an Assistant Fire Chief with the Central Fire District. His work is mostly in public relations and research. The Los

Lyman Feathers, Police Chief from 1939 to 1943. While on the police force during the Depression in the early 1930's he helped many "down-and-outers" at the famous "Feathers Hotel." He entered the taxi business after he resigned his position as Chief of Police in 1943. *(Courtesy Mrs. Louise Feathers Rodgers)*

Gatos Fire Department is no more, but the fire protection is as good, if not better than ever before.

FOOTNOTES

1. Addicot, James E. *Grandad's Pioneer Stories,* p. 46ff.
2. Sawyer, Eugene, *History of Santa Clara County,* p. 168.
3. *Ibid.* Also Library *Collection,* Bk. 34.
4. Library *Collection,* Bk. 34.
5. *Ibid.*
6. *Ibid.*
7. Town Board *Minutes,* Bk. II, p. 124.
8. Library *Collection,* Bk. 34.
9. Town Board *Minutes,* Book IV, p. 434.
10. Los Gatos Weekly *News,* November 23, 1888.
11. Los Gatos *Mail,* July 29, 1891.
12. Los Gatos Weekly *News,* August 14, 1891.
13. Town Board *Minutes,* Bk. II, p. 253.
14. Los Gatos *Mail-News,* February 7, 1930.
15. Town Board *Minutes,* Bk. III, p. 464 ff.

CHAPTER IX

Early Business and Financial Institutions

Hotels

DESPITE the fact that the Los Gatos Hotel—later the Lyndon Hotel—had been in existence for a number of years, the local press, in 1885, expressed the hope that "a good hotel, large enough to accommodate 200 persons" would soon be built in Los Gatos. The railroad was bringing hundreds of people into Los Gatos during the latter part of the 19th century. The Weekly *News* in October 1885 lamented that "people are constantly turning their attention to other points because there is not such facilities here as they demand." It would be a paying investment to have a hotel "and it would add largely to all other business." The *News* felt that the South Pacific Coast Railroad would be interested in having such a hotel established "since it would get people to patronize its line."

The first response to this suggestion was the Wilcox Hotel, opened in early 1887. It had 35 rooms "all provided with water, gas, electric bell-calls, and sunshine." A new feature of the hotel was the finish which "left the grain of the native wood unpainted but preserved by the use of shellac or varnish." Even before the opening, Mr. Queenan, a hotel keeper "of much experience in San Francisco," reported that a party of 15 eastern tourists had already engaged rooms for a season. As far as can be determined the Wilcox was located on

the south side of the bend on East Main Street, near College Avenue.

In 1881 a small hotel known as the Coleman House had been built at the foot of El Monte Hill on East Main Street. It was managed by the father of Zepf Macabee, the inventor and manufacturer of the gopher trap. It was later the Alpine Hotel. In 1889 it was enlarged, a third story added, and renamed the Rockhaven Hotel. The Los Gatos Weekly *News* gave great praise to the new hostelry in its issue of November 17, 1889. "The new hotel on East Main Street," it said, "has been leased by S. R. Mathewson, who will furnish it in the best modern style." Mrs. M. A. Hardesty of Santa Cruz was the housekeeper for the hotel. Mr. Mathewson provided bus service to carry passengers to and from the hotel and the depot. Other hotels had similar service, and old timers remembered seeing the horse and buggy "hacks" at the station, each seeking customers for his particular hotel.

The Rockhaven had a gala opening on December 7, 1889. Everyone was invited to partake of the refreshments and to dance to the music of an orchestra imported from San Francisco for the occasion. The local press commented: "The Rockhaven bids fair to become one of the prominent institutions of our young and thriving city."

However, the Rockhaven found itself in diffi-

The El Monte Hotel at East Main Street and Pleasant St. at the foot of El Monte Hill. Built in 1881 as the Coleman House, it became successively the Alpine Hotel, the Rockhaven and, on April 20, 1891, the El Monte. *(Library Collection)*

The elegant El Monte Hotel in its hey-day in the early 1900's. Destroyed by fire on July 3, 1909. *(Library Collection)*

culty from the start. Thomas Guilford sued the owners for $16,000 he claimed was owed him for repair work on the building. The case went to court, and Guilford was given judgment in the amount of his claim. When the Sheriff came to enforce the judgment, Mrs. Mathewson sued the Sheriff and his men for taking her personal property to satisfy the claim. That week the Rockhaven was leased to T. J. Rice and the name was changed to El Monte Hotel.

Under the new management the hotel's policy was to cater to families and "those who wish to stop a week or a few months in this most beautiful town in California." Garten Keyston, a former early resident of Los Gatos, recalled the El Monte in a letter to Miss Dora Rankin, as "a large, red, wooden structure, L-shaped with long verandas on all stories extending the entire length of the building." It had, he said, one of only two tennis courts in town––the other being on the Dr. W. S. McMurtry place.[1]

There was always danger of a fire at the hotel because of its all-wooden structure. Predictably, on July 3, 1909 the El Monte Hotel was totally destroyed by fire. No one was injured in the spectacular blaze and the greater part of the furnishings and personal belongings were saved. Thus ended the life of the widely-known hotel which had been the scene of many local social functions. It was never rebuilt.

After the fire of 1891, which destroyed most of East Main Street, a new brick building, known as the Beckwith Block, was constructed. This later became the Rex Hotel and, in its early days, housed the Post Office and other business establishments. The fire of 1901 damaged the rear of the building but otherwise left it intact. It is still used as a hostelry, and business establishments occupy the ground floor.

There were other small hotels or "boarding houses" in Los Gatos. One of these was the

HOTEL EL MONTE,
CAPT. S. S. AUSTIN,
PROPRIETOR.

––––––o––––––

Positively the only First-Class Hotel
–in Los Gatos.–

Los Gatos,   **Santa Clara Co. Cal.**

Los Gatos *Mail*, June 1, 1893.

Greeley House, located on Church Street. In the late 1860's and 1870's the Greeley House served as an overnight stopping place for teamsters hauling tan bark to San Jose. The house, with its 8 bedrooms and large attic, gave accommodations to many a teamster going to, and coming from, San Jose. The building was later purchased by Mrs. Mary C. Knowles, the mother of Dr. Frank Knowles, who maintained his office on the ground floor near the front entrance. The E. C. Yocco family purchased the building in 1883, and it later became the home of Mr. and Mrs. E. C. Yocco.[2] Mrs. Yocco lived there for many years after the

The Perkins Hardware Store, 1886. In the picture are Mr. Perkins, Mr. Sweeney, and Mr. Lingley. (Identification made by Miss Hulda Erickson) *(Library Collection)*

Lewis and Son Store before the fire of 1891. Originally the Perkins & Son store until Sept. 1887 when it became Lewis & Hood, and, in 1888, Lewis & Son. This building escaped the fire of 1891 only to be destroyed by fire in 1943. *(Library Collection)*

death of her husband. The building was torn down in 1957 to make room for the new Methodist Church Sanctuary and grounds.

Some Early Stores

We have already noted some of the early businesses such as Lyndon's store and lumber yard, McMurtry's store, etc. But some of the best known old-time businesses came later. The A. F. Place Furniture and Undertaking establishment became a landmark business in Los Gatos. Mr. Place started the business in 1884. It was originally located on East Main Street, about where the Masonic Temple now stands. By 1887 the business had grown so that new quarters were obtained in the Willey Block on the north side of East Main Street. In the fall of 1887 A. F. Place left the business and moved to San Benito County, where he was killed in an accident. His son, Elvert Ernest Place, conducted the business himself. The Willey Block was destroyed by the fire of July 27, 1891. Mr. Place, undaunted by his loss, immediately opened in a building at 13–15 North Santa Cruz Avenue. In 1920 he purchased the old Cogswell home at 115 North Santa Cruz Avenue, where the business remains to this day.

In 1922 Mr. Place disposed of his furniture business in order to concentrate on the funeral and ambulance service. His son George became associated in the business with him in that year, but E. E. Place remained the head until his death in June 1937. The Place Funeral Home became well-known under the leadership of George Place, the third generation to head the business. When he retired in 1966 the business came under the management of someone other than a member of the Place family for the first time in 85 years.

Another three-generation enterprise in Los Gatos is the H. J. Crall Store. It started in 1890 when a young man by the name of Henry J. Crall came with his bride from San Francisco to visit his brother in Los Gatos. His bride fell in love with the town, and the result was that Henry J. opened a store, "Crall's Palace of Sweets" in a building at 120 West Main Street. Mr. Crall was no stranger to the candy business, having previously worked with the Townsend Candy Factory in San Francisco.

Along with candy Mr. Crall began gradually to stock toys, children's books, school supplies and stationery. The Great Fire of October 13, 1901 destroyed the Crall store, as well as many other

Edw. C. Yocco's Los Gatos Meat Market on corner of East Main and Wilcox (now College) Avenue 1890. *(Photo courtesy Mary Yocco Rugh)*

91

Advertisements in early newspapers. From original files. *(Courtesy the Leland Walker family)*

business houses. Everything was a total loss, and at 56 years of age Henry J. Crall started over again. He located in one side of Fred Knowles' Candy and Ice Cream Parlor in the Rex Hotel. He gave up the candy and toy business and concentrated on books and stationery.

Later, when the town was rebuilt after the fire of 1901, the store moved to the Ford Block---later Crider's and now the Opera House Antiques. Crall persuaded Mr. Knowles to move to the new location with him. When Knowles retired several years later, Mr. Crall bought his part of the business.

After J. Walter Crider purchased the Ford Block in 1916, Crall moved to the present location at 21 North Santa Cruz Avenue. His son, Henry C. Crall, recalled in the 75th Anniversary Edition of the Los Gatos *Times Observer,* May 11, 1965, that the Crall store was the last store on the street, just on the edge of the business district.

Henry J. retired in 1916. However, the War came along and his son, Henry C., went into the Army, which brought the founder out of retirement and into the business again. He stayed in the business until the son returned from overseas, in April 1919. Back on the job again, Henry C.

decided to expand the business. He bought out George Rasmussen, who not only had a book store but operated all the newspaper routes in Los Gatos. Crall's delivered newspapers in Los Gatos for 29 years. Henry C. added new items to his merchandise, including greeting cards and various gift items and some imported articles. Picture framing has also been added, and it has grown rapidly in recent years.

The third generation Crall, Henry L., became a partner in the business in 1964. It almost seems that Crall's is as much a part of Los Gatos as the Main Street Bridge or the very foothills themselves.

But no account of Los Gatos business undertakings would be complete without mention of Green's Pharmacy. It began when T. E. Johns established a drug store in the Rex Hotel building in 1893. It soon became the Johns and Johnson Drug Store. The first prescription was written in June 1893. This prescription was still on the books when Mr. and Mrs. Fred Callis, its subsequent owners, retired in 1964. In 1904 George Green bought the pharmacy, continuing in the same location until 1914. In that year Green moved to a building at 11 East Main Street, next to the bridge. Here the drug store remained for over 40 years. Mr.

Los Gatos Agricultural Works, located on the north side of East Main Street about where the Methodist Parking and Recreation Office are today. This, the building next to it, and the Seanor Opera House all burned down in 1890. The men are John Erickson, Thomas Tobin, Mr. Dow, Geo. Seanor and Harry Ball. (Identification by Miss Hulda Erickson) *(Library Collection)*

Green built the new building which is now the Dental Laboratory.

In 1946 Fred and Lucia Callis bought the pharmacy and operated it in the same building until 1954, when they moved to North Santa Cruz Avenue. When they retired in July 1964, Green's Pharmacy had been a landmark for over 60 years.

Other early business ventures could be mentioned. There was the Yocco Meat Market on East Main Street. The Yocco barn was across the street on Villa Avenue, about where the Civic Center is now located. Miss Hulda Erickson recalled that two boys, John Purviance and Jack Hill, slept in the barn to guard it.

Then there was the Schomberg Piano Factory. Few people know that pianos were once made in Los Gatos. The Schomberg family produced pianos on the ground floor of the house on the corner of Wheeler and San Jose Avenue---the Mullins house. Schomberg exhibited his piano in Chicago, and it received a ribbon for excellence. Again, Miss Erickson remembers one of the Schomberg girls as a fellow student in the Los Gatos schools.

Store on Main Street near the bridge in 1890. The men in the picture are: Robt. Wilson, Mr. Lewis and Mr. Gibson. *(Museum Collection)*

The Farmers' Union became a large and well-known store in Los Gatos in the 1890's. It was incorporated in March 1890 with the following Directors: W. D. Tisdale, C. Roemer, F. M. Farwell, H. B. Edwards, E. B. Howard, and J. A. Brachett. The building was a 65 x 100 foot structure that fronted on Santa Cruz Avenue with the rear bordering on the railroad tracks. It was a two-story building, the upper story being used as the Masonic lodge rooms. The building was torn down in 1967 to make room for a series of one-story shops and offices.

Financial Institutions

There were no banks in Los Gatos prior to 1883. In that year the Los Gatos Weekly *News* stated that Los Gatos had need for a banking house. "There is enough idle capital lying around to start a respectable bank." Two Los Gatans, Mr. Conklin and Mr. Kirkland accepted the challenge and organized a bank in 1883. It was incorporated in November 1883 as the Bank of Los Gatos with a capital stock of $50,000, and occupied a brick building on the south side of East Main Street and College Avenue "on the A. Berryman property." Some of the leading stockholders included A. J. Stanfield, Robert Walker, A. E. Wilder, H. H. Kooser, A. Berryman, W. C. Shore, George Seanor, J. W. Lyndon, D. D. Holland, George Holland, James Hamilton, Charles Milliken, J. S. Fowler and Mack Davis. George Turner was President, A. J. Stanfield, Vice-President, and Eben C. Farley, Cashier. In 1891 the bank moved to the Theresa Lyndon Building on the corner of West Main Street and Santa Cruz Avenue, the present Park Plaza Building. This corner of Los Gatos became known as the Bank Corner since a bank occupied the location from 1891 until 1963, when the Bank of America left it for its new quarters.

Edw. C. Yocco's Los Gatos Meat Market on Santa Cruz Avenue. Geo. Yocco on right and E. C. Yocco in center. About 1896. *(Los Gatos Museum and Mrs. Mary Yocco Rugh)*

Commercial Bank Building, 1890's. Located on southeast corner of West Main Street and Oak Street (Front Street and now Montebello Way). Destroyed by fire in October 1901. *(Library Collection)*

Original location of the Bank of Los Gatos in the early 1890's. Building was on East Main Street between College Avenue and Pageant Way. *(Library Collection)*

The second bank founded in Los Gatos was the Commercial Bank, of which Joseph Ryland was Cashier and leading stockholder. It opened for business on July 2, 1889 and was located on the corner of West Main and Front Street---now Montebello Way. The building burned down in the great fire of October 13, 1901 but the fireproof vault survived the fire. The assets of the Commercial Bank were then purchased by the Los Gatos Bank.

The Bank of Los Gatos was purchased by S. D. Balch and J. A. Case in 1904 and continued as a locally-owned bank until 1926, when it was purchased by the Bank of Italy, which shortly thereafter changed its name to Bank of America. A new building was erected on the Bank Corner. In November 1963 it moved to its new and larger building at 333 North Santa Cruz Avenue where it has ample off-street parking. Mr. Walter Adams is the local manager.

The third bank in Los Gatos was the First National Bank, which was organized in June 1911 and opened its doors on September 5, 1911. Dr. Charles Cooper of Campbell was the first President and Milton Allison the first Cashier. In 1913 Zedd Riggs became President and the Board members included Dr. F. W. Knowles and C. F. Hamsher. The bank was originally located in the building on the south side of Main Street, later occupied by the Los Gatos Telephone Company. In February 1912 it moved to the Fretwell building on the corner of University Avenue and Main Street.

In 1918 the First National Bank purchased the building on the east side of the railroad track on Main Street, which was occupied by the Nuss and Hayes Hardware Store and the G. S. McMurtry Realty Office. The bank moved into the new quarters over the Labor Day weekend in 1918. The Los Gatos *Mail* reported that "C. F. Hamsher, the Cashier, stated that the new Quarters would give ample room, and that as soon as some of the leases expired in the quarters, the bank would be further expanded."[3] But instead of a large remodeling job the bank decided to build a new building in 1920. The First National Bank Building was a beautiful building and served as a bank until 1955. It became the Village Floor Covering store, owned by Robert Brouwer, and is now the London Oyster dining room.

In 1927 C. F. Hamsher was elected President of the First National, Dr. F. W. Knowles was elected Vice-President, and Herbert Roberts became the Cashier. In the early 1930's the First National became the victim of the Great Depression and was reorganized under government regulation. Paul Curtis became manager, succeeding C. F. Hamsher, D. L. McKay was President, and the Directors included Arch Cilker, F. F. Watkins, Leland Walker, Dr. F. W. Knowles, D. T. Jenkins and Dr. J. H. Pond. In December 1939 S. D. Balch purchased McKay's interests in the Bank and became President. The American Trust Company purchased the First National Bank on February 1, 1955. American Trust built a new building on the corner of Royce and Santa Cruz Avenues and moved into the spacious building on October 24, 1955. Mr. William Balch, who had been with his

First National Bank before the new bank building was constructed. *(Museum Colleetion)*

father in the reorganized First National, remained for a number of years with the American Trust Company. In 1960 American Trust merged with the Wells Fargo Bank and since that time the Wells Fargo Bank has served a growing clientele in the Los Gatos area. Mr. J. C. McCarthy is the manager of the local branch.

Since World War II, new branch banks have been established in Los Gatos. The First National Bank of San Jose came to Los Gatos in 1954. Mr. Charles Hayes of Saratoga was the first Manager of the Los Gatos Branch. In 1955 the bank moved into its new building at 308 North Santa Cruz Avenue, with its ample off-street parking.

The Valley First National Bank came to King's Court Shopping Center on Blossom Hill and San Jose Avenue in 1959. After ten years in Los Gatos, the Valley First National was sold to Barclay's Bank on December 14, 1969. Mr. Dick Ward is the manager of the local branch.

The last banking corporation to establish a branch in Los Gatos is the Crocker Citizens

National Bank, which came in April 1967. It constructed a beautiful building on the site of the former Wright's---later Fanning's---Motel on Saratoga and Santa Cruz Avenues. The local manager of this bank is Mr. Frank Fratto.

Savings and Loan Associations

On April 23, 1889 a group of "representative men of Los Gatos" organized the Los Gatos Building and Loan Association. Mr. A. Berryman was the leading figure and served as Secretary for a number of years. Its capital stock was $100,000 in 500 shares of $200 each. Among the other "representative men" on the Board of Directors were C. F. Seamon, Magnus Tait, E. W. Potter, J. H. Lyndon, Thomas Gibson and C. F. Wilcox.

The Association prospered and was an established savings institution for many years. It ceased operation in the late 1920's.

Just as banks built branches in Los Gatos during the great growth of the 1950's and 1960's, so did the large corporate Savings and Loan Associations.

The First National Bank Building built in 1920. *(Library Collection)*

Lobby and staff of the First National Bank before 1920. C. F. Hamsher in the foreground and Herbert Roberts in the middle cage and W. A. Riggs in the rear cage. *(Courtesy W. R. Hamsher and the Museum)*

95

James J. Stanfield, an early businessman and banker in Los Gatos. He became connected with the Bank of Los Gatos in 1887 and later served as its Vice–President. *(Courtesy Sheila Stanfield Heid)*

The first of these was the American Savings and Loan Association. It came to Los Gatos on February 28, 1958. After doing business in a temporary building, the Association moved into its large new quarters on the corner of Saratoga and Santa Cruz Avenues in December 1959. Its beautiful spacious building is located where once there was an old cannery warehouse. Mr. W. L. Doyle is the local manager.

In December 1965 the Eureka Savings and Loan Association established a branch in Los Gatos. It was housed in a temporary "mobile" office until its new building was completed in August 1967, on the corner of Santa Cruz and Bachman Avenues. A number of shops and a Title Insurance Company occupy parts of the two-story building. Mr. Ronald H. McCubbin has been the local manager from the beginning of the Los Gatos branch.

A Film Company in Los Gatos

Few people will believe that at one time Los Gatos was the locale for a moving picture. The Essanay Moving Picture Company and its cowboy star-producer, "Bronco Billy" Anderson, came to Los Gatos in 1906 to make a movie. The Old Stage Coach Road and the rear of the Hotel Lyndon were used as settings. Vic Potel and others were here for the filming. The company made its headquarters in the Hotel Lyndon.

The company came originally to San Jose to take pictures, but were "tipped off" about the little town of Los Gatos that "nestled at the foot of the Santa Cruz Mountains" and which had rugged scenic opportunities. When they arrived in Los Gatos "we were enchanted, especially when we went into the mountains over what you term the Old Stage Coach Road."[4]

The company used Los Gatos people as extras. A teen-age girl from Los Gatos made such a good impression that they asked her to join the company. They gave her the name of Veda Nertram.

C. F. Hamsher of the First National Bank. Long-time civic leader and collector of historic items on Los Gatos. *(Courtesy Clarence A. Hamsher)*

Los Gatos *Mail,*
August 6, 1896.

She passed away before she could become a big star.

Essanay had its headquarters in Niles, where Anderson had associated himself with a Chicago millionaire, George K. Spoor, who developed the first movie camera. In 1907 they formed the Spoor and Anderson (S & A, hence "Essanay") Film Manufacturing Company, with headquarters in Chicago. The company produced many famous movies in Niles, among them "The Great Train Robbery" in 1903, and numerous Westerns. By 1912 Anderson was established as the Hopalong Cassidy of his day. He made more than 700 movies during his career. Some of the heroes of the Essanay company productions included Ben Turpin, Charlie Chaplin and Wallace Beery. The last film in Niles was made in 1916. Anderson died January 20, 1971.

Mrs. William Hatch Craddock, whose father, Eldon Hatch, was one of the "extras" in the Los Gatos movie, sent Bronco Billy a copy of a

Group that was in the Western movie filmed in Los Gatos by "Bronco" Billy Anderson in 1906. Eldon Hatch, father of Mrs. Camille Hatch Craddock, is on the right at the top. *(Courtesy Mrs. Wm. Craddock)*

picture of the actor-producer, which had appeared in the Los Gatos *Times-Observer* on the occasion of his receiving the Special Oscar Award in 1958. She received a reply from Bronco Billy stating that he valued the picture very much and that it would no doubt "be in demand by all foundations as U.C.L.A. and the Eastman Foundation and others."[5]

Other Early Business Enterprises

A catalogue of all the business establishments of early Los Gatos would consume volumes. But there are a few that must be mentioned. One of the oldest lumber yards in the county was the Sterling Lumber Yard, which occupied a site on University Avenue just off Main Street for more than 80 years. The business traces its ancestry back to the 1880's and the establishment of the Santa Clara Valley Mill and Lumber Company, which opened its plant on the University Avenue site. Later it was purchased by the R. W. Adams Company, a chain enterprise concentrating on lumber and building materials. In 1916 it became the Adams and Johnson Lumber Company. However, it was still a chain store controlled by the Adams corporation.

Mr. Edwin R. Haller began to work for the company in 1919 and in 1922 became the local manager. He remained at that post until his retirement in 1961 after 42 years with the company. Ed Haller and the lumber business were almost synonymous, for he was a familiar figure to all amateur builders and local contractors.

After Ed Haller's retirement his son Frank, who had been his "understudy" in the business for some time, became the manager. In 1968 the Sterling Lumber chain sold all of its yards and the local plant was purchased by Max Walden of Old Town, who made a parking lot out of it.

Frank Haller had lumber in his blood and he and two other former employees of Sterling, Jack Vodden and Walt Pierce, joined forces to form a new corporation, The El Gato Building Materials Inc., located at 565 University Avenue. Here they are giving their customers the benefit of their wide experience in the building materials field.

One of the most unique enterprises in Los Gatos was the Hubbell Pigeon Farm. This was originally located between Santa Cruz Avenue and the railroad, a site now occupied by Rao's Market and the

Milligan Meat Market 1905. Building stood on corner of East Main and Wilcox (now College Ave.). Note interurban rails in street. *(Library Collection)*

97

The Place Grocery Store at 125 East Main Street. This was destroyed by the fire of July 26, 1891. *(Library Collection)*

The Cogswell House purchased by E. E. Place for his Funeral Home in 1920. Enlarged and remodeled, it still serves the Place Funeral establishment. *(Courtesy Mrs. Wm. Craddock)*

Times-Observer office. Dr. G. M. Hubbell developed the famous Hubbell strain White King breed of pigeons. The male of these was not sold for meat but was particularly suited for the wholesale florist trade. These perfectly white male pigeons were prepared and mounted as if alighting, and were ideal for floral decorations. These were shipped to all parts of the United States and Canada in boxes containing 6, 12 or 18 doves. The Hubbell White King Doves were in such demand that he could not supply all of the requests.

In 1923 the Hubbell Pigeon Farm moved to a five-acre site on University Avenue, extending to the Los Gatos Creek. Besides selling doves to the florist market, Dr. Hubbell sold squabs for food.

Alexander F. Place, left, who started the Place Store and Furniture business in 1884. He left the business in 1887 and his son, E. E. Place, lower left, carried it on until his death in 1937. His son, Geo. Place, below, became a partner in the undertaking business in 1922 and continued until 1966 when he retired. *(Courtesy the Place family)*

As many as 50,000 squabs were sold a year. A quick deep freeze system was built into the plant. This burned down only recently.

Shortly before his death Dr. Hubbell moved his Pigeon Farm to the Old Cooney Ranch near Almaden.[6]

Another unusual business venture in Los Gatos was the apricot kernel plant. One of the big agricultural crops of the valley was apricots. These were either canned or dried for the market. But what about the apricot pit? Was it useless, to be thrown away? Well, Sewall S. Brown and Howard Scott didn't think so. They established the apricot kernel plant near Vasona Junction on Winchester Road. The firm was established in 1925 as the Scott and Brown Apricot Kernel Company. Both men had been employed by the California Prune and Apricot Growers Association (Sunsweet) so they were not strangers to the apricot and its possibilities.

Apricot kernels were processed at the Vasona plant---the large red building was a landmark---and its products sent to all parts of the world. At the plant the pits were dried in the open and then taken by a conveyor system into the plant for cracking. The kernels were sent to Europe for the most part, where they were used in the manufacture of almond and apricot kernel paste, which in turn was made into cakes, candies and cookies. Because the apricot kernels were cheaper than the almonds, the Europeans often substituted apricot kernels in the manufacture of "almond" paste.

The shell of the apricot pit was also used. A plant in San Jose made wood alcohol and ascetic residue in the form of charcoal. The pit charcoal was of very high quality. Its value had been known in World War I, when it was used extensively in gas masks. A number of other valuable products were made from the apricot kernels. Oil was extracted, and it compared favorably with the oil of sweet almonds. This oil was used extensively in the cold

The Hans Nielsen Eatmore Ice Cream factory on North Santa Cruz Avenue and Elm St. Now the Beatrice Foods Co. offices and plant. *(Library Collection)*

cream and cosmetics trade. The better cold creams were made of almond and apricot kernel oil. The apricot kernel was also used in the manufacture of hair dressing.

Another by-product of the apricot kernel industry was Apricot Kernel Meal fertilizer which sold for $2.50 a 100-pound sack. However, the fertilizer was not very strong chemically and thus did not become very popular with orchardists and gardeners.[7]

The Sewall Brown Company had a branch plant in Santa Paula to handle the pits from the southern part of the state. The company dissolved on the death of Mr. Sewall Brown Sr. in May 1952.

Los Gatos was noted also for the excellent ice cream manufactured here. Mr. Hans Nielsen, a native of Denmark, came to Los Gatos in 1922 and started his ice cream business. He personally manufactured it under the trade name of Eatmore Ice

Cream in a building at 104 North Santa Cruz Avenue. Since he operated the business alone he often worked at night making his ice cream, and delivered it in the daytime. A well-known employee was Richard Swanson, who joined the firm in 1929 and was with the company until his death in March 1958. The local plant produced over 1100 gallons of ice cream a day. The company expanded so that it had plants in Watsonville, Santa Cruz, San Jose, and Palo Alto.

In 1944 Beatrice Foods bought the Los Gatos plant and Hans Nielsen remained as manager. The company plant and offices are still in the same location on North Santa Cruz Avenue. Distribution is handled by the Meadow Gold Company, whose dairy products are delivered all the way from Santa Maria to the Oregon Coast and eastward into Arizona.[8] It delivers over 5 million gallons of ice cream to the retail stores in the area.

In 1925 another unusual business was started in Los Gatos, when Fred Hitt and Sam Young began to manufacture fireworks at their Daves Avenue plant. Fourth of July celebrations just were not complete without the Hitt and Young spectaculars. Later they manufactured railway fuses and highway flares. For over 30 years the Hitt Company manufactured fireworks and fuses in Los Gatos. It sold out in 1941 to the Central Railway Company of Boston, which changed the name to Pacific Railway Signal Company. Later it was sold to the Olin Mathieson Company. In September 1953 the

Sewall S. Brown looks over a handful of apricot kernals at his Vasona Plant. *(Courtesy Sewall Brown family)*

Theresa Block built by J. W. Lyndon in 1890 and named after his wife. Stood until 1931 on the northeast corner of West Main St. and Santa Cruz Ave. At the time this picture was taken the Bank of Los Gatos occupied part of the street floor. Park View Building located here today. *(Library Collection)*

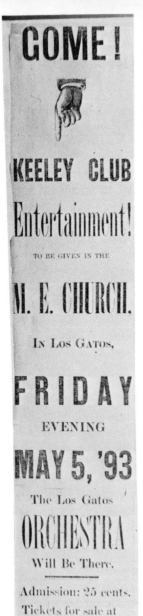

COME!

KEELEY CLUB

Entertainment!

TO BE GIVEN IN THE

M. E. CHURCH.

IN LOS GATOS,

FRIDAY

EVENING

MAY 5, '93

The Los Gatos

ORCHESTRA

Will Be There.

Admission: 25 cents,

Tickets for sale at

Holladay's Drug store

STOP! READ THIS!

Save your Friend OR Relative

If he is SUFFERING from the effects of

WHISKEY, MORPHINE,

OPIUM or TOBACCO.

A GUARANTEED CURE in three weeks time at

THE American Institute

of California, situated at

Los Gatos, Santa Clara County, Cal.,

——— AND AT ———

Hanford, Kings County, Cal.

Hundreds of testimonials furnished on application. Endorsed by the leading medical men of the State. Our Remedies are entirely free from the dangerous minerals used at other institutes. We invariably guarantee a perfect, complete and permanent cure, or make no charge whatever. Terms, $90, complete cure. For full particulars apply to

H. J. BUTLER,   Dr. J. W. WALKER,
Manager,   Medical Director.
Box 397, LOS GATOS, CAL.

Keeley Cure advertisements in the Los Gatos *Mail*, Sept. 20, 1894. From original files. *(Courtesy Mrs. Leland Walker)*

John H. Stanfield, son of J. J. Stanfield, a graduate of Los Gatos High School and Santa Clara College. After three years as a mining engineer in Alaska, he returned to Los Gatos and later became Supt. of Plant #13 of the California Prune & Apricot Growers' Association in 1919. *(Courtesy Sheila Stanfield Heid)*

West Main Street, 1915. Lyndon Hall in left foreground. *(Museum Collection)*

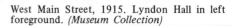

Rankin Block in 1904. Built after the fire of 1901 on the site of the Commercial Bank building on the corner of Main Street and Montebello Way, it housed the Post Office from 1917 to 1948. Still stands and serves a number of business enterprises. *(Library Collection)*

Henry J. Crall in front of his "Palace of Sweets" at 120 West Main Street, 1900. This store was destroyed by the fire of Oct. 13, 1901. *(Library Collection)*

Henry C. Crall, the second generation operator of the Henry J. Crall Co. book and stationery store at 21 North Santa Cruz Avenue. *(Courtesy the Crall family)*

Henry L. Crall, the third generation in the H. J. Crall Co. store. He became a partner with his father Henry C. Crall in 1964. *(Courtesy the Crall family)*

Garage on Main Street 1907. *(Museum Collection)*

local plant was heavily damaged by a spectacular fire which caused more than $75,000 damage. In 1955 the company moved to Morgan Hill.[9]

The Keeley Institute

Alcoholism was a concern of the people in the early days of Los Gatos, as we have seen in a previous chapter. Various techniques were advocated for the cure of alcoholism. But one of the most unique was that of the Keeley Institute which came to Los Gatos in December 1891. Herman Sund, the building contractor, constructed a building for the Institute on the west side of East Main Street, about where the Masonic Temple is today.

The Keeley Institute was supported by the American Institute of California, whose purpose was to cure people of the alcohol, narcotics and tobacco habits. Men came to the Los Gatos Keeley Institute from long distances. They were given lectures, demonstrations and literature. Over 1000 patients, fifty of them from Los Gatos, came to the Institute during the three years of its existence in Los Gatos. The testimony of people on leaving the Institute was that their appetite for intoxicating drinks had been overcome, and that they were free of the habit. An average of 50 "students" attended the Institute and the expense amounted to $50 a week.[10]

After leaving the Institute many of the "cured" patients from out-of-town would go to the saloons before leaving town to test the effectiveness of the cure. Then too, the Keeley "students" were often the objects of jibes from the local tipsters. They were taken to the saloons and teased into drinking. The Town Board thought this so serious that it considered passing an ordinance on October 17, 1892 prohibiting the sale of liquor to persons taking the cure.[11]

The Keeley Institute ended its work in Los Gatos in 1895. "Hard times have interfered very largely with the liquor habit," and this was the best cure of all. After the Keeley Institute left, the building was used as a Town Hall until 1913 when the new Town Hall---prior to the present one---was completed.

FOOTNOTES

1. Los Gatos Weekly *News,* April 17, 1891.
2. Information from Mrs. Mary Yocco Rugh in conversation with the writer.
3. Los Gatos *Mail,* September 5, 1918.
4. "Bronco Billy Anderson's Own Story," Los Gatos *Times-Observer,* July 29, 1958.
5. Letter to Mrs. William Craddock, quoted in Los Gatos *Times-Observer,* September 2, 1958.
6. Information obtained from an interview with Attorney Carl Hubbell, one of the sons of Dr. Hubbell.
7. Information furnished by Sewall S. Brown Jr.
8. Library Collection, Book 9. Also *Times-Observer,* August 10, 1958.
9. Library Collection, Book 9, October 19, 1955.
10. Los Gatos Weekly *News*, April 7, 1893.
11. *Ibid.,* October 21, 1892.

One of the early grammar school buildings in the 1870's. It was located off of East Main Street on University Avenue, near the site of the later University Avenue School. (*Library Collection*)

CHAPTER X

Schools and the Library

Grammar Schools

THE people of Los Gatos have always had great pride in their schools. As early as August 2, 1859 they formed the Los Gatos School District. The first grammar school was located on the crest of the hill on Saratoga Avenue, later the Cleveland estate. The school was opened on January 19, 1863. It was a one-room, one-teacher school with 25 pupils. When the building burned down in 1874 classes were held in a home on the corner of Bean and Santa Cruz Avenues---later the location of the home of Dr. Gober and John Bean.

The next location was near the Ten Mile House on Oak Street---Montebello Way. There was a second section in a home in East Los Gatos at 179 Market Street---Loma Alta Avenue. Here Miss Rena Ott taught second grade and some old-timers are still living who attended this school which existed until after the beginning of the 20th century. Among these old-timers are Miss Hulda Erickson and Mrs. Ella Case Angell.

An interesting sidelight in connection with the early schools in Los Gatos should be mentioned. Mr. George Teasdale was a fairly well-to-do man who had no children. When he died on September 12, 1872 he left $300 in trust, the interest of which was to be used to buy candy for the school children of Los Gatos. He conditioned this with the proviso that the school children decorate his grave each year on Decoration Day. Once a year the children were given a treat of candy. Another local citizen, Mr. Edward A. Johnson, left a similar bequest to the school children when he died in 1905. Year after year, generally at Christmas time, the elementary school children were treated with candy, the money coming from the interest on these two bequests. But the children became too numerous, so the annual candy distribution was stopped. The money was then used for the purchase of playground equipment, which the Board felt was more valuable to the children than candy. However, Miss Ruth Rigby, who began her teaching career in Los Gatos in 1919, recalled in a conversation with the writer, that the children were treated to candy at Christmas from the fund as late as the 1920's.

At the end of 1970 the "Teasdale Fund," as it was known, amounted to $1200. Mr. Don Eddy, the District Superintendent, was puzzled as to what to do with this mysterious fund about which a bank was sending him reports. When he learned that the School Board had used some of it for playground equipment as early as 1897, he had the answer. The fund would help to buy playground equipment, and Mr. Teasdale's desire to make the

An addition to the original school was built in 1881. When the school opened on August 8, 1881 it had two rooms and 98 pupils. *(Library Collection)*

103

Grammar School, erected in 1885. The section on the right behind the trees is the high school wing built in 1893. The high school moved to its new location in 1908. *(Library Collection)*

children of Los Gatos Grammar School happy would be fulfilled.

In 1881 the main elementary school moved to the University Avenue site which had been purchased from the Mullen family. A two-room building was built and served for a number of years. The editor of the Los Gatos Weekly *News* was favorably impressed with the Principal, Mr. T. W. Whitehurst, who conducted a reading lesson in his presence. Editor Walker thought the Principal's statement to the children that "if you learn to read one lesson well you can read a hundred others just as well," was good advice. The editor also thought that Mr. Whitehurst and his assistant, Mrs. Hoyt, "are doing all they can to educate the children of this place, and fit them for duties that will devolve upon them in later years."[1] The first school bell was purchased in 1881 by funds raised by entertainments the children put on.

The small building soon became overcrowded. In 1884 a Citizens' School Expansion meeting was held to discuss the question of better school facilities. But a division of opinion arose. Some wanted a school on the "East side" of the Creek, and proposed the Peter Johnson property on Market Street (Loma Alta Avenue) as a second school. Others felt that it was unnecessary to have two schools---one for east and one for west of the Creek. The fate of the $8000 school bond issue was at stake. Should Los Gatos have an East Los Gatos school and a West Los Gatos school? Common sense finally prevailed and the $8000 bond issue for a new wing on the University Avenue site was approved. It was built next to the earlier building, but it faced University Avenue. A two-story building, it had four classrooms.

The old elementary school on University Avenue, built in 1885. *(Library Collection)*

By 1892 the school census for the Los Gatos Elementary School was 472. The county apportionment was $4 per student, or $1888 from the county. By 1893 the school population was 710 and the county funded $6 per student, or $4,200. This assistance from the county helped Los Gatos solve its school growth problem.

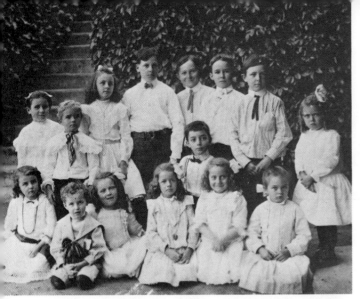

Group picture of early-day birthday party. Picture taken at Dr. Frank Knowles' at the junction of College Ave. and Reservoir Road in 1904. *Front row:* Linda Roberts, Alfred Lewis, Faith Williams, Lucille Macabee, Raymond Macabee, Mildred Williams, Bertha Edwards. *Back row:* Mary Yocco, (?), Roma Roberts (Mrs. Chandler), Nelson Mullen, DeWitt Emerson, Edw. S. Yocco, Knowles Emerson. *(Courtesy Mary Yocco Rugh)*

The University Avenue Grammar School served for many years. Another elementary school held classes on Farley Road near John's Nursery. This was the old Vineland School, and it consolidated with the Los Gatos School District in 1905. The Vineland school house was later moved to 269 San Jose Avenue, where it still serves as a residence.

In 1886 the Los Gatos Grammar School had three teachers and a Principal---Mr. W. H. Sisson, who also taught first and second grades. Miss Lily Love taught the 3rd and 4th grades, and she had 68 pupils. Miss Flora DeWolfe taught the 58 pupils in the 5th and 6th grades, while Mrs. Sisson taught the 55 seventh and eighth grade pupils.

By 1894 the total enrollment in the Grammar School was 571. Interestingly enough, this was 99 more pupils than were on the census rolls.

One of the long-time teachers in Los Gatos was Miss Louise Van Meter, who started teaching here in 1893, after four years in the Union District and Pacheco Pass schools. She taught for 35 years in "Miss Van Meter's Room," the sunny southeast side of the old school. She was a popular and progressive teacher. Long before a kindergarten became part of the public school, Miss Van Meter advocated a "pre-first grade" class for Los Gatos children. The matter came up for discussion at the Town Board meeting on July 16, 1888. Mr. Henry Meade Bland, the Principal, explained the general character of the kindergarten and the benefits that could be derived from it. Mr. Herman Sund favored the system, but Mr. Fisher said that while he favored the principle of a kindergarten, he opposed making it a public charge against the school system. He said he had never seen a kindergarten anywhere supported by the public, but only by private subscription.[2]

A private kindergarten was organized in Los Gatos by Miss Harrison. It was located "in the Lewis Cottage on School Street." On September 9, 1892 the Weekly *News* reported that the kindergarten conducted by Miss Harrison was "well-worth visiting by parents. It is hoped that the kindergarten will be liberally sustained by Los Gatos."[3]

It was not until July 20, 1916 that the Los Gatos *Mail-News* could report that it had received assurances from the Board of School Trustees that a kindergarten for Los Gatos was an assured fact. Miss Van Meter's idea had finally taken hold. Her service to education in Los Gatos is memorialized by the Louise Van Meter School on San Jose Avenue.

One of the big events for the educators of Los

Austin School District 1886. Those identified include, Maude Shoumaker, Frank Lemmon, Eddie Baker, Susie Lancaster, Miss Starbird (teacher), Jimmie Merriam, Lottie Lancaster, Charlie Lemmon, Harold Lancaster, Thedie Beckwith and Ruby Gish. (others unidentified) *(Library Collection)*

Miss Louise Van Meter's first grade class of January 1896. One of the members of this class---Mr. George Place---still lives in Los Gatos, and Leland Walker, another member, passed away in March 1971. *(Museum Collection)*

Gatos and the townspeople was the visit to Los Gatos of a group of delegates from the National Education Association Convention. On July 21, 1911 eight railroad passenger cars carrying 415 delegates came to Los Gatos. The Chamber of Commerce served fruit and punch on the porches of the Hotel Lyndon. After this they were taken on a tour of Los Gatos and the surrounding country in automobiles furnished by local teachers and businessmen. The reception given the N.E.A. delegates rivaled that given to President Benjamin Harrison when he visited Los Gatos in 1892. This was due no doubt to the short time the President spent here. But hundreds of Los Gatans had come to the railroad depot to see their President. J.W. Lyndon, the President of the Board of Trade, introduced the President who spoke from the rear platform of the railroad car. Miss Annie Reid, on behalf of the Young People's Society of the Christian Endeavor of the Presbyterian Church, presented a basket of flowers to the President. It had the inscription "The Young People's Society of Christian Endeavor of the Los Gatos Presbyterian Church sends greetings to our noble Christian President. While others honor you as a great statesman, we shall think of you, and pray for you, as a Christian Elder in our beloved Church." Mrs. Harrison was given a basket of flowers and a "luscious basket of Los Gatos oranges."[4]

The 1886 building could not for long fulfill the needs of the growing community and the increase in enrollment. More land and a larger building were needed. On September 7, 1916 the Los Gatos *Mail-News* reported that Mr. J. D. Farwell had given to the school district "two strips of land

extending from the school grounds of the Grammar School to the Creek. Through this grant the school grounds can be enlarged about 150 feet in length and 50 feet in width, narrowing down to about 10 feet."

In 1922 the people of the district passed a bond issue by a vote of 722 to 143 to provide for a new and larger grammar school building. The old school was sold to a San Francisco Wrecking Company for $1336 in November 1923. The new building was dedicated on November 10, 1923.

For a number of years the need for additional playground space for the grammar school had been keenly felt. There was "no room on the ground for baseball, soccer, etc." Across the Creek from the grammar school was an open field that was ideal for a playground. In 1926 the School Board obtained this land and built a bridge across the creek to make it accessible to the pupils. This low swinging footbridge was completed in April 1926 and dedicated with pomp and ceremony.

When the Freeway went through and the creek was diverted through huge concrete pipes a new and higher bridge was constructed. It was completely enclosed by safety wire to make the

Crowd at the depot to greet President and Mrs. Benj. Harrison on May 1, 1891. "Mayor" J. W. Lyndon on the decorated flatcar, welcomed the official party. *(Library Collection)*

crossing to the play area safe for the pupils. This bridge still serves as a short-cut to Old Town and to Forbes' Mill, recently converted into a "youth hang-out."

A new era of growth for the elementary school began with the coming of Raymond J. Fisher as Principal in June 1928. His contribution to education in Los Gatos is best summarized in an editorial in the Los Gatos *Times* on the occasion of Mr. Fisher's retirement in 1959. The editorial said, in part, "Mr. Fisher has been able to swing into and cope with the new era of tension pressure, and expanded school population very well . . . The good condition of our educational program today is largely due to his guidance."[5]

Mr. Fisher, who replaced Mrs. Cecil M. Hall, who had been Principal since 1918, helped the schools to meet the needs of our growing community. The new Louise Van Meter School was built on San Jose Avenue in 1959, and Ralph Berry was the first

First group to take the post-graduate course after grammar school, in June 1891. Principal Henry Meade Bland on left, upper row, and Edw. C. Yocco, a Trustee, on upper right. *(Library Collection)*

Principal. It is still one of the show-places of Los Gatos. When the old Lexington school, which had come into the Los Gatos Elementary district, was torn down and the site taken over by the Lexington Reservoir, a new school was built for the district. The Los Gatos Union School District purchased property from the Redwood Estates Mutual Water Company for the site of the new Lexington school in 1952. The school was completed in 1953 with Ellis Crosby as Principal.

On June 6, 1952 the voters approved a bond issue for $320,000 for a new school on Daves Avenue. This opened in the fall of 1953 with Kenneth McCoy as the teaching principal. In June 1956 a five-acre site was purchased on Shannon Road and a District Administration Building was erected. It has been expanded under the leadership of Mr. Don Eddie, the District Superintendent, and is one of the most complete office buildings and teachers' workshops and audio-visual centers in the county.

In February 1957 a $600,000 bond election was passed to provide for a fifth school---the Blossom Hill School. This was completed in 1958. With the growth of the Vasona Area, it was necessary to build a new school on Oka Avenue. Another bond election for $460,000 was passed for this project. Mr. Ralph Berry, who had been a teacher and administrator in the schools, was honored by having this school named after him. His death on February 14, 1961 was a shock to the community.

In February 1959 the Board purchased 24 acres on Roberts Road for an intermediate school. This was completed in 1961 at a cost of $938,214 and was named the Raymond J. Fisher School.

Raymond J. Fisher became District Superintendent full-time in 1953. In that year Art Thimann became Principal of the Louise Van Meter School and Ralph Berry took over as Principal of the University Avenue School in place of Mr. Fisher.

Second year class 1895, Los Gatos High School. *Back row:* Arthur Waller, Harriette Sage, June Merriam, Nat Symonds, Dora Johnson, Mr. Kelley, Myrtle Roberts, Miss Cilker, Ruth Wilham, Fred Lobdell, June Millbery. *Bottom row:* John Crummey, Erma Simons, Edward Waller, June Willis, Frank Foster, Myrtle Sporleder, Junie Tobin. *(Library Collection)*

Class of 1897, Los Gatos High School. *Back row:* Frank Foster, Jane Willis, H. Brodie Atkinson, Harriette Sage, Edw. J. Waller, Erma I. Simon, Arthur J. Waller. *Front row:* Ethel Holliday, Nathaniel Symonds, Ruth A. Killam, J. D. Crummey, and A. Irene Milbery.

Thus, by 1970 the Los Gatos Elementary School had grown from a one-room school of 25 pupils in 1863 to a unified system comprising six schools with a total of 3,720 pupils.

High School

There was no high school in Los Gatos until after 1890. This type of school had not yet found favor in many parts of the country. But the people of Los Gatos saw the colleges and universities in the area as an opportunity for their children. Leland Stanford Jr. University, San Jose State Normal College, and the College of the Pacific and Santa Clara University in Santa Clara, were all ready to accept students from area schools by examination. But the question was how to prepare students for these examinations. For this purpose a number of private academies had been established. One of these private schools was the Los Gatos College, which was started before 1892. It offered courses in Latin, Greek, and other college prepara-tory courses as well as some commercial or "practical" courses. But the question still remained: Why should not the grammar school have a "post-graduate" course to prepare those students who are willing and able to go on to college? In July 1887 the people voted to establish

a "grammar school", course to prepare students for college entrance examinations. The Los Gatos Weekly *News* stated that only those who passed an examination were admitted to the course. And then the *News* continued, "This course differs only in name from the high school course."[6]

Henry Meade Bland, later to become a famous poet, was the first Principal of this "graduate course" in the fall of 1887. He was responsible for developing the idea of a public high school for Los Gatos. At the end of the 1888-89 school year, Mr. Bland left Los Gatos for the College of the Pacific, and Mr. C. H. Crowell became the Principal. In June 1891 the following people "graduated" from the two-year post-graduate course: Ida Sund, Harry Trantham, Paul Mason and Hattie Howell. Three people were promoted from the Junior to the Senior class by examination: Clinton Trip, Cora Finnie and Archie Stidston.[7]

But the people of Los Gatos wanted a full-fledged high school. In April 1891 a petition requesting the establishment of a high school was circulated. On October 2, 1891 the Los Gatos *Mail* lamented the lack of a high school in Los Gatos. "A large number of our young men and young women are going to San Jose when they should be educated at home."

It was not until June 10, 1893 that an election was held on the proposal to establish a high school. It was to be a three-year course after the 8th grade and was to prepare students to enter college or university. It was reported that there were between 32 and 35 scholars ready for high school. The election resulted in unanimous approval of a high school, the vote being 102 to 0.[8]

The Los Gatos *Chronicle* on October 19, 1893 stated that the contract for the high school wing would be let the next day. The building was to be "two stories in height and contain four classrooms, a chemical laboratory, a philosophy room, a dark

Los Gatos High School building in 1908. *(Library Collection)*

108

University Avenue Elementary School in 1918. *(Library Collection)*

University Avenue Elementary School built in 1923. *(Library Collection)*

room, office and library." (Not bad for a beginning!) The building was to be located on the University Avenue site "adjoining the old building on the east and extending south about 30 feet, with entrance on the south."

But difficulties arose over the matter of financing the new structure. California had passed a law making it legal to levy taxes for construction of a high school. However, before Los Gatos could sell the $6000 bonds the people had voted, the law was declared unconstitutional. But this did not stop Los Gatos from getting its high school. The people signed the bonds themselves and completed the building.[9]

The high school opened on September 3, 1894 with 20 students enrolled. The first class graduated in 1897 and it had among its 12 members Mr. John D. Crummey, later of Food Machinery fame, who was President of the class. It published the first Yearbook, the "Wildcat", which contained a class history, poems, prophecy, etc. Nathaniel G. Symonds was editor, John D. Crummey was business manager, M. B. Atkinson, athletic editor; A. J. Walker, assistant editor; and Janette Tobin, artist.[10]

In 1897 the school district---grammar and high school---had a deficit of $802.58 for the school year ending June 30. Salaries of teachers could not be paid in January of that year.

In 1898 the first school newspaper was published. It was a monthly 8-page paper and was called "Lambda Gamma" (Greek for L.G.). Mamie Skinkle was editor and Claude Pollard the business manager.[11] The first alumni association banquet was held at the Lyndon on June 8, 1900. N. G. Symonds '97 was the first president, Mary Spence '99 was vice-president, Ruth Kellam, secretary and Joseph Mini, treasurer.

The high school remained a three-year school only a short while. In 1900 Stanford raised its credit requirements to 15 and to meet this, Los Gatos High School added the fourth year. There were 50 students in 1901 and 75 students in 1906.

The University Avenue school remained the high school until 1908. In 1907 the local press expressed the feeling of many when it said, "Our high school students cannot make good progress while the school is within a block of the railroad and near the business district." The editor of the *Mail* urged action on a new high school. A bond issue had been voted on February 16, 1906 in the amount of $30,000. On February 20, at a mass meeting, the trustees were instructed to buy the Nicholson Tract of four acres and, in addition, the house and lot on Church Street owned by Mrs. Lees. This new site was a block and a half "from Main Street and well away from the railroad." The school Board planned to extend 6th Street (High School Court) as an access to the new school.

In 1906 the people also voted to separate the high school from the grammar school Board of Trustees and have a separate Board for the high school. The first high school Board of Trustees consisted of Mr. George Lewis, Mr. H. B. Wheeler and Mr. F. H. Milligan. This new board awarded the contract for the new two-story building in July 1907, the building to cost $20,000. On July 22, 1907 a faculty of five was selected, with Frank Kerr as principal at a salary of $100 a month. Others were to receive a salary ranging from $40 to $90 a month.

The new school was dedicated on March 10, 1908 with Dr. David Starr Jordan, President of Stanford University, as the main speaker for the occasion. After Mr. Kerr's resignation in July 1908, Mr. Allen B. Martin was elected principal at a salary of $1800 a year. After much controversy, and over the objections of the Clerk, the Board of Trustees agreed to buy a mirror for the girls' cloak room.

Even in the early days there were conflicts between students and administrators. In 1908 the Board was called upon to settle the complaint of a Dr. MacGraw about a school regulation. At that time the school had a rule that a boy could not participate in school sports unless he had a passing grade in three subjects. The son of Dr. MacGraw had not met this requirement and was therefore forbidden to participate in athletic events. However, he disobeyed the rule and for this he was suspended from school. His father, Dr. MacGraw, challenged the rule and the suspension and took the case to the Board. The Board upheld the school rule and the suspension.[12]

The new school broadened its curriculum to include a commercial course. Miss Mildred Fosdick was employed as a part-time teacher for this "practical course" at $50 a month. In 1909 Los Gatos High School was accredited by the University of California.

The first debate team was organized in 1910 and the first question debated was: "Resolved: That selection of candidates for city, county and state officers by direct primary is superior to a system of caucus." The affirmative was upheld by Henry Crall and Miss Lela Stanley; the negative by Alvin Hambly and Walter Wallace. On Saturday December 10, 1910 a debate team from Los Gatos debated a team from San Jose High School on the question, "Resolved: That United States Senators should be elected by direct vote of the people." Glen Thompson and Alvin Hambly of Los Gatos upheld the affirmative and Ruth Bennett and Arthur Johnson of San Jose upheld the negative. It can be seen that Los Gatos began its successful forensic program early in its history.

With the expectation of an expanded building program, the High School Board proposed a bond issue to buy more land for the high school. On October 21, 1911 a bond issue in the amount of $10,000 was passed and the Board purchased land fronting East Main Street "from 6th Street east to the Tom Barbano property" for $7,500. In September 1913 a shed "for horses and automobiles" was built. This remained a faculty parking shed until it was torn down in 1968 to make room for the new science building.

Principals came and went in rapid succession for a number of years. In June 1915 C. F. Blayney replaced Frank Watson. In January 1916 W. F. Walton became Principal and served until June 1918. Eli N. Mabrey came next, but he resigned in January 1920. I. W. Snow followed and he served until May 1922, when he resigned to accept a principalship in San Francisco.[13]

Raymond J. Fisher, Principal, and later Superintendent, Los Gatos Elementary Schools from 1928 to 1959. Also active in many community affairs. *(Photo courtesy Fisher family)*

Prentiss Brown, Principal, Los Gatos Union High School, 1931–1956, longer than any other person to serve in this capacity. *(1946* Wildcat *picture)*

The area was growing and the need for a unified high school district was great. An election was held on March 31, 1922 which resulted in the formation of the Los Gatos Union High School District. It included Los Gatos, Saratoga, Austin, Booker, Lakeside, Lexington, Wrights and the Guadalupe schools. The first Union High School District Board members were George Shaner, Mrs. A. G. Williams, Dr. E. M. Miller of Los Gatos; Dr. R. L. Hogg of Saratoga, and Miss A. Bessie Walker of Lexington. Mr. George Osmer replaced Miss Walker in late 1922. Dr. Miller was chosen President of the Board. Mr. J. Warren Ayer came in as Principal to succeed I. W. Snow in 1922.

In line with an expanding program and increased attendance the District called a bond election for a new classroom building and a gymnasium. Bonds in the amount of $250,000 were approved and the contract was let in January 1923. The new building was dedicated on January 17, 1925. Henry Meade Bland, the first principal, and by then a famous poet, gave the dedicatory address.

After the completion of the new building with its beautiful and expansive lawn, the old high school building behind it became the wood shop. It was torn down in 1954 to make room for the new high school library and classroom building.

Another expansion program took place in 1935 when the music wing and a three-story classroom wing were added with the help of W.P.A. funds. The Federal Government provided 45% of the cost, and a bond issue in the amount of $60,000 helped pay for the balance. Incidentally, it was during the construction of the music wing that a near tragedy occurred. The contractor was in the basement of the new wing with a lantern to inspect some pipes.

Douglas Helm, long-time coach and later Vice Principal. Served Los Gatos High from 1923 to 1953. Helm Athletic Field named in his honor. *(1943 Wildcat picture)*

Mrs. R. D. Robertson for many years Dean of Girls and instructor in History, 1925–1952. *(1943 Wildcat picture)*

Mr. Fred Canrinus, Athletic Coach, Vice–Principal and Principal, Los Gatos Union High School 1957 to 1970. He came to Los Gatos Union High School in 1938. *(Photo from the High School Yearbook* The Wildcat)

Evidently the lamp shade broke and the flame touched off accumulated gas in the basement. The explosion blew him out of the building and did considerable damage to the uncompleted structure. What made it so near a tragedy was that at the time of the explosion more than 600 students were in an assembly next door to the new wing. Only the calm handling of the situation by Mr. Brown, the principal, and the faculty members prevented a panic and injury to the students.

The Los Gatos Union High School expanded again in 1954 when a $500,000 bond issue was approved for an Industrial Arts building, Home Economics building, a new Boys' Gymnasium and a swimming pool. The second high school in Saratoga was completed in 1959, after a successful bond election in the amount of $3 million. Dr. Vernon Trimble, who had been Director of Guidance and later Assistant Principal, became Principal of the Saratoga High School. In 1963 the Library-Science Building was completed and in 1970 the new Science classroom building was ready for occupancy.

Mr. J. Warren Ayer served as Principal from 1922 until May 1931. Mr. Prentiss Brown followed him, and he served during a period of great growth in the student body and faculty. He served longer than any other man as Principal of the Los Gatos Union High School District, his tenure lasting from 1931 to 1956. Loren Critser followed Mr. Brown. He resigned in June 1961 and was replaced by Dr. B. Frank Gillette.

Coach Douglas Helm became Assistant Principal in 1938 after the death of Charles Eichelberger in 1937. He served in this capacity until his death on September 28, 1953. He was loved by everyone as a coach and administrator. The new athletic field has been named Douglas Helm Field as a memorial to him.

In 1955 Mr. Fred Canrinus, who had taken over Douglas Helm's coaching duties in 1938, became Assistant Principal. When the offices of Principal and District Superintendent were separated in June 1957, Mr. Canrinus became Principal of the Los Gatos Union High School and Loren Critser became the first Superintendent of the Los Gatos Joint Union High School District.

PRINCIPALS OF LOS GATOS HIGH SCHOOL

Henry Meade Bland	1887–1889
C. H. Crowell	1889–1891
H. E. Shumate	1891–1895
A. M. Kelley	1895–1898
Louis K. Webb	1898–1899
George C. Russell	1899–1901
W. W. Wilson	1901–1905
Charles I. Kerr	1905–1908
Allan B. Martin	1908–1909
Frank M. Watson	1909–1915
Edwin Forrest Blayney	1915
W. F. Walton	1916–1918
E. N. Mabrey	1918–1920
Irving W. Snow	1920–1922
J. Warren Ayer	1922–1931
Prentiss Brown	1931–1955
Loren A. Critser	1955–1957
Fred Canrinus	1957–1971

Under Dr. Gillette the Joint High School District weathered many storms and has continued to meet the requirements of a changing society. Today there are more than 2000 students in the Los Gatos Union High School and about 1800 in the Saratoga High School. A parcel of land on Karl Avenue in the Monte Sereno area was purchased in 1963 as a site for a possible third high school for the district.

Front view of the Los Gatos High School building today. *(Photo by Bert Donlon)*

Los Gatos High has always drawn to itself an excellent administrative and teaching staff. This is due to the ideal climate and the excellent class of people in the district. Teachers like to come here and stay. Some of the teachers who had long terms of service in Los Gatos include Mrs. Ralph D. Robertson, who taught History and served as Dean of Girls from 1925 to 1952; Miss Pauline Clark, the librarian, who came in 1925 and endeared herself to hundreds of students and retired in 1954; and Miss Grace Wood, who came in 1922 and stayed until her retirement in 1960. And of course, Miss Winnie Chamberlin, who taught art from 1915 until her retirement in 1945.

The Los Gatos Union High School has also been fortunate in its student body. Not only have Los Gatos students attended the school, but for many years students came from the Willow Glen district in San Jose; which at the time was outside of any high school district. They arrived each morning on the Interurban electric train and went home on the Interurban in the evening. Saratoga students came to Los Gatos High School, furnishing some of the subsequently famous people such as movie stars Olivia de Havilland, who graduated with high honors in 1934, her sister Joan Fontaine and Audry Long. National honors were won for Los Gatos High School when William Wollin Yabroff won the National American Legion oratorical contest in 1946.

In recognition of its high scholastic standards the California Scholarship Federation granted a Charter for a local chapter of that organization in April 1937. A group of local students made application and drew up the constitution. Those in the original group were Jack Webster, Sarah Kimball, June Breschini, John Dimeff, Denny Robertson and Student Body President Warren Smith.

Adult School

The Adult Education Department of the Los Gatos Union High School had its beginning in 1923 with two classes in Americanization, which were begun at the suggestion of the American Legion. The *Mail-News* reported on November 1, 1923 that 37 "enthusiastic and industrious pupils" were enrolled in the Americanization classes of the high school. Two teachers met these foreign-born twice a week to prepare them for their naturalization and the responsibilities of citizenship in a democracy.

Along with the Americanization classes the school offered classes in English for foreign-born. Gradually, under the direction of Mr. Charles Eichelberger, the Assistant Principal, the program was expanded to include sewing, wood-working and typing. After Mr. Eichelberger's death in 1937, Dr. George G. Bruntz took over the Adult Education program.

During World War II the Adult Education program was expanded to meet the war-time needs. Classes in Pattern-Making, Metal Work, Welding, etc. were offered. More than 1700 students attended the evening and daytime adult classes.

When Dr. Bruntz became Professor of Social Science and Teacher Education at San Jose State College in 1946, Mr. Claude Hampton became Adult Education Director. Dr. Thomas Damon succeeded Mr. Hampton in 1957, and when Dr. Damon went to Palo Alto as Head of the Adult School there, Mr. Jerry Zappelli took over for a whort while. Mr. William Cunningham was named Director in 1959, and he began an expanded program. Citizenship and English for foreign-born are no longer the large classes they once were. The fine arts classes are the most popular today.

One of Mr. Cunningham's great accomplishments has been the accreditation of the adult program for high school graduation. In 1969 the Los Gatos Adult School granted high school diplomas to 25 students, most of whom would not have received these had it not been for the Adult School classes.

In 1970 there were more than 2000 adults in the District Adult classes and 56 teachers.

Mark Twain High School

In 1965 the California State Legislature passed Assembly Bill #2240, which requires every school district to have a continuation program. The law also requires that every student must go to some kind of high school until he is 18 years of age or graduated. Since the law also stated that no student can be suspended for more than 10 days during a school year, it became necessary for every high school district to have a continuation education program. The students were to be provided with a second educational opportunity. This second chance was to be structured in a small, counseling-oriented environment free from the pressures of the typical large high school.

The Los Gatos Union High School District established a Continuation Education program on January 1, 1965. On August 23, 1967 the State Department of Education granted the request of the local Board of Trustees to operate a Continuation High School under the "necessary small high school classification." On August 5, 1968 the Board renamed the Continuation High School the Mark Twain High School.

The school is housed in a home at 224 Wilder Avenue. In 1970 there were 4 staff members, consisting of Dr. Jack Lucas as Principal, Mrs. Jane Adams, Mr. Delbert Pfister, and Mr. Charles Rogers. The hours are limited by law to three, and last from 8 A.M. to 11:15 A.M., giving time for those students who are employed to go to their jobs.

Dr. Lucas stressed the purpose of the school when he said, "We want to try to help them keep from dropping out. Without a high school diploma today the student has very little chance for success or a full life." The work at the school is programmed for each student according to his individual ability and needs. The school had a small beginning. In June 1970 it held its first graduation exercises at which four students received their high school diplomas.[14]

Private Schools

Montezuma School for Boys. In 1909 a young man who had recently graduated from Gustavus Adolphus College in Minnesota, came to California. His family joined him in 1910 and the father purchased a ranch on Bear Creek Road, formerly owned by the Bissell and Rankin families.

Young Ernest Andrew Rogers had always dreamed of conducting a school for boys that would help build good character and have a wholesome effect on the lives of young men. And so the old ranch, located in the Montezuma School District, became the Montezuma Mountain School for Boys. From one ranch house and several buildings, moved from a neighboring ranch, the school's building program eventually included three low, wide-spread Pueblo-type buildings.

The first classes were held in January 1911 with an enrollment of 12 boys. Prof. Rogers---as he became affectionately known by his students---and Prof. William Meredith of Palo Alto were the first instructors. Prof. Meredith taught English and History and remained at Montezuma for many years.

Dormitory of Montezuma School for Boys, 1934. *(Library Collection)*

View of the campus of the Montezuma School for Boys on Bear Creek Road. The school existed from 1910 to 1955 and was nationally recognized for its excellence. *(Museum Collection)*

In 1912 Prof. Rogers was joined by John Lloyd as part owner, Secretary, and Business Manager. Much of the school's success was due to the able management and enthusiasm of Mr. Lloyd.

A new concept of education was introduced at Montezuma. Classes were held only in the mornings. The afternoons were given over to extra-curricular activities such as swimming, hiking, horseback riding or athletics. The school's horses of Peruvian blood were widely known and Mr. Lloyd took particular pride in them.

One of the great national movements started by Prof. Rogers was that of the Junior Statesmen. Backed by leading business and professional people throughout America, Junior Statesmen had as its function the education of students in good citizenship. Local Chapters were established all over the United States and Summer Seminars were held at Montezuma.

In 1953 a disastrous fire destroyed the buildings which housed the school's dining room, kitchen, assembly hall, book store, supply rooms and practice rooms for music. This loss came at a time when Prof. Rogers' health was failing. The result was that the school was closed in 1955 and the property sold to the Sisters of the Presentation. After 45 years of outstanding service, Montezuma faded into history. Prof. Rogers died in 1957 and Mr. Lloyd in 1962. But their influence in the lives of young men from all over America will no doubt live for a long time.[15]

Hillbrook School. In 1935 Miss Mary Orem, a New England-educated teacher, came to Los Gatos and founded a school for children "in an environment conducive to learning." The first school was located in a large house on Rose Avenue. Seventeen children between the ages of three and ten made the Rose Avenue school their home. A summer camp program drew more children, and the school grew to the point where larger quarters were needed.

In 1936 the Children's Country School moved to the Colonel James Parker Ranch in the foothills east of Los Gatos. This was a perfect setting for a school of the kind Miss Orem dreamed of. It contained rolling foothills, beautiful vistas, plenty of room for riding, hiking, nature study, gardening and the keeping of pets. As the school grew, new and modern buildings which reflected the tradition of "an environment conducive to learning" were added.

> "The countryside, the wide expanse of hills,
> The soul-inspiring closeness of nature,
> The contact with the soil, without which
> No child's life is complete
> This is a legacy."

Each year a new grade was added, and each year a summer camp for children brought youngsters from all parts of the country to enjoy the camp. Miss Orem was joined by Miss Elizabeth Glassford and Mrs. Nathalie Wollin in the operation of the school.

The school was chartered by the State of California in 1945 as a non-profit institution. The resident school became a day school where children were transported from their home to and from school by bus. The school had grown so much that it could no longer accommodate all who wanted to attend as a residence school.

In 1960 the Children's Country School became the Hillbrook School. It has an enrollment of over 300 from the nursery through the 8th grade. The school has activities of interest and value to all children, including drama, singing, and art, as well as nature and sports, all of which are a part of the environment of Hillbrook, as they were a part of the Children's Country School.[16]

Since the retirement of Mrs. Wollin and Miss Glassford, Dr. William Wollin Yabroff has been the Director of the school, and he shares the progressive ideas of the school's founders.

General view of Hillbrook School, Marchmont Avenue.

Junior High classrooms, Hillbrook School.

Memorial Library

Thomas Jefferson once said, "Books constitute capital. A library book lasts as long as a house, for hundreds of years." Early in the history of Los Gatos, a library was considered an absolute necessity. Talk of a public reading room took definite form on February 4, 1898 when the Board of Trade appointed a committee composed of George Lewis, B. J. Gregory and F. J. Davis to look into the possibility of fixing up a place for a town library. The Board of Trade was to furnish the books and furniture, and the project was to be under the management of the Town Board of Trustees.

On March 4, 1898 the Los Gatos Floral Society voted to turn its assets over to a reading room, on condition that a library worth $400 be established. Such a reading room was set up in the L. A. Wilder store on the south side of Main Street, just west of the bridge. Miss Dora Rankin, in her column "As It

Was" February 18, 1965 recalls that "the town library hung over the creek. It was built on stilts on the west side of the creek." Also in 1898, the W.C.T.U. gave "their excellent library of 350 volumes of choice books" to the library. On May 16, 1898 the chairman of the Library Committee reported to the Town Board that it would cost $16.00 to fix up the room. The Board of Trade wanted to use the room as a monthly meeting place.

Upon the recommendation of the Board of Trade, the town Trustees adopted the following rules on August 15, 1898:

"1. All residents of the town; all members of the Board of Trade, Floral Society, W.C.T.U. Improvement Society and other open organizations whose work is wholly in the interest of the town, although such member may not be a resident within the limits of the town, are to have free access to the library.

2. Others pay $2.00 for six months in advance. No more than three books per family at one time. Books can be kept 2 weeks and a fine of 5 cents a day for over-time.

3. Users of library must be recommended by a member of the Library Committee, an officer of the Board of Trade, or other responsible person. Reading room open 10 A.M. to 9 P.M. weekdays and from 2 P.M. to 6 P.M. Sundays."[17]

The first librarian was Miss Case, and she reported 846 volumes in the library on November 7, 1898. Most of the books were donations. Money for the maintenance of the reading room and for books came from donations and special events by town groups. On September 19, 1898 the Town Board began discussing the possibility of levying a tax of 5 cents on $100 evaluation for the support of the library.

Miss Case resigned on November 29, 1899, and Miss Willa Hazen was appointed by the Town Board to succeed her. On March 18, 1901 Miss Bessie Cooper replaced Miss Hazen, and the Board ordered the library to be open from 9 A.M. to 9 P.M.[18]

The question of a permanent library was discussed throughout 1901 and 1902. A site had to be selected, and in 1901 the Town Board had accepted the Opera House block on East Main Street as the best location for the library. But on January 20, 1902 a new offer was made by the owners of lots on University Avenue. The actual transfer of these Carlin-Robershotte-Lyndon lots was delayed by Lyndon, who insisted that the town allow him a 14-foot right-of-way to the railroad track. Trustees Lewis and Sullivan said they were tired of the "dilly-dallying." They pointed out that, in the original offer and in the actual diagram of the site, it was specifically understood that Lyndon had no claim to the 14 feet. Lewis moved that the Board rescind the motion to accept the title to the site. It carried. Then the motion was made to accept the Opera House block on East Main Street, provided clear title could be presented.

In the meantime, Mr. F. H. McCullagh presented a petition with 61 signatures, asking the Board to reconsider its motion to accept the Opera House lots. On April 7, 1902 the Board, ignoring the petition, accepted title to the Opera House block and designated it as the site for the new library. But a new Town Board took office on April 21, and it rescinded the East Main Street acquisition and accepted the University Avenue site. The town paid $4.14 in back taxes the owners owed to the county.[19]

The town had been corresponding with the Carnegie Corporation that was giving money to towns all over America for library buildings, expressing its desire for a grant for Los Gatos. On December 2, 1901 the Carnegie people outlined the steps to be taken to qualify for a grant. A lot had to be purchased; the town had to guarantee 10% of the donation for maintenance; and the architect's plans had to conform to the Carnegie standard.

The Town Board appointed a Citizens Committee on the type of building---each Board member to select two citizens. Those selected were C. L. Ford, W. H. B. Trantham, Dr. Robt. Gober, Dr. Richard Urquhart, Mrs. Urquhart, Mrs. Pearce, Mr. E. C. Farley and B. P. Shuler.

The Carnegie Foundation agreed to give $10,000 toward the building on condition that the town pay at least $1000 a year for its upkeep. The Town Board accepted these conditions and called for bids on May 8, 1902. The contract was let on August 14, 1902 at a cost of $9,411.00. The new library opened its doors to the public on September 25, 1903 with Miss Bessie Cooper continuing as librarian.

Civic organizations and other groups sponsored money-raising projects for the purchase of books and magazines. The women of the Los Gatos History Club sponsored a lecture on May 24, 1903 by Prof. H. Morse Stephens of the University of California. His lecture on "India" netted enough to supply "60 volumes of choice reading" for the library. When Miss Cooper died in 1904, there were more than 1160 volumes in the library. Miss Henri

Rankin succeeded Miss Cooper as librarian, and in 1909 Mrs. Martha Proctor was appointed, and she served until 1919.

A regular library board then took over the control of the library. The first Board was appointed on September 21, 1903 and was composed of A. Berryman, R. R. Bell, J. W. Lyndon, B. P. Shuler and W. H. B. Trantham.[20] On April 20, 1903 the Town Board received the first bill for library books from P. F. Collier & Company in the amount of $28.80. If paid immediately a 10% discount would be realized. The Board paid immediately!

An interesting sidelight on the library is that in 1910 the Library Board shut out the comic sections of the daily and Sunday newspapers. They did not want to corrupt the minds of the young people.

The library became more popular and increased its volumes under Miss Caroline Bailey, who succeeded Mrs. Proctor in 1919 and served until 1926, when she became a librarian at San Jose State College. Miss Grace Smith---later to become Mrs. Tomlinson---served from 1926 to 1946, when she retired because of ill health. Miss Ruth Whitehill became first acting, and in 1948, head librarian with Miss Elizabeth Blakey and Kitty-Lou Willard as her assistants. After 26 years with the library Miss Whitehill resigned in June 1953. Miss Blakey and Kitty-Lou Willard also resigned in that year, and Mr. John Schmuck, a library assistant at San Jose State College, was appointed librarian.

When the University Avenue Carnegie Library building was condemned, the library moved to the Legion building on East Main Street---ironically, the disputed Opera House site. The town purchased this building in 1954 for $34,000 and sold the lot on which the old library had stood to the Episcopal Church for $20,000.

The Legion Hall proved inadequate for the growing community. The newly established Recreation District needed a building, and the Legion-Library building seemed the best suited to its needs. With the completion of the New Civic Center in 1965, Los Gatos had its excellent library building. One of the features of the new Library is the Children's Library Wing. This was under the direction of Mrs. Mary Alice Greene---now Mrs. H. D. Long---until she became Assistant Librarian in 1965. Mrs. Mary Dilles succeeded her as Children's Librarian. The Reference Room of the Main Library is well-supplied with reference material and is staffed with well-trained librarians.

Another new addition to the library is the Art Section. Future growth of this department is assured by a gift from Dr. Ansten Ness, a promi-

Carnegie Library on University Avenue. Built in 1902. Torn down in 1954. *(Library Collection)*

nent **Los Ga**tos physician, who donated four lots in **Santa Cru**z, valued at $10,000, to the library as a **Memorial to** his wife Clelles Ness. The fund is to be **known as the** Clelles Ness Memorial Fund and is to be **used for** the purchase of art books and related **materials.** Later that year (1961) the Los Gatos **Business** and Professional Women's Club added **$600 to thi**s fund in memory of Mrs. Ness.

The Los Gatos Memorial Library is one of the **finest in the** State for a town the size of Los Gatos. This is due not only to the excellent leadership of John Schmuck, the head librarian, and his staff, but also to the cooperation and hard work of the Library Board. Mrs. George (Ethel) Kretsinger, a retired teacher from the Elementary School, was chairman of the Board for 17 years during the library's great growth period. She spent many hours in hard work for the library. She instituted microfilming of newspapers and historic documents. She established a record library and set up the Art Section. In recognition of her work, Mrs. Kretsinger was named "Library Trustee of the Year" by the California Library Association at its annual Convention in Long Beach in October 1954. Although retired from the Board, Mrs. Kretsinger still keeps her interest in the library and works hard for its improvement. William Balch, a long-time resident of Los Gatos, took her place as chairman of the Library Board in August 1965.

From a small reading room, sitting on stilts over the Los Gatos Creek on Main Street, with 350 volumes, in 1898, the Los Gatos Library has grown to a modern, well-equipped building with more than 70,000 volumes. The distributions average over 8,000 books each week. Besides the books, the 20 librarians and employees provide a large selection of records, reference works and government documents.

FOOTNOTES

1. Los Gatos Weekly *News*, September 3, 1881.
2. Town Board *Minutes*, Bk. I, p. 35.
3. Library *Collection, Schools*, Bk. I, p. 9.
4. Los Gatos Weekly *News*, May 1, 1891.
5. Los Gatos *Times*, June 2, 1959.
6. Weekly *News*, July 22, 1887.
7. "History of Los Gatos High School" by students of Mr. T. P. Schweitzer's three history classes in 1969. The writer is indebted to the students for some of the information in this section.
8. Weekly *News*, June 19, 1893.
9. Shortridge, Chas., *Santa Clara County* p. 80–81. Also the 1897 Yearbook "The Wildcat" p. 9. Copy of this rare book is on file at the Los Gatos Union High School.
10. 1897 "Wildcat" p. 12.
11. Library *Collection, Schools*, p. 19.
12. *Ibid.,* p. 34.
13. A complete list of Principals is given in Schweitzer's students' "History of Los Gatos High School."
14. Information obtained through interview with Dr. Lucas.
15. Information from memo to the writer by Mrs. John Lloyd.
16. Information supplied to the writer by Mrs. N. Wollin.
17. Town Board *Minutes*, Bk. II, p. 79.
18. *Ibid.,* Bk. III, p. 170 and p. 242.
19. *Ibid.,* Bk. I, pp. 322ff.
20. *Ibid.,* Bk. I, pp. 449 and 487.

The old Methodist Church, built in 1889. A familiar landmark, it was torn down in 1965 to make room for the new church complex and church parking lot. *(Courtesy Mary Yocco Rugh)*

Sketches of the three different church buildings in the history of the Los Gatos Methodist Church. *(From "A Century of Faith and Service" First Methodist Church of Los Gatos)*

Church of the Immaculate Conception built in 1880 on the corner of Bean and North Santa Cruz Avenues, served as a Catholic Mission Church until 1912. *(Library Collection)*

CHAPTER XI

Churches and Cultural Organizations

Early Churches

METHODIST Episcopal Church. The first religious congregation in Los Gatos was the First Methodist Episcopal Church, which was founded in 1866. For 15 years it was the only church in Los Gatos. The first minister was Dr. William Morrow, a physician, not an ordained minister. But he had the fervor of a missionary. On September 1, 1867 William Bramwell Priddy, who had just graduated from the College of the Pacific in Santa Clara, was appointed to serve the small congregation of Los Gatos Methodists and a group in New Almaden. Mr. Priddy described his work in a letter to Rev. C. V. Anthony, author of *Fifty Years of Methodism* as follows: "When I went there I found no church property of any kind at Los Gatos. There was a church in New Almaden but no parsonage on the work. I held services under a live oak tree just above the old stone (Forbes) mill as long as the weather would permit but in the meantime I had a church and parsonage in the process of erection. I moved into the parsonage in November. The church was dedicated, I think, in January 1868 by Dr. Thomas."[1]

Shortly after William H. Rogers purchased Forbes Mill, he took Mr. C. G. Harrison as one of his partners. Having obtained more land than they needed these two men deeded "land lying near the Los Gatos Flour Mill known as M. E. Church and parsonage lots ... containing one acre more or less." The Methodists paid $1 in "gold coin" for this land, part of which is still the property of the church. Both Mr. Rogers and Mr. Harrison were members of the Board of Trustees of the church.

Early church pastors did a great deal of traveling. For example, Rev. James Corwin was pastor in 1869. "One Sunday he would preach in Los Gatos at eleven o'clock and ride to the summit for a service at four in the afternoon. The next Sunday morning he would preach two sermons at Union School House and one at New Almaden in the evening."[2]

In 1879 the Annual Conference of the Methodist Church reported 32 members in the Los Gatos church. It created Los Gatos as a separated church entity, and from then on it was no longer a circuit

charge, although the pastor continued to serve Guadalupe and Alma. The church grew in membership until 1882, when a smallpox epidemic closed all churches for a while. At the same time, the Guadalupe Mines shut down and many members moved away to seek other employment. Then too, the Presbyterian, Christian, Episcopal and Baptist churches organized in the early 1880's, with the result that the membership of the Methodist church dropped to 48.

In 1889 the congregation built a new church, which was dedicated on December 29. The successful completion of this building, which served the church continuously for more than 76 years, was due in large part to the hard work of the building committee. Among the members were such men as W. G. Alexander, E. E. Dow, Thos. Hayselden, and D. C. Crummey, the father of John D. Crummey, "who pumped the pipe organ by hand for three of his boyhood years."[3]

In 1923 the Methodists purchased the property across the street in front of the church for $10,500---now the parking lot. The reason for the purchase was mainly "to rid the area of old buildings and the disreputable old town jail."

A big event in the history of the local Methodists was the burning of the mortgage on February 6, 1944. The Finance Committee that completed this task was composed of A. C. Ellis, chairman; Ross Page, financial secretary; W. F. Burke, treasurer; Bernard Hardwicke, secretary; Paul Curtis, H. E. Burke, Orin Weed, Leland Walker, R. W. Lloyd and the pastor Samuel Chaney.

After World War II and the influx of new people into our valley, all churches increased in membership and faced new responsibilities. For instance, the membership of the Methodist church stood at 211 in 1939, 470 in 1956, and at 888 in 1965.

Rev. Romain Swedenburg came as pastor in 1955, and he gave new life and vigor to the entire congregation. A trained organist and Choir Director were employed. A long-range program for expansion was adopted. New Sunday School classrooms, an Administration building and a Sanctuary were among the projects included in the plans. The new plant was built in separate units, the first being the Kindergarten wing and administrative offices, which were completed in 1958. Then came the education unit in 1961 and the new Sanctuary in 1965. The final unit was the Youth Center and Social Hall, completed in 1970.

The new church complex changed the picture in the Church Street area. The Yocco house and the other old-time residences were torn down. The Church Parsonage, which had stood between the Presbyterian Church and the old Methodist Church for over 70 years was removed. The old pipe organ, which had been installed in June 1889 and had "900 pipes," according to the Weekly *News,* was given to the University Lutheran Church of Palo Alto.[4]

In January 1964 Rev. Swedenburg resigned to accept the pastorate of the American Church in Beirut, Lebanon, and Dr. Robert Boswell came to the Los Gatos Church. Dr. Boswell continued the process of expansion begun by Rev. Swedenburg. An Assistant Minister, Rev. Robert Schwartz, was called in in June 1965 to help with the youth program. He left in 1970. Mr. William Balch became Minister of Visitation in 1964, giving his time as a service to the church. Dr. Boswell

MEMORIAL SERVICES

In Honor of The Late

PRESIDENT WILLIAM M'KINLEY

AT BUNKER HILL PARK, LOS GATOS, CALIFORNIA,

THURSDAY, SEPTEMBER 19, 1901, AT 10 O'CLOCK A. M.

———

PROGRAMME.

Procession will form at 10 o'clock in the following order: Grand Army of Republic, Women's Relief Corps, Clergymen, Masonic Order, Odd Fellows, Knights of Pythias, on Santa Cruz avenue north of Main street; other Orders, School Pupils and Citizens, on Main street east of Santa Cruz avenue. LINE OF MARCH—North on Santa Cruz avenue, east on Gray's lane, south on University avenue, east on Main street to Bunker Hill Park. MARSHAL—J. G. Fitch; Aids, J. H. Lyndon, J. H. Pearce.

Introductory Remarks, - - - JAMES H. LYNDON

Quartette, "Lead, Kindly Light."

Invocation, - - - - REV. J. C. ROBBINS

Scripture Reading, - - - REV. S. C. KEETCH

Prayer, - - - - - REV. C. W. JOPSON

Hymn, "Nearer, My God, to Thee."

Address, - - - - REV. A. H. BARNHISEL

Hymn, "America."

Prayer and Benediction, - REV. C. E. WINNING

The Public is Invited to Attend.

Order of Services at Memorial Services for President Wm. McKinley at Bunker Hill Park Sept. 10, 1901. *(Los Gatos Museum)*

This sketch of the First Presbyterian Church appeared in the Los Gatos Weekly *News* for January 31, 1890.

The First Presbyterian Church on Church Street after being remodeled in 1938. *(Photo by Hazel Wintler, Courtesy Mrs. Ruth Yocco)*

resigned in February 1971, and Dr. George Parr became the interim pastor.

Presbyterian Church. Mr. G. W. McGrew, an Elder in the Santa Clara Presbyterian Church, came to Los Gatos early in 1881. An ardent Presbyterian, he was anxious to have a Presbyterian Church in Los Gatos. Calling on people in the neighborhood, he found many of like mind. A meeting was held in the Methodist Church at 4 P.M. on June 26, 1881 at which Rev. J. N. Newell, the pastor of the Santa Clara Presbyterian Church, preached the sermon. After the service it was decided to organize a church in Los Gatos. A formal application, signed by 23 people, was made to the Presbytery Committee on Home Missions. In the meantime Mr. R. C. Moodie, a recent graduate of Auburn (N.Y.) Theological Seminary, and his wife, had arrived in Oakland. Rev. Newell invited him to come with him to Los Gatos. A meeting was held the following Sunday in Lyndon Hall where Mr. Moodie---then not yet ordained---preached.

Rev. Newell then organized a church with the 23 members. Mr. McGrew served as the only Elder. Trustees were elected the next Sunday, and it was decided that Elders should serve for 3 years. A Sunday School was organized on July 17, 1881 with Mr. C. W. Mills as Superintendent. Mr. Moodie was ordained and installed on November 8 as the

Rev. H. H. Wintler, pastor of the First Presbyterian Church from 1908 to 1934. *(Courtesy Edw. S. Yocco family)*

Present Sanctuary, First United Presbyterian Church, completed in 1958.

first pastor. Mr. W. S. Butler was elected as the second Elder on November 20, and on December 10 the Session held its first meeting. The first person taken into membership, after the original 23, was Miss Nellie McMurtry, who was admitted upon Confession of Faith on December 10, 1881. Mrs. Moodie and Mrs. Z. Riggs were received on certificate at the same Session meeting. Thus, the membership on December 10 was 26.

Church services were held at the Lyndon Hall for three years. Dr. W. S. McMurtry donated a lot on Church Street to the church. Rev. Moodie had a house built on part of this lot. Additional land was purchased in 1882 at a cost of $1400, most of the money for this having been raised by the women of the church. One money-raising affair was a big lawn party at the McMurtry home on Friday, September 10, 1881 which was attended by more than 250 people, some coming from as far away as San Jose.

The church was chartered on July 23, 1883 and the Session was enlarged to 4 members. A church building was erected on the Church Street site in 1884–1885 at a cost of $5000, including furniture, organ, chairs, carpets, chandelier, fence and sheds. The new church was dedicated on May 3, 1885. The Los Gatos Weekly *News* reported the event as follows: "On Sunday at 3 p.m. May 3, 1885 a large audience assembled for the exercises dedicating the new Presbyterian Church. Rev. H. C. Minton of San Jose delivered the sermon. The church was erected and furnished at a cost of $4,700, not including the lot." The article also told of the lawn parties the ladies of the church held to raise money for the furnishings and carpeting. "The National Board of Church Erection gave $600 and at the dedication services pledges were made in the amount of $276.35, enough to make the congregation debt-free and have $6.35 left."[5]

In 1894 the church was overhauled and furnished with opera chairs. These opera chairs remained until 1938, when the church was again remodelled and pews installed. The writer remembers sitting in the opera seats on a Sunday and hearing the squeak-squeak of the seats as the occupants changed position.

The church bell was procured by subscriptions through the efforts of Mr. W. G. McGrew. It was this bell that served as a "fire bell" for the town, calling the volunteer firemen to their posts whenever there was a fire.

Rev. Moodie left Los Gatos on May 19, 1889 and was succeeded by Rev. James Gardiner as a supply pastor until Rev. Frank Bush came as a regular pastor on May 4, 1892. Several others came in rapid succession until Rev. Henry H. Wintler was called on September 27, 1908. Rev. Wintler served longer than any other minister, holding the pastorate until his retirement in 1934 after 26 years in the Los Gatos church. Rev. Everett Clay Thomson followed him, and it was during his pastorate that extensive alterations were made in the Church Street building. This remodeled church was dedicated in December 1938. In that month Rev. Nottley Stever Hammack became pastor, Rev. Thomson having accepted a call to the Palo Alto church.

The need for expanded facilities became acute after World War II. Five acres on Shannon Road were purchased from Charles Torrey in 1948. Two more acres were added later to give more room for expansion and parking. The first section of the over-all plan was the Fellowship Hall, which was completed in 1953. Services were held in this building until 1958, when the new Sanctuary was completed. Rev. Hammack resigned in April 1954, and Dr. C. James Miller saw the completion of the new Sanctuary before he resigned to go to the San Francisco Theological Seminary at San Anselmo. Dr. Thomas Gee became pastor in 1959. During his tenure another building program was undertaken, which provided the Youth Center Building and an addition to the Choir Room.

The membership in the First United Presbyterian Church in 1970 was over 1200. The youth program was under the direction of the Associate Pastor, T. Royal Scott. The church boasted five choirs, taking in all ages from the very young to an Adult Chancel Choir under the direction of Mrs. Kent Padgett.

St. Mary's Catholic Church. Although Mass was celebrated in Los Gatos before 1880 by Father Testa and Father Young, there was no Catholic congregation until sometime after 1881. The first church building was erected in 1881 and was located on the corner of Bean and Santa Cruz Avenues---now a parking lot---on property belonging to the College of Santa Clara. At that time St. Mary's was attended by Jesuits from the Sacred Heart Novitiate. It was a Mission Church until 1912. In 1913 the building was moved two blocks west, to the southeast corner of Bean and Tait Avenues, where it became part of an enlarged church complex.

In September 1912 St. Mary's Parish was turned over to the Most Rev. Archbishop Hanna, and he appointed Rev. Chas. R. Raschab as pastor. A parochial residence was built in 1912, and a new church was erected on the new site in 1914. The Rev. Raschab was succeeded in 1917 by Father O'Hara, who remained until 1925. Rev. W. F. Keller came next, and under his administration the parish grounds were beautified with trees, flowers and shrubs. Under his direction a large Sunday School chapel was built and the Rectory was completely renovated.

St. Mary's School was built on Lyndon Avenue in 1954, during Father Dougherty's tenure. This school originally contained the first through the fifth grades only. Later all eight grades were included. The first class graduated in the late 1950's, and by 1970 more than 500 pupils had graduated from the school. In 1970 St. Mary's had an enrollment of 250 students.

Sacred Heart Novitiate, though located in the hills above Los Gatos, played an important role in the history of the area's Catholic Churches. Santa Clara College prepared Novices for some time after it was founded. But the Jesuit Fathers began to look for a quieter place for a novitiate. After being disappointed by three prospective sites, they were

The Novitiate and vineyards in the hills above Los Gatos, left, 1890, and right, about 1950. *(Library Collection)*

The old Episcopal Church next to the library on University Ave., 1910. The library is gone and the church has remodeled and expanded. *(Library Collection)*

invited to view the property of Mr. Harvey Wilcox, which stood just south of Los Gatos at an altitude of 700 feet. The prospective site contained 39 acres, including a vineyard and an orchard with 1200 orange trees and a variety of other fruit. The Society of Jesus was pleased with the site and on March 18, 1886 paid $15,000 for the nucleus of the present Sacred Heart Novitiate.

The "middle building" was completed in April 1888 and the novices moved in on June 14. The first Mass was celebrated the next morning at 5:30 A.M. Father Pinasco was the Novitiate's first Superior and Master of Novices, and he was soon succeeded by Fr. Paul Mans, who served until his death two years later. Fr. Dominic Giacobbi was assigned to the helm, and he guided the destinies of the young men entrusted to him for 14 years. It was largely to his foresight and competence that the Novitiate owed its stature and effectiveness. By 1893 the property holdings of the Novitiate had reached 247 acres, and in 1910 the Carlsen Ranch of Guadalupe was purchased.

With the increase in novices the complex was expanded. In 1914 a building program was undertaken, and in 1926 a large new Novitiate wing and another Juniorate wing were added, making the building complex one of the most complete and beautiful in the area.

In 1934 the Society purchased the famous estate of Dr. Harry Tevis. This was a 50-acre tract, plus fee title to 212 additional acres, and was obtained for $85,000. Dr. Tevis had spent more than a million dollars developing the estate. This became Alma College and was the first house of Theology in the West in which members of the Society of Jesus received the last 4 years of their 13 years of training. By 1940 there were 120 Jesuits at Alma College.

In 1969 Sacred Heart became the head office of the California Province of the Jesuits, which included California, Nevada, Arizona and Utah, plus five high schools and three universities---San Francisco, Loyola and Santa Clara.

Alma College announced, on October 17, 1967 that it would move its entire operation to Berkeley, after 30 years at the Alma Campus. The move was made so that this training center could be near the Graduate Theological Union of the University of California. Thus Los Gatos lost an important educational institution for Catholic Priests.

One of the most beautiful settings for an educational institution is that of Guadalupe College, above Los Gatos on Foster Road. This 2½ million dollar novitiate of the Sisters of Charity of the Blessed Virgin Mary was built in 1963 and dedicated on December 12, 1964. The Sisters of Charity is one of the large and long-established teaching orders of the Catholic Church. It was to train teaching nuns. However, lack of students forced the closing of the college in 1968. In March 1968 it sought a use permit for a cultural Educational Center. However, the poor road conditions leading to the buildings led to the refusal of such a permit by the County Planning Commission on April 17, 1968. The beautiful campus and imposing buildings now serve as a locale for retreats.

St. Luke's Episcopal Church. The first church service for a group wanting to establish an Episcopal Church in Los Gatos was held in the Presbyterian Church on the afternoon of May 21, 1882. The Rev. R. M. Chapman conducted the service and helped to organize a congregation. Services were later held in the AOUW Hall and in the Masonic Hall. A site was acquired on University Avenue next to the Elementary School in 1883. Here the new congregation built the first church.

They held their first service in the new building on September 9, 1883.

In 1901 the church was burned during the great fire of October 13, 1901. The sum of $5000 was raised by voluntary contributions, and a new building was erected in 1902. At the time the church was consecrated, on May 23, 1902, only $400 was left to be raised. The Guild Hall was built in 1904. By 1911 the ladies of the church had accumulated a substantial sum of money for a Parish House. However, before it could be used, the institution in which they had invested the money failed, and they had to start all over again. The Parish House was built in 1912.

After Rev. Chapman, the Rev. Dr. Lewis became the Rector. When he tendered his resignation in February 1890, the Vestry urged him to stay until September. Rev. Mr. H. E. Clapham came in 1891, and he resigned in 1897 to go to San Francisco. Among the later Rectors at St. Luke's were the Rev. John A. Collins, Rev. David Todd Gillmor and Rev. Stanley Clapham. Rev. Gillmor came in January 1931. When World War II broke out, he was called into active service and resigned from St. Luke's in May 1942. Rev. Stratton became Rector until Rev. Stanley Clapham arrived.

In 1967 the Vestry made plans for a new church building in the Monte Sereno area. But residents of Monte Sereno objected to a church on the Oak Knoll Drive site. Despite this, a permit for a church building was granted in January 1968. However, objections were still voiced, and the Vestry decided to give up the plans for a church in Monte Sereno. The building on University Avenue was remodeled in 1969. Rev. Father Edward Jacobs is the Rector, and Father Livingston is part-time assistant. Membership in St. Luke's was 260 in December 1970.

The Baptist Church. The first Baptist Church was organized in 1883 by 16 people who had been members of the First Baptist Church in San Jose. They elected officers and held regular services, with one of their number reading a sermon. A retired minister, Dr. Abbott, visited the group and persuaded them to adopt the New Hampshire Confession of Faith.[6]

In 1884 Rev. W. H. Latourette became the first pastor and he was followed by Rev. F. L. Sullivan in 1889. During his pastorate a church was erected on West Main Street near Lyndon Avenue. The new church was dedicated on Sunday May 26, 1889 and was paid for in full by that date. The sanctuary had opera chairs and a seating capacity of 400. A "Blymer" bell weighing 1100 pounds, with a reach of 40 inches across, was placed on the belfry. It was said that it could be heard for 7 or 8

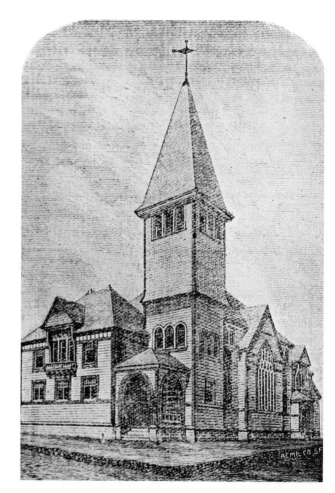

This sketch of the First Baptist Church on West Main Street appeared in the Los Gatos Weekly *News* for January 31, 1890.

miles. However, a defect in its construction resulted in a deep crack, and the bell could not be used. In 1895 a new bell costing $300 was purchased.

Not only did the church have a bell, but it acquired the second pipe organ in Los Gatos in 1899. The organ had originally been built by J. Mayer for the First Baptist Church of Oakland, but that church wanted a larger organ so they sold it to the Los Gatos church.[7]

The church was heated by a wood stove. The Los Gatos *News* reported on January 17, 1890 that "plenty of dry wood is expected to make the Baptist church warm next sunday."

The Baptist Church grew in numbers, as did all the churches in Los Gatos. Ministers came and went without causing much disturbance. However, in September 1909 Rev. Robert Whitaker arrived, and then things began to liven up. Rev. Whitaker edited and published a pocket-size magazine, "The Insurgent," and he had also written numerous articles and has had a book of verse published. The title of this was "The Gospel at Work in Modern Life," and it pleaded the modern viewpoint in

Two churches on West Main Street in 1927. The one on the right—the automobile in front—was the original Baptist church built in the early 1880's. The farthest, with the tower, located on Lyndon Avenue and West Main Street, was built by the Baptists in 1889. The Christian Church purchased these in 1917 and moved the nearest building to Lyndon Avenue where it served as a Social Hall. The buildings were torn down in 1958. The A.O.U.W. Hall, foreground, was built in 1881, originally located on the corner of West Main Street and Santa Cruz Avenue. It was moved to this location in 1894 and served, for a number of years, as a Scout Hall and Boys' Club meeting place. It was torn down in 1930. *(Information supplied by Henry Crall. Picture from Library Collection)*

religion. His magazine also emphasized the modern viewpoint in religion, politics, and sociology, and in general preached the "social gospel."

Rev. Whitaker was a "heretic" as far as the conservative Baptists were concerned. He got a majority of his congregation to pass a resolution, in June 1910, to the effect that "we can no longer feel that we can make any matter of ritual a barrier to church membership, and we believe that the use of baptism should be left to be determined by the individual believer, and should not be forced upon anyone as a condition of fellowship with other believers in the Church of Jesus Christ." Membership in the Church, said Rev. Whitaker, should be based, not upon ceremony, but entirely upon the spiritual.[8]

The church split as a result of this resolution. Two factions, each contending it should control the property of the church, quarreled. The case went to court and Judge Welch decided that "a church, independent of higher authority, is governed in temporal and religious matters by majority rule; that the majority expelling minority is a church action and not a corporate action and that therefore both should share the property by dividing it among them."

The Whitaker faction continued to be called the First Baptist Church until 1921. Rev. Whitaker served until that year after which he became a free-lance writer and nothing more was heard of his group.

The minority faction continued to be recognized by the Northern Baptist Convention and the San Jose Baptist Association, and it held meetings in the home of Mrs. H. M. Dickenson. They called Rev. N. L. Freeman of Turlock to become pastor and held meetings in the Montezuma Block until

their new church on Main Street and Wilcox (College) Avenue was completed. The new church was dedicated on May 6, 1917. The original Baptist Church building on West Main Street and Lyndon Avenue became the home of the Christian Church.

After Rev. Freeman left in 1917, Rev. T. S. Lovell came, and he served until 1923. Rev. B. F. Stump came in 1923 and served for 28 years before he retired in 1952. The First Baptist Church grew steadily under Rev. Stump. However, in 1948 a group of dissidents broke away and organized the Calvary Baptist Church. In 1953 this new group built a large Sanctuary, seating 850; church offices, Sunday School wing and an Educational and Social center at 16330 San Jose Avenue. Under the leadership of Dr. Blaine Bishop, the congregation grew from the original 90 members in 1948 to more than 1700 by the end of 1970. From a one-pastor congregation the church has grown to require a staff of eight. Dr. Bishop's sermons are broadcast over radio station KEEN on Sunday mornings.

The First Baptist Church on East Main and College Avenue was torn down in 1958 to make room for the Penthouse Apartments. A new church was built on Farley Road and dedicated in March 1963. H. O. Van Gilder was pastor after Rev. Stump retired. He was succeeded in 1963 by Rev. A. R. Rutledge. In 1970 Dr. Irving Penberthy served the congregation, which numbers 170 members.

The Christian Church. Because there were seven saloons in Los Gatos in 1884 and "no Protestant Church on the west side of town," twelve staunch churchmen founded the Los Gatos Christian Church "to counteract the evils of the wet days." The 12 staunch churchmen were Mr. and Mrs. John

The Christian Science Church, built in 1930. *(Photo by the author)*

Montgomery, Mr. and Mrs. John Berry, Mr. and Mrs. Will Mack, Mr. and Mrs. John Mack, Mr. and Mrs. T. B. Proctor, Miss Caroline Belscher, and Josiah Royce. They met in the Odd Fellows Hall over what is now the Corner Drug Store and laid plans for the new congregation.[9]

Rev. W. A. Malone, who had taken up ranching near Los Gatos, became the first pastor. Needing a permanent place to worship, the group looked around for a suitable site. In 1886 they purchased a building on West Main Street for $1185, making a down payment of $85 and mortgaging the rest. This building was remodeled and enlarged in 1899, most of the expenses for this being donated by Mrs. R. Smith. When the new Baptist Church was completed on East Main Street and Wilcox Avenue in 1917, the Christian Church purchased the West Main Street Baptist Church and used it as a Sanctuary. Their original lot on Lyndon Avenue was sold and the building was moved down to become the Social Hall of the Church.

The Christian Church grew rapidly once it had a permanent home. One of its most progressive pastors was Rev. Myron Cole, who came in 1933. New life was injected into the church in the short time he was here. He drew young people into the church. He organized a baseball team; had his church sponsor various youth activities; organized a men's quartet, and participated in many local civic affairs. It was with regret that his church and the people of the town saw him leave in 1936 to become Chaplain at Chapman College in Los Angeles. His successor was Rev. W. L. Mellinger.

In 1956 the church realized that it would have to move away from the downtown area. Property was purchased on Daves Avenue, and a Fellowship Hall was erected for worship and classes. The Sanctuary was completed in 1961 at a cost of $67,453 plus pews, carpets, pulpit, and communion furniture. In 1967 the Sunday School wing of 9 classrooms was completed and extensive remodeling undertaken at a cost of $55,000. A residence and an acre of land west of the sanctuary was purchased in 1969 for church offices, three classrooms and a Fireside Fellowship hall. A custodian's residence and two acres behind the parking lot were purchased in 1965 for $39,000.

The church had grown to a membership of 1200 by December 1970. Rev. Marvin Richard is the pastor and he has a youth minister and a minister of Christian Education assisting him.

The Christian Science Church. In 1904 two Christian Science Practitioners, Mr. and Mrs. J. J. Harding, began to read the lesson-sermons in their apartment. To accommodate the increase in attendance they met at various places---Ford's Opera House, the Beckwith Block and finally, in 1908, the IOOF Hall.

In March 1909 they built a chapel and reading room on two lots on Broadway. This was also used for the Sunday School and church services. It had a seating capacity of 130 and had every modern convenience such as "lighting by Tungsten electric lights." The building cost $3,500 and was formally opened on April 4, 1909.[10]

A new and larger church was needed for the growing congregation. In February 1929 two lots on Main Street, across from the high school, were purchased as the site for a new church. A dignified colonial style building, with Corinthian portico, was erected. The first service in this beautiful new building was held in February 1930. The building is still one of the most striking in all of Los Gatos. The old building on Broadway was sold to the Seventh Day Adventists.

More Recent Churches

Seventh Day Adventist Church. The members of this denomination used the old Christian Science building at 57 Broadway until 1957. On June 5 of that year a fire destroyed much of the building. A new church was built and dedicated in March 1957. It was debt free at the time of dedication. Pastor Don E. Duncan is the minister and the congregation numbered 225 in December 1970.

Faith Lutheran Church. In 1949 Rev. Bernard Hanson came to Los Gatos to organize a Lutheran Church here. At first it was a Mission Congregation of the Evangelical Lutheran Church, which merged in 1969 to become the American Lutheran Church. Rev. Hanson established a strong congregation and was instrumental in the building of a beautiful

Sanctuary on Ferris Avenue, which was completed in 1965. Rev. Harold W. Pennington succeeded Rev. Hanson in 1969. In December 1970 Faith Lutheran Church claimed more than 800 members.

Mormon Church. The Church of Christ Latter Day Saints, a ward of the Mormon Church, had been established in the Los Gatos area shortly before 1957. In that year a 5-acre site was purchased on Rose Avenue off Saratoga Avenue. An imposing church building was erected at a cost of $355,000. This church serves Los Gatos, Saratoga, Campbell and the Cambrian Park area. The chapel has a seating capacity of 322, and there is a classroom wing of 22 rooms. The Los Gatos Ward had more than 1000 members in December 1970.

Jehovah's Witnesses. In the 1940's a group of 8 or 10 people met regularly to worship in the manner of Jehovah's Witnesses. For a while they met on Santa Cruz Avenue, then on Wedgewood Avenue. Early in 1967 two separate congregations were formed. One was the Los Gatos Central Unit and the other the Blossom Hill Unit. The presiding minister of the Los Gatos Central Unit is Mr. Daniel Davidson, while Mr. Nicholas Garrett is the presiding minister of the Blossom Hill Unit.

In 1967 a new Kingdom Hall was built on Blossom Hill, and this was dedicated by the two congregations on October 11, 1967. Mr. Nicholas Garrett, in his remarks at the dedication, said, "It is our hope to make Kingdom Hall a center of pure worship in the community, contributing to the spiritual uplift and welfare of the city."

Both congregations meet at the 15980 Blossom Hill Kingdom Hall. One group meets at 9:30 on Sunday mornings and the other at 3 o'clock in the afternoon. Week-night meetings are also shared. Early in 1971 the membership in the two congregations was about 250.

Unitarian Fellowship. The Unitarians came into Santa Clara County as early as 1865. In 1893 a group met to hear a sermon by J. Herndon Garnett, Assistant Minister of the Unitarian Church in San Jose. This was the first Unitarian service in Los Gatos.

The Unitarian movement declined in the early 1900's, and it wasn't until 1949 that a Unitarian Fellowship was organized in Los Gatos. The leaders of this organizing group included Mr. and Mrs. Merritt Cutten Sr., Dr. Norman Dolloff, Maurice Hinman, Elinor Allen, Pat Beaudry, Ruth Duval, Ida Florendo, Lillian Gishin, Marg. Piercy, Maggie Rees, and Mr. and Mrs. Paul Madsen.

The Unitarian Fellowship met at the Los Gatos History Club for a while and later moved to the main hall of the Recreation building on Main Street. Speakers are brought in to discuss war,

Admission Day Parade 1892. Some 7,000 visitors came to Los Gatos in special trains to help the Native Sons and Native Daughters celebrate. *(Library Collection)*

peace, poverty, foreign entanglement, government spending, drug abuse, ecology etc. It is an active group, believing that people should act on their convictions if they want the world to be a better place in which to live.

Mr. H. T. Faaland was the program coordinator for 1971. At that time the group had 112 members. Meetings are held on Sunday mornings at 10:30 A.M.

Cultural Activities

Opera Houses. Very early in its history Los Gatos became known for its cultural activities. Lyndon Hall had been the scene of numerous performances in the field of music and drama. In 1885 Seanor's Opera House was completed on East Main Street between Main and Church Street. It opened on July 4, 1885 with the Pierce and Mitchell Opera Company performing afternoon and evening. The Los Gatos Weekly *News* hoped that the public would support Mr. Seanor's Opera House. However, Seanor's Opera House was destroyed by fire in the fall of 1890. This left the town without a hall for cultural events. The *News* again urged people to get behind a move for a new opera house. "If people are looking for a profitable investment," said the editor in the July 30, 1891 issue, "they should look into the matter of an opera house or entertainment hall."

In May 1892 a new corporation was formed that had as its purpose the purchase of a site and the erection of a suitable building. A vacant lot, owned by Miss L. L. Dinsmore, fronting on Main Street and extending through Church Street, "next to C. A. Morgan's Carriage Painting establishment" was available. The price was $1,800. The corporation proposed to dispose of 300 shares of stock at $25 a

G.A.R. lineup for the Memorial Day Parade. The Los Gatos Chapter of the G.A.R., known as EOC Ord Post, always led the town's Memorial Day parades. Organized July 17, 1885, the last member, James A. Thom, of Culver City, died March 28, 1937. Mr. Henry Crall has the complete roster of members with biographical sketches. *(Library Collection)*

share, making a total of $7,500. Miss Dinsmore subscribed to 72 shares, and in a short time more than 237 shares were sold.

At a stockholders' meeting on May 23, 1892 Chas. Wilcox was elected chairman and Fen Massol secretary of the corporation. It was decided that the corporation should be known as the Johnson Opera House Association. The corporation was to "erect, own and hold a public hall or opera house, and for this purpose to acquire, own and hold such real estate and personal property as may be necessary and convenient, and to lease, let, mortgage or convey any and all real or personal property of the corporation and to conduct any and all business pertaining to the premises." The 68 stockholders comprised the "solid citizens" of Los Gatos.[11]

There was a long delay in starting the project and the local press was impatient. On October 21, 1892 the *News* lamented that "Six months have passed since the enterprise was initiated, but as yet nothing has been done." The contract was finally let on November 19, 1892 and Ralph de Clairmont, a noted scenic artist, was given the contract to paint the scenery, including the drop curtain. When the theater part was completed, it was leased to Butler and Gelatt for $60 a month. The Native Sons of the Golden West rented lodge rooms in the building at $17.50 a month the first year and $20 a month thereafter. Other stores in the building were leased to bring the rental income to $100 a month, on an investment of $15,000.

Because the corporation was unable to pay for the furnishings, a judgment went against it. Despite this, the opera house opened on Monday evening, March 5, 1893 when Clay Clement presented "The Bells." On Thursday of that week "The New Dominion" was presented, with Clay Clement playing the part of Franz Victor Von Hoffenstauffen.

The Johnson Opera House continued to bring good performances to Los Gatos. The admission charge was 50 cents for adults and 25 cents for children. But the night of August 24, 1894 proved a disaster. The opera house burned to the ground. The fire was so intense that it threatened the J. J.

Nichols house. Mr. Nichols was forced to move his sick wife to a neighbor's house for safety. Dr. Frank Knowles, who lived across the street, first spotted the fire when he got up early to go on a hunting trip. He ran to the Presbyterian Church and rang the fire bell. He kept his house wet with blankets and a bucket brigade. The Los Gatos *News* reported that the Johnson Opera House "was a beautiful structure and the pride of Los Gatos ... Just before the fire Mr. Augustine Duncan had entertained an audience with singing and a reading. The lessee and Manager, Mr. G. A. Butler, was the last in the building and put out all the lights. A little after 12 an explosion rocked the Opera House and neighborhood. Inferno resulted."[12]

The damage amounted to $16,000, and the fire was thought to have been of incendiary origin. The fire also destroyed a blacksmith shop, a house, and two barns. It was only due to the hard work of firemen and citizens that the Methodist and Presbyterian Churches were saved.

Ten years after this fire another opera house was built. The pavilion at the Los Gatos Cannery had been used for entertainments since the Johnson Opera House fire. But in May 1904 Mr. George Hooke, the owner, announced that the pavilion would no longer be available because of expansion plans for the cannery. A new meeting place had to be built. Mr. E. L. Ford decided to build an opera house. The Ford Opera House---now the Opera House Antiques---at 140 Main Street was completed in October 1904. The "Sweet Clover" Company gave the opening night performance. Young Henry Crall managed the opera house, "doing all the jobs from publicity, selling tickets to cleaning up."

The Ford Opera House became the center of activity in the town. Traveling players, chautauqua performances and lecturers came there. High School plays were presented and school graduations were held there.

Chautauquas. In 1873 John H. Vincent and Lewis Miller were attending a Summer Sunday School Institute of the Methodist Church in

Chautauqua, New York. They conceived the idea of expanding the program to include secular as well as religious instruction. An eight-week program was offered in the summer of 1874, including courses in the arts, science and humanities. Lecturers were sent out to home study groups. Soon other communities were inspired to form local Chautauquas. Authors, explorers, musicians, and political leaders were brought to local communities. In 1912 the movement was organized on a commercial basis and lecturers and entertainers were furnished to local groups, much like the "Concert Associations" that today make contracts for concert series.

Los Gatos looked into the possibility of a Chautauqua series in 1915. On March 16, 1916 the Ellison-White Chautauqua Company assured Los Gatos that it would have a Chautauqua in 1916. On May 12, the Chamber of Commerce announced that a Chautauqua would be held in Los Gatos from May 25 through June 3. A local Chautauqua Association was appointed with J. D. Farwell as President, C. F. Hamsher, Vice-President; K. H. Erickson, Secretary; and S. D. Balch, Treasurer.

On Sunday evening, May 28, the Comus Players presented selections from Shakespeare and a Canadian classic of frontier life, "Carson of the North Woods." Since the Chautauqua Company did not charge for Sunday performances, all seats were free that night. On Monday the 29th the National Operatic Singers presented the comic opera "Martha." Another program featured the concert violinist Alexander Skibinsky.

By 1924 the Chautauqua had lost its appeal throughout the nation, and Los Gatos was no exception. Blake Franklin, President of the Chamber of Commerce, writing in a column in the *Mail-News* on May 12, 1924, expressed regrets that

"Frontier Days" Pageant, 1935. L to R Evan Heid, George Bruntz and Prentiss Brown. *(Courtesy Mrs. Roberta Heid Blake)*

PROGAM
Afternoon of June 21, 1919
Los Gatos' First Annual Pageant
"Fulfillment"

2 P. M.—Opening of Entertainment.
Band Concert on Plaza in front of Hotel Lyndon.
Flag raising by Boy Scouts.
Address of Welcome by Mayor Godfrey.
March to High School Grounds for Baseball and Tennis Contests.

2:30 P. M.—Baseball: Bean Spray Pump Co. Team vs. Los Gatos Firemen.
(Two Best Teams in Santa Clara County)

2:00 P. M.—Tennis Tournament: High School Court, Osburn Court, Case Court. Direction of H. G. Osburn. Players from San Francisco San Jose, Campbell, Los Gatos. Prizes.

4:30 P. M.—Automobile Parade. Start at Santa Cruz Ave. and Main St. to Hill Climbing Contest.

4:45 P. M.—Auto Hill Climbing Contest: Glen Ridge. Local and outside drivers. "Lots of Fun." "Something different."
Prizes.

Band Concert all afternoon opposite Hotel Lyndon.

7:45 P. M.—Pageant Gates open.

8:15 P. M.—Band Concert at Pageant Grounds.

9:00 P. M.—Pageant "Fulfillment" by Wilbur Hall.

Bunker Hill Park open all day for picnics.

Pageant Information Bureau and Ticket office in front of Bank of Los Gatos open all day.

Pageant and reserve seat tickets can be secured at both drug stores or at special ticket booths.

EATS

Cafeteria dinner, 12 M. to 7:30, at M. E. church, off Pageant grounds; Hotel Lyndon, the Ideal Restaurant, Park Cafe, Graeb's.

All Day Nickle Dance at W. O. W. hall.
Street Dance in evening before and after Pageant upon West Main St.

Ladies' Rest Room—Town Hall, Chamber of Commerce, W. O. W. hall, M. E. church.

Program for first Los Gatos Pageant in 1919. (Notice misspelled heading.) *(Library Collection)*

the 100 people who had bought season tickets would be forced to fork over another $7.50 each to make up the deficit. He also questioned the value of the Chautauqua to Los Gatos, since San Francisco and Oakland were close enough to offer good entertainment for those who wanted it.

Los Gatos Pageants. Even before the demise of the Chautauqua programs in 1924, Los Gatos was providing entertainment with local talent. An outdoor pageant took over and became very popular. Credit for the idea of a pageant for Los Gatos belongs to Wilbur Hall, noted Los Gatos author. He converted the old winery behind the Town Hall

"Frontier Days" Pageant 1935. *(Courtesy Mrs. Roberta Heid Blake)*

into an outdoor theater and presented the first pageant there in 1918. He wrote and directed "The Pageant of Fulfillment." This was a symbolic story of earth's creation and development down to the present.

The pageant of 1920 was on a larger scale and was in the form of a play, "The Californian," again written and directed by Mr. Hall. Many notable people attended one or the other of the two performances given on June 18 and 19. Governor William D. Stephens and the famous writers Gertrude Atherton, Ruth Comfort Mitchell Young, Helen Hoyt, Mrs. Fremont Older and John D. Barry, all of national note, and living in or near our town, witnessed the performance in 1920. So impressed was Governor Stephens that he remarked after the performance, "As an illustration of history, the pageant was the finest thing I have ever witnessed. The entertainment as a whole was well worth going any distance to see. The story was well-told and a tribute to Mr. Hall."

The San Jose *Mercury* said about the performance of 1920, "It presents in dramatic spectacle the vital movements in the history of the Commonwealth. The acoustics in the natural amphitheatre where the pageant was given are remarkable . . . and with a dusky canopy overhead, brilliant with a million stars, the rugged setting and faithful costuming of the players went to make a vivid glimpse into the past, reflecting credit to both Mr. Hall and the city of Los Gatos."[13]

Wilbur Hall produced the pageants from 1918 through 1926. After that various other local people wrote or directed them. In 1928 Henry Crall, a local businessman, wrote and directed "Tashida," and it proved very successful. Vivian Johnson had charge of the dances. The success of this performance was lauded by the local press when it said, "The perfect evening, with the sky set with glittering stars and a half crescent moon, added to the marvelous stage set with its modern turrets, minarets, arches, latticed balconies, and oriental bazaar, made the performance one to be long remembered."

The popularity of the Los Gatos pageants became such that people came here from great distances to see them. Famous people continued to come. In 1925 Governor Richardson and his family came to see the performance. In 1929 more than 200 bankers from five Bay Area counties, while meeting in Los Gatos, attended an evening performance of "The Magic Lamp," their wives accompanying them.

In 1920 it looked like the pageant would die before it had a chance to live. A party in San Francisco was dickering to buy a piece of land from Mr. Vedova. This was needed for the pageant stage. A group of citizens got together and purchased the land, thereby saving the pageant. The *Mail-News* said of this, "The action of these men deserves the highest commendation from citizens."[14]

At a meeting in the Town Hall on September 21, 1921, the organization of the Los Gatos Annual Pageant Association was completed. A committee composed of Mrs. Sanborn Young, Henry Crall, and W. G. Lidley, presented a proposed constitution and by-laws. These were accepted unanimously. Membership in the association was of four kinds---contributing, subscribing, sustaining, and general. The property belonging to the association amounted to $3,000.

The pageants were held in an area behind the Town Hall which presented a perfect setting for the outdoor performances. In July 1935 the L. G. Cassaletto lot was purchased for $900, the town paying $250 and the Pageant Association paying the balance.

W. W. Clark, the Secretary of the Chamber of Commerce, envisioned a real bowl for the pageant productions and other dramatic and musical entertainments. When the San Jose Water Company put in larger pipes on San Jose Avenue (Bascom), Mr. Clark got them to haul the excess dirt to the pageant ground for a bowl. Once the dirt was in, the local people volunteered to help. They installed seats and put the bowl in shape for performances. The Bowl was dedicated on August 16, 1940. It could seat more than 2,500 people.

High School art students were invited to draw up plans for a waterfall to be installed on the hillside of the pageant grounds. Miss Jeanette Owen won first prize and Miss Camille Hatch second prize. Frank Ingerson, the famous artist, resident of Alma, advised the committee on landscaping, etc. When completed, the waterfall was lighted at night with vari-colored lights. It was a most artistic sight.

The Los Gatos Bowl Association was organized in April 1941, with Dr. Ernest Colvin as President. This group planned to have Sunday concerts and dramatic and operatic performances. However, the war interfered with these plans. By 1950 the Bowl Association had become inactive. Efforts were made in 1955 to reactivate it, but greater plans for a civic center were in the cards.

In 1957 the *Fiesta de Los Gatos* took the place of the Bowl activities. This was a one-day affair offering games, a parade, coronation of a queen, etc. But it was not the same as the good old days of the pageant, where community cooperation and fellowship prevailed.

The Los Gatos Concert Association. The idea of bringing famous performers to Los Gatos dates to 1946, when a representative of Columbia Artists Bureau came to Los Gatos and met with Mr. and Mrs. Morton Harvey and Dr. Gustav Fassin, who was then President of the Los Gatos Bowl Association, to discuss their program. The plan was well-received, and a Concert Association was organized. Volunteers went to work to enlist membership in the Association, and in a short time 750 members had signed up. The original officers were Robert Hamsher, President; Dr. Gustav Fassin, 1st Vice-President; Mrs. Tom Haire, 2nd Vice-President; Mrs. Effie Walton, 3rd Vice-President; Mr. Howard Olson, Secretary; and Martin LeFevre, Treasurer.

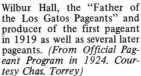

Wilbur Hall, the "Father of the Los Gatos Pageants" and producer of the first pageant in 1919 as well as several later pageants. *(From Official Pageant Program in 1924. Courtesy Chas. Torrey)*

Dr. Ernest F. Colvin, first President of the Los Gatos Bowl Association. Active in Many cultural activities. *(Courtesy the Colvin Family)*

The first performance of the Concert Series was the Mia Slavenska Dance Company. During the years of the Concert Series such artists as Nadine Conner, The Trapp Family Singers, George London, Leontyne Price and Cesare Siepi have performed in Los Gatos.

Originally the membership was $6 per person for four concerts. Season tickets now cost $10. The concerts were held in the old auditorium of the high school, which accommodated more than 800 people at a concert. In 1964, when the auditorium was condemned, the concerts were held in the West Valley College auditorium in Campbell, and the membership had to be limited to 500. In 1968 the concerts returned to the Los Gatos High School auditorium, which had been remodeled and named the Prentiss Brown Auditorium. The membership is now around 550, the most that can be accommodated.[15]

Programs are selected by a committee, and the members are given a chance to choose the type of program they prefer. The Community Concerts have become a vital part of the cultural life of the community, and no doubt more people would join the association if a hall large enough to accommodate them were available.

The Los Gatos Museum. On May 26, 1965 a group of citizens interested in a museum met to discuss the possibility of a museum for Los Gatos. Thirty people came, and attorney Norman Stoner was elected chairman. Thirteen people volunteered to serve on a committee to complete an organization. Regular meetings were held at the home of Dr. and Mrs. John Atkinson. Out of these meetings the non-profit Los Gatos Museum Association developed. A constitution and by-laws were

The Los Gatos Museum on West Main Street and Tait Avenue. Mrs. W. R. Hamsher, one of the hostesses, is ready to greet visitors to the Museum. *(Photo by the author)*

Mr. William Allaway, Director of the Los Gatos Museum. *(Photo by Dr. Ethel Dana)*

adopted and a Board of Directors chosen. The original Board consisted of Norman Stoner, President; George Lagomarsino, 1st Vice-President; Art Thimann, 2nd Vice-President; Dr. Ethel Dana, Secretary; and Miss Catherine Smith, Treasurer. Other members were Wendell Hammon, Robert E. Lee, Mrs. Leonard McCammon, Mrs. Margaret McDaniel, Mr. Hammond Smith, Mr. Roland Perry, Mr. Lawrence Moitazo, and Mr. George Kane, publisher of the *Times Observer.* A short time later Dr. Dorothy Kautcher, Dr. George G. Bruntz, John Lincoln, Mrs. Robert Smith, Mrs. Susan Faaland, Mrs. John Lincoln and Mrs. Henry L. Crall became members of the Board.

The search began for suitable quarters for the Museum. On May 16, 1966 the Town Council voted to lease the old Fire House on West Main Street and Tait Avenue to the Association for five years. A token payment was to be made. A fund drive was begun. Donor memberships of $100 or more, as well as regular membership fees of $10 or more, a year were accepted. Display cases were either donated by local merchants, purchased by the association or constructed. Everyone helped--- including teenagers, the women of the History Club and P.T.A. groups. The building was remodeled, and the young people helped to paint the interior with paint donated by local merchants.

The History Club gave the Museum a good start when it sponsored a two-day museum show at its clubhouse, to demonstrate what a museum could do for our town. The Board of Directors set up four departments for the museum: Local History, headed by Dr. George G. Bruntz, assisted by Mrs. William Craddock and Mrs. Donald L. Sweeney; Science, with Mrs. Leonard J. McCammon, assisted by Mr. William Allway, Mrs. Robert Lee and Mrs. Judy Whitney; Fine Arts, originally headed by Mrs. Hammond Smith and later by Mrs. Henry L. Crall, assisted by Mrs. Jerry Price; Classroom Collections, by Dr. Ethel Dana, assisted by Mrs. Evelyn Jaca.

The Museum opened its doors on May 20, 1967. It is staffed entirely by volunteers who act as attendants and who help in other ways to make the museum attractive and worthwhile. Mrs. Alan Ryan (Shirley) was the first coordinator of volunteers, and she got together a large corps of workers. Mrs. H. T. Faaland succeeded her in this responsibility. Mrs. Maryanne Cottrell is chairman of public relations and publicity.

Early in 1971 Mr. William Allaway, who has had considerable experience in museum work in the middlewest, was appointed Director of the Los Gatos Museum.

The Museum is open to the public free of charge from 1 to 5 daily and from 2 to 4 on Sundays. School classes may make arrangements for morning visits if they cannot schedule visits during the regular hours. Scout Troops, Campfire Girls and many other groups have taken advantage of the fine educational and cultural exhibits. Attendance has averaged about 25 people on an afternoon, and on some days it reaches as high as 50. Many out-of-town visitors have come to the Museum, which is proving to be a great cultural boon to our town.

FOOTNOTES

1. *First Methodist Church of Los Gatos,* a Century of Faith and Service, 1886–1966.
2. *Ibid.*
3. *Ibid.*
4. *Ibid.*
5. Los Gatos Weekly *News,* May 9, 1885.
6. Library *Collection,* Bk. 17, p. 1.
7. *Ibid.,* p. 8.
8. Los Gatos *Mail,* July 14, 1910.
9. Library *Collection,* Bk. 17, p. 15.
10. *Ibid.,* p. 19.
11. Los Gatos Weekly *News,* May 27, 1882.
12. *Ibid.,* August 31, 1894.
13. Sawyer, *History of Santa Clara County,* p. 291.
14. *Mail-News,* October 7, 1920.
15. Information from a memo to the writer from Mr. Harwood Warriner, President of the Community Concert Association, 1971.

CHAPTER XII

Service Groups and Clubs

Postal Service

MAIL was first distributed in Los Gatos at Forbes' Mill in 1854. Later a corner in the Los Gatos Store owned by Dr. W. S. McMurtry was used as a mail pick-up point. The mail was brought in by a stage line running from San Jose to Santa Cruz, with stops at the Lexington Stage barns where they changed horses. On December 8, 1864 the first post office was established in Los Gatos in the Ten Mile House, near the end of what is today Montebello Way. H. D. McCobb was appointed the first postmaster on April 6, 1865.[1] The building was also used as a stage office.

The second postmaster was Dr. W. S. McMurtry, who took over from Mr. Cobb in 1869. Among the other early postmasters were W. E. Rogers and B. G. Allen. At that time the position was a political plum, given to faithful workers of the party in power in Washington. The tenure of the Republicans ended when Grover Cleveland, a Democrat, took office as President in 1885. He appointed a local Democrat, F. M. Jackson, to be postmaster. The local press said of his appointment, "He has

weathered the storms of defeat for years and now he steps up to the front and takes his reward."[2] By 1885 the salary of the Postmaster for Los Gatos was $1000 a year, compared to the $12 a year received by Dr. McMurtry in 1869.

After Jackson's short term the Republicans again took over the local post office with J. H. Lyndon, who was followed by Anna Gaffney. In October 1885 the Los Gatos *News* reported that the question of the location of the post office had been settled. The Los Gatos Store planned to build a two-story building, and the entire lower room was to be used as a post office. The building was built by Herman Sund and was to cost $700, including the boxes and furniture. The press rejoiced that the boxholders would be able to pick up their mail any time of day or night.

In 1894 the Rankin Building---where the Rex Hotel is today---was chosen as the post office site. New boxes were installed and rented. There were more than 450 boxes, which prompted the *News* to comment that "Los Gatos now can boast of fine post office facilities." There was only one omission---no Sunday mail distribution, but it hoped that this would soon be remedied.

One of the early pictures of our town showing the foothills and the valley before the days of freeways and smog. Taken from Loma Alta Ave. (then Market Street.) *(Library Collection)*

Lewis Torrey, Mountain Area Mail Carrier, 1906 to 1931. *(Courtesy Chas. Torrey)*

Miss Elsie Torrey, Mountain area mail carrier 1906 to 1928. She had many harrowing experiences. *(Courtesy Chas. Torrey)*

Mr. Lee Darneal, local Democratic leader and businessman. Served as Postmaster 1916–1920 and from 1933 to 1942. *(Library Collection)*

W. C. Campbell became postmaster in 1899, and W. W. Lyndon was assistant postmaster. In May 1902 the local postmaster's salary was raised to $1800 a year.

The local post office still lacked a permanent home. Buildings were leased for short periods of time. After the big fire of 1901, which destroyed the Rankin Block, the post office moved to the site of the Foothill Hotel and later to the Montezuma block on West Main Street---into a building which had been successively a saloon, a butcher shop and a movie house. In 1918 the post office moved to Main Street near Montebello Way, where it remained until 1948.

Los Gatos had no free home delivery within the town limits until after April 1, 1920, although rural free delivery had been in operation for many years. As early as 1907 the local press was urging a free delivery system. The postal receipts, said the press, far exceeded the $500 minimum to give such service. It hoped that "next year will see free delivery, not only in the mountains but right in town."[3]

Before free delivery could be granted, the town had to have a house-numbering system. In July 1911 the Town Council finally adopted Ordinance 149, which authorized the Town Clerk to block-map the town and provide for numbering of the houses. The Clerk could employ helpers at $2.50 a day for this task.[4] In February 1912 the Chamber of Commerce asked the Federal authorities to establish free delivery, calling attention to the fact that the town had set up a house-numbering system. On June 23, 1913 the Town Board, disgruntled over the delay, appointed a committee to look into the reasons why Los Gatos had no free mail delivery as yet. The committee reported on July 7, 1913 that the local postmaster, Mr.

Campbell, suggested that the city file a new application.[5] It was not until April 1, 1920 that Los Gatos was given free mail delivery service within the town limits.

An exciting event, in 1920, was the arrival of the first air-mail letter in Los Gatos in September of that year. Miss Winnie Chamberlin, an art teacher in the Los Gatos schools, received the air-mail letter from New York on September 13. The letter had left New York on September 8 at 2:30 A.M., reached San Francisco September 11th, and was delivered to Miss Chamberlin on Monday September 13. The message to the Los Gatos teacher read: "Greetings. I have crossed the continent on that first trans-continental Aero mail to bring you greetings from the San Francisco *Bulletin,* on the successful culmination of the long flight to put you into quicker communication with the great cities of the east.

"This epoch-making event is one which will be long remembered and frequently referred to in centuries to come."[6]

The mountain areas around Los Gatos had free mail delivery from the beginning of the century. Many heroic tales could be told about this tough job, for delivery of mail in some parts of the mountains was not easy. Two well-known rural carriers were Lewis Torrey and his sister Elsie. Both joined the post office staff in 1906 as rural carriers. When Elsie Torrey retired in 1928 the Postmaster, Lee Darneal, revealed some of the harrowing experiences of the lady letter carrier. "Swollen streams and bad weather, and petty illnesses were no barrier between herself and her job," said Mr. Darneal. "During the last ten years of her connections with the post office she lost only 2 days of work---once when thrown from her buggy while fording the Los Gatos Creek during a

This building on the corner of Main Street and Montebello Way served as the Post Office from 1918 to 1948. Photo taken in 1910. *(Library Collection)*

downpour, and again when she fell while getting out of her buggy. Once when her horse balked at crossing a swollen mountain stream, Miss Torrey, undaunted, took off her shoes and stockings, got out of her 'rig' and waded across the stream, leading her horse."

Mr. Lewis Torrey also had some hair-raising experiences. He had the dangerous and difficult Route #2 in the Santa Cruz Mountains. On one occasion his rig and horse plunged 100 feet over an embankment, but he escaped without injury and took the mail through. He did not know until he reached home that he had suffered two fractured ribs in the accident. Mr. Torrey retired in 1931.

There were other old-time letter carriers in the Los Gatos Post Office. The man with the longest period of service was Mr. Arthur W. Bassett, who joined the post office staff on February 1, 1902 as assistant postmaster. He held this post for 18 years. When city delivery was instituted he became one of the first carriers. In 1923 he became a rural carrier and served in that capacity until his retirement in 1948 after 46 years of service.

Another old-time carrier was Louis L. Pettingill, who started in 1906. He became a rural carrier in 1913. When free delivery was started, he had a route in East Los Gatos. His was a familiar figure on Loma Alta Avenue and neighboring areas for many years. He retired in October 1939. Mr. Pettingill estimated that in his 33 years of service he walked more than 50,000 miles delivering mail.

After a string of Republican appointees, Mr. Lee Darneal, a Democrat, was appointed postmaster by the Wilson Administration. The Los Gatos *Mail-News,* on January 21, 1916, announced, "Lee Darneal, having been appointed postmaster, it will be necessary for him to give up his work in the grocery store owned by Darneal Brothers. It is reported that Darneal Brothers will dispose of their business."

After the victory of Harding in 1920, a Republican was again appointed postmaster in Los Gatos. Mr. Ed Vodden succeeded Darneal. However, with the election of Franklin D. Roosevelt, Lee Darneal again took over the post office in our town.

A new post office building was needed for Los Gatos. In 1918 the *Mail-News* urged people to write to congressman Hayes, urging him to support a new post office building for the town. Indeed, the editor even suggested that a Federal Building be built in Los Gatos. "Now that the government has located a branch of entymology here, there is still greater reason for a Federal Building."[7]

Since the lease for the post office building was to expire in 1934, many thought it a good time to erect a new building for a permanent post office. Lee Darneal asked people to get behind the movement for a new post office building. However, a new three-year lease was signed for the old location. When Postmaster-General James Farley came to Los Gatos on October 18, 1937, to inspect the postal facilities here, he was treated royally. He was made an honorary member of the Los Gatos Chamber of Commerce, the presentation being made by Raymond J. Fisher, President of the Chamber that year. But Los Gatans had to wait until 1947 before they got their new building.

In June 1938 postmasters of first, second and third class post offices were taken out of politics and the positions made permanent. Lee Darneal of Los Gatos and Miss Lutheria Cunningham of Saratoga benefited from this new law. Mr. Darneal retired on April 30, 1942. Mr. Ed Roberts was acting postmaster for four months. Mr. John Whisenant was made acting postmaster on August 21, 1942. Examinations for the new postmaster were held in May 1943. Erwin Freudenthal, Cliff Hammontree, and Don Eldridge were the high point men. Cliff Hammontree was appointed in May 1944.

135

The hoped-for post office building was finally completed and the new quarters occupied in May 1948. This new building on North Santa Cruz Avenue, near Royce Street, gave relief to the crowded conditions that had existed in the rented Main Street structure.

Ralph Wanzer became the first Superintendent of Mails in March 1949, a post that was newly created at that time. Mr. Wanzer had been with the local post office for 29 years, having joined the staff in July 1920. He was the second carrier in the town limits after Mr. Bassett. He retired in 1966 after almost 46 years of service.

In 1952, after the death of Cliff Hammontree, E. E. Briggs, the acting postmaster, was appointed to the position of postmaster in May of that year. When Mr. Briggs retired in 1966, John (Jack) Panighetti became postmaster. He had started with the local post office at the age of 16. He was selected from a list of ten candidates who took the examination in 1967. John Dudley was assistant postmaster.

In 1964, after considerable pressure, a new post office building was erected on the corner of Santa Cruz Avenue and Broadway. It stands at the end of the Civic Plaza, whose fountains grace the front of the building. This plaza and the post office are located where once stood the Southern Pacific depot and freight office, and the plaza occupies the area of the tracks where once the railroad passed through the town.

The Los Gatos Post Office today is a far cry from the "little corner" in the McMurtry Store, or the space in the Ten Mile House of early years. Besides the new post office building, there are three sub-stations---one in the Blossom Hill area, another in Monte Sereno, and a third in the La Rinconada Shopping Center on Pollard Road. There are 88 full-time employees in the local post office, handling some 3 million pieces of mail a month. Thirty-three mail routes are served from Los Gatos.

Service Groups

From Board of Trade to Chamber of Commerce. The Chamber of Commerce traces its history to the old Board of Trade, which was born the latter part of the 1880's. In March 1887 some men met at Jordan & Company's office to discuss the possibility of a Board of Trade. The Weekly *News* supported such an organization, declaring, "We need a Board of Trade so that our section may be properly represented in the tidal wave of prosperity that is sweeping over the state."[8] On October 16, 1890 another meeting was held at the City Hall to take steps toward the organization of a

John "Jack" Panighetti, Postmaster of Los Gatos since 1966. *(Courtesy Panighetti family)*

Board of Trade. The temporary officers were: J. H. Lyndon, President; F. M. Jackson, Vice-President; G. S. McMurtry, Secretary; and the Bank of Los Gatos, Treasurer.

A constitution was adopted the latter part of April 1895 and a permanent organization completed. The object of the Board of Trade was "To promote the mercantile, manufacturing, transportation, agricultural, viti-cultural and home features of Los Gatos and vicinity." Also to see "to the public improvements and buildings; to advise with the town officers and others in authority; to advise in regard to 'deadbeats' that the members may be on their guard against giving them credit; to provide for the entertainment of visitors and do whatever may come before the organization."[9]

The second Monday of each month was set as the time for meetings. Fees were to be 50 cents plus 25 cents monthly dues. Any person, firm or organization was eligible to join. At the second meeting of the organization on April 26, 1895 in the Town Hall, A Skinkle Jr. was elected President; W. A. Pepper, Vice-President; R. R. Bell, Secretary; and J. W. Riddle, Treasurer. The Directors included E. C. Yocco, A. Skinkle Jr., W. A. Pepper, S. Syverson and Paul C. Roemer.

In August 1895 the Board of Trade asked the Town Board to provide "suitable street crossings" in the business district. The members complained that the wet streets and the mud made crossing the streets hazardous. The Board of Trade was interested in civic improvements as well as business and financial affairs. It supported every bond issue for a city hall, a sewer system, electric light plant, parks and a water system. It gave unstinting support to the establishment of a public library and fought for the elimination of the old cemetery

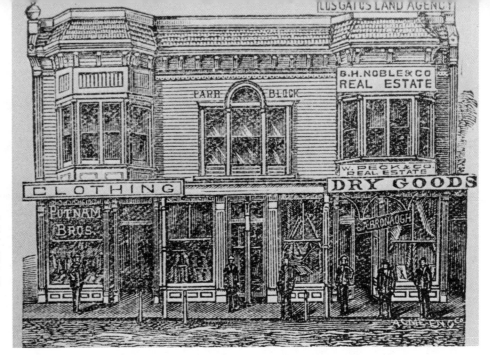

Sketch of the Parr Block before 1895. Located at 140 West Main Street on the north side, it was destroyed by the fire of October 13, 1901. Ford's Opera House, later Crider's Department store, and today the Opera House Antiques located here. *(Library Collection)*

on North Santa Cruz Avenue. It worked untiringly for a broad gauge railroad to Los Gatos.

It also took an interest in the activities of the Town Board. At a special meeting on May 28, 1905 it endorsed the town ordinance prohibiting drums and noise on the streets without permission. (See Ch. V.)

However, lack of money seemed to restrict its activities at the beginning of this century. The Los Gatos *Mail* suggested that the Board of Trade be reorganized and given new life. On August 15, 1904 it asked the Town Board for $250 to be matched by an equal sum from the members of the Board of Trade. The Town Board took no action.[10]

In 1908 the Board of Trade adopted the slogan "Los-Gatos-of-the-Green-Hills." This was the last flickering light of the Los Gatos Board of Trade. The Los Gatos Chamber of Commerce was to replace it in 1911.

On June 13, 1911 a meeting was held in the real estate office of D. H. Milligan Bros. & Company for the purpose of organizing a Chamber of Commerce. The Los Gatos *Mail* reported that the purpose of the meeting was to have "some sort of Civic Improvement organization, and that something should be done to bring our charming section to be better known."[11] The temporary chairman was W. Drummond-Norie and the temporary secretary was K. H. Erickson. Another meeting was held on June 23 at the Lyndon Hotel, at which time 33 members signed up. Herbert L. Kent, of the Lyndon, was elected President; H. K. Erickson, Secretary; and S. D. Balch, Treasurer. The membership fee was set at $4.00 per year, payable quarterly. Each person present at this meeting was asked to seek two new members.

By-laws were adopted at the June 30, 1911 meeting which was held at Kyle's Hall. The second Monday of the month was designated as the regular meeting time. A. B. Smith was elected Vice-President and J. Walter Crider, E. L. Wilder, F. F. Watkins, C. W. Gertridge and Frank Watson were elected Directors.

The important issue at the time was a state highway between San Jose and Santa Cruz via Los Gatos. An effort was made to get a slice of the $18 million appropriated for highway purposes by the Legislature. The final first link of this road to Glenwood was begun in 1920. In June 1913 the Chamber went on record as opposing an 8-hour law for women in the canneries. In July 1913 fourteen Directors of the Chamber of Commerce of the United States, headed by President Harry A. Wheeler of Chicago, visited Los Gatos. The Los Gatos Chamber was elected to membership in the National Chamber in July 1918.

The Chamber has interested itself not only in the economic life of the town, but it has taken an active part in all phases of life---off-street parking, youth activities, better citizenship, and even the religious life of Los Gatos. In 1924 and for several years thereafter, it sponsored union church services. It was hoped that these would be held once a month, on the third Sunday evening of the month. Services were held in the auditorium of the grammar school. In February 1941 the Chamber conducted a "Go to Church" campaign. This was supported by the *Mail-News* in an editorial. "Liberty," said the editorial, "is a spiritual heritage of America. Our freedom of speech, of thought, worship and expression are spiritual rights that formed the basis of our Constitution. George Washington, Thos. Jefferson and other forefathers

Members of the Ancient Order of Union Workers (A.O.U.W.) brotherhood. *Top row:* Robt. Green, Frank Jackson, L. A. Cole, Fred Suydam, Lewis Trailer, Jules Shannon, George Bailey, Frank Reynolds and Herman Sund. *Bottom row:* James Lyndon, Thos. Clelland, Thos. Jenkins, Wm. Lingley, John Erickson, Wm. Spencer, Thos. Cox, Jackob Sachet, Harry Ball and Fred Taylor. *(Library Collection)*

held the conviction that such non-material things come only from the Creator." And later it said, "It would do little good to safeguard the material values and surrender the spiritual." Also, in 1941, the Chámber sponsored a Thanksgiving Service in "our beautiful Town Bowl."

From 1923 on, the Chamber of Commerce took on new life. Dr. Blake Franklin was President in that year, and Mrs. Lynn Lobdell was the Secretary. Paul Curtis followed Dr. Franklin, serving two terms---1924 and 1925. Major Harry Hostetter served for two terms---1926 and 1927. Sewall S. Brown served the longest as President, holding that office from 1932 through 1936. W. W. Clark was Secretary from 1937 through 1942, and it was through his untiring efforts that the Los Gatos Bowl was built behind the Town Hall on Pageant Way.

In the years from 1923 to 1971 the Chamber had 33 Presidents and 14 different Secretaries. Mrs. Mary Powell served the longest as Secretary, having held that position from 1955 to 1968. During her term the "Clean Sweep" campaigns which won two first-place awards for Los Gatos were inaugurated. Winston King took over as Secretary on March 1, 1968.

Junior Chamber of Commerce. A Junior Chamber of Commerce existed for some time in Los Gatos after World War II. But it disappeared in the early 1950's and was not revived until early in 1963. On Monday April 6, 1964 the new Junior Chamber celebrated its first anniversary at a banquet at which time it inaugurated its new officers. Dr. Hugh Schade was President; Ben

Reichmuth, external Vice-President; Ray Eastburg, internal Vice-President; Clayton Bruntz, external Director; Barry Baxter, internal Director; Leslie Petulla, Treasurer; and Bob Bowman, Secretary.

The Junior Chamber is open to young men between the ages of 21 and 35. It has two goals: community service and leadership training. It took an enthusiastic part in community activities from the start. It conducted a seat-belt clinic every month in 1964; it donated $1000 to the Town for playground equipment for the Oak Hill Play lot; it supported the fund-raising campaign for the Billy Jones Wildcat Railroad; and it planted trees in the center islands on Saratoga Avenue between Santa Cruz and University Avenues.

The J.C.'s hold an annual Distinguished Awards Banquet at which they recognize individuals who have contributed time and effort to community service. In 1969 Emmette Gatewood, Los Gatos Realtor, Wm. E. Mason, who was most responsible for the Billy Jones Wildcat Railroad, and Dr. George G. Bruntz were recognized. The President of the Los Gatos High School Student Body, David Grais, was also recognized. In 1970 Ben Reichmuch, Chairman of the Parks Commission; Russell Cooney, Town Manager; Pete Denevi, coach at Los Gatos Union High School; and Ralph Phillips, retiring Chief of Police, were recognized.

The Junior Chamber of Commerce co-sponsors, with the Los Gatos *Times*-Saratoga *Observer,* and the Los Gatos Recreation Department, the annual Fourth of July celebration at Oak Meadow Park.

Although the membership of the Los Gatos J.C.'s is not large, the enthusiasm of the members makes up in spirit what they lack in numbers. Their spirit is aided by the Jaycettes, the auxiliary of the Junior Chamber of Commerce. These ladies are also very active in the civic affairs of Los Gatos.

Kiwanis Club. Wendell Thomas was a member of the San Jose Kiwanis Club who lived in Los Gatos. He had heard rumors that some Los Gatos businessmen were hoping to start a Rotary Club. He is said to have remarked, "If they think they can form a Rotary Club in town I will show them that I can form a Kiwanis Club while Rotary is thinking about it, and if there is anybody left for Rotary they can have him." Evidently some people agreed with Thomas, for they organized the Kiwanis Club the latter part of 1923. They were given their charter at a gala Charter Night Banquet and program at the Vendome Hotel in San Jose on Saturday night, March 7, 1924. More than 450 Kiwanians from the entire Bay Area attended.

The first officers of this first Service Club of Los Gatos were Jack Collins, President; Cecil Dickinson, Secretary; and Eugene Rounds, Treasurer. The Directors included Blake Franklin, J. D. Farwell, Dr. E. M. Miller, C. F. Hamsher, J. Warren Ayer, A. W. Templeman, Fred Berryman, J. R. Burtner, W. G. Irons, Lewis Neuman and Henry Kissinger.[12]

The Kiwanis Club has sponsored Scout Troops and sponsors the Key Club, a service group at Los Gatos High School. The faculty advisor to this group is Mr. Ted Schweitzer, instructor in History. The Kiwanians have contributed liberally in time and money to the support of worthwhile projects. In November 1966 the club donated $750 to the Town to help defray the cost of the flagpole on the lawn of the new Civic Center. It contributed $1000 and many man-hours to the Billy Jones Wildcat Railroad. These and other activities, too numerous to mention, are proof of the civic-mindedness of this Men's Service Club.

One of the most interesting things the Kiwanis Club did was to help out a Negro school in Mississippi. The local Kiwanians had, for a number of years, a wooden mule mascot named "Spiritus." The Piney Woods School for colored people in Piney Woods, Mississippi, lost by death their only mule, used in their agricultural projects. Without a mule they could not educate their pupils properly. Having heard of "Spiritus" and seen pictures of the famous mascot, the Piney Woods school people asked the Los Gatos Kiwanis Club if they would be willing to contribute toward the purchase of a new mule. The local club responded that they would be glad to provide the money for a mule if the animal were named "Spiritus." Thus the mascot of the Los Gatos Kiwanis Club became the means by which a poor colored school in Mississippi obtained

The old Massol House on Massol and Saratoga Avenues. First acquired by F. H. McCullagh and later the home of S. D. Balch. The people in the group include (l. to r.) Katherine Cosgrave; Lucy Stiles (grandmother of Mrs. S. D. Balch); Fanny Reiniger (sister of Mrs. S. D. Balch); Lucy Balch; S. Dean Balch and C. A. Cosgrave. *(Photo and identification courtesy William Balch)*

a live "Spiritus" and kept the school's program alive.[13]

In 1970 there were 70 members who met every Thursday noon for luncheon and fellowship.

The Rotary Club. In 1923 Edwin H. Melvin was a young Funeral Director and Dr. Ernest F. Colvin was a local dentist. These two men had become acquainted with Rotary Clubs in other communities, and they got the idea that such a club was needed in Los Gatos. They talked it up among friends and found them responsive to the idea.

As early as 1922 Melvin had corresponded with the Secretary of International Rotary in Chicago and with the District Governor, John Williams. Williams thought Los Gatos was too small for a club, and that it was too close to San Jose which already had a club. Edwin Melvin and Dr. Colvin argued that although Los Gatos had fewer than 2,300 people, a club would draw from the surrounding areas, which commanded a population up to 6000 or more. They also pointed out that the Chamber of Commerce had a business and professional group of from 60 to 80 members. It was during that delay that the Kiwanians jumped the gun on the Rotarians and were organized first.

Dr. Colvin and Edwin Melvin talked often about plans for a Rotary Club while they were together on vacations. After much correspondence and more talking, the San Jose Rotary Club offered to sponsor a club in Los Gatos. It received its Charter #1601 on January 16, 1924. The first officers were Edwin H. Melvin, President; Prof. Ernest A. Rogers of Montezuma, Vice-President; Forrest Meyers, formerly of Shanghai Rotary Club, Secretary; J. A. Case, Treasurer; and J. Walter Crider, Sergeant at Arms.

Shortly after the local club was formed, Prof. Rogers issued an ultimatum to the effect that either the club put a ban on smoking at its meetings or he would resign. He resigned. At another time, when the speaker for the day did not show up, a visiting Rotarian started to entertain with off-color stories. A number of members followed his example, and this irked a number of other members, who left the club. The Board of Directors brought peace by issuing an order that such stories were taboo.

But not all of Rotary's activities are geared to levity. It sponsors a Scout Troop and supports all worthwhile projects in the town. It has been especially active in support of work for crippled children and for young people in general. In 1968 the club donated $200 to the Los Gatos Parent Nursery School and gave $1000 to the Billy Jones Wildcat Railroad project.

The club meets every Tuesday noon, when outstanding programs and speakers are presented. Some 80 members enjoy the weekly fellowship of Rotary in Los Gatos.

The Lions Club. One of the newer men's service groups is the Lions Club of Los Gatos. Sponsored by the San Jose Lions Club, it was organized on February 22, 1946. Charter night ceremonies were held on Saturday, February 27, 1946 at La Rinconada Country Club, with Loren Critzer, then District Governor, and later Superintendent of the Los Gatos Union High School, as the installing officer. The original officers were Le Roy H. Halverson, President; W. J. Fremier Jr., 1st Vice-President; Chas. Butler, 2nd Vice-President; George Gianola, Secretary-Treasurer; John L. Suhlett, Lion Tamer; Dr. Edwin D. Kilbourne Jr., Tail Twister. The Directors included James F. Thompson, Dr. L. S. Wilder, Donald A. Wetzel and L. A. Lincoln. There were 37 members on the original roster of the club.

The Lions Club meets every Wednesday noon for luncheon—in 1970 at the Grog and Sirloin. John D. Smart was District Governor in 1962-63 and was given a lifetime appointment as International Counselor of Lions International in July 1963.

The Lions Club has been always busy doing things for the community. It purchased more than two dozen trash containers for use in the business district; financed the band stand at Oak Meadow Park; furnished play equipment for the park and the authentic fire truck at Oak Meadow Park. Along with other Lions Clubs, it gives financial support to Guide Dogs for the Blind at San Raphael, helps give books and typewriters for children with sight problems in elementary and

Col. Edwin H. Melvin, one of the organizers of the Los Gatos Rotary Club, chairman of the local Red Cross chapter for many years, a leader in many civic activities, and mortuary owner. *(Courtesy Mrs. E. H. Melvin)*

high schools, and furnishes eyeglasses to needy children. It also sponsors an annual glaucoma clinic for children, and helps to educate young people on the drug problem. Like other service clubs, it too has donated money to the Billy Jones Wildcat Railroad.[14]

Indeed, the Lions Club has done much to make our community a better place in which to live. In 1970 there were more than 70 members in Lions.

The Optimist Club. This club is one of the newer groups in Los Gatos. In keeping with its motto, "Friend of the Boy," it sponsors an annual oratorical contest for young people, a Cub Scout Pack, and a Little League baseball team. It also sends boys to Optimist-operated Summer Camp "Boysville" and sponsors "Youth Appreciation Week" each year in November.

The Los Gatos History Club. One day in 1897 Mrs. Richard A. Urquhart asked a group of six women to meet in her home to study history—ancient and modern. This group increased in number, and the interest was so great that three years later they formed a club, choosing as their name "The Los Gatos History Club." At first they limited the membership to 20. The first officers were: Mrs. R. A. Urquhart, President; Mrs. J. W. Lyndon, Vice-President; and Miss Emily Cohen, Secretary-Treasurer.

Later the membership was enlarged to 30 and six sections set up—History, literature, civics, current events, domestic science and music. The club met every Wednesday afternoon in the home of a member.

A clubhouse was needed. Mrs. Urquhart proposed that funds be raised to buy a lot for a building. She suggested that each member pledge to raise five dollars a year. But almost the entire amount was raised in one evening at a meeting with "husbands, brothers, fathers and mothers all con-

Paul Curtis, prominent banker and civic leader. Served on the Town Board from 1936 to 1940 and was active in the Red Cross and American Legion. *(Courtesy the Curtis family)*

tributing." A lot on San Jose Avenue and Simons Way was purchased from Mr. D. P. Simons for $350, although he had originally set the price at $500.[15]

Money for the clubhouse was raised in various ways. Miss Adeline Mills offered to lend, without interest, the money to build the clubhouse. The sum of $3000 was borrowed and the club signed a contract with Chas. N. Wheeler to build the building. It was completed in July 1908 and dedicated on September 4, 1908. The debt was paid in a short time by the hard work of the women, who held rummage sales and made everything from knitted wash cloths to mustard pickles to sell to their friends.[16]

The club was incorporated on July 9, 1907 with the following officers: Miss Emily Cohen, President; Miss Mary McMurtry, Vice-President; Mrs. F. A. Wilder, Secretary; and Mrs. R. P. Gober, Treasurer.

From the start the History Club became active in civic affairs. It planted the deodar tree opposite the Lyndon Hotel, which still stands in the Civic Plaza on Santa Cruz Avenue and is decorated with lights each Christmas. It removed the old wooden watering trough on Santa Cruz Avenue across from the Lyndon and replaced it with a granite trough. The club was instrumental in helping secure the grounds on which the high school stands, secured expert help from the University of California to pass on plans for the grammar school in 1923, paid for planting the lawn and trees on the University Avenue Library grounds and furnished a room at the Veterans Hospital in Palo Alto.

The club has supported many youth activities and cultural events in Los Gatos. The Los Gatos Museum owes a great deal to the History Club for its financial support and active help in getting the museum on its feet. It is still a willing helper for that educational and cultural organization.

As the membership in the club grew, the need for a new clubhouse became acute. In 1959 additional land was purchased and a new clubhouse was built. This is not only a center for meetings of the History Club, but it is the scene of many other activities from church meetings to dances and wedding receptions. In 1971 the club had 160 members—a far cry from the six which started the organization in 1897.

Business and Professional Women's Club. Thirty women met on September 18, 1930 at the home of Miss Lora Cooper to discuss forming a Los Gatos chapter of the national Business and Professional Women's Clubs. This had been organized in 1919 to promote the interests of business and professional women. Members from the San Jose branch were present to explain the purposes and functions of such a club and to assist in establishing a branch in Los Gatos. Mrs. Ida Bruegge was the temporary chairman and Miss Edna Stump the temporary Secretary.

Another meeting was held on October 18 at which the following officers were elected: Ida L. Bruegge, President; Blanch Young, Vice-President; Henri Rankin, Corresponding Secretary; and Martha Williams, Treasurer. The Directors were Miss Nell Berryman, Miss Pearl Hook, Mrs. Viola Carrol and Mrs. Margaret Graun. The first dinner meeting and installation of officers was held at the Lyndon Hotel on Tuesday evening, October 25, 1930. More than 80 women from Peninsula Chapters of B.P.W. attended the affair. Thirty-seven local women became charter members.

The Club has dinner meetings twice a month. The membership consists of owners of businesses, office workers, teachers and other professional women. The local Chapter has sponsored a Girl Scout Troop, which was organized by Ruth Reid, a member of the club. It awards the Ruth Comfort Mitchell Scholarship annually to a deserving high school student, and supports all worthwhile civic projects. In 1968 the club gave $600 to the Library's Art Fund in memory of Mrs. Clelles Ness.

One of the main objectives of the club is to promote recognition of women's place in the business world and in today's economy. Meetings discuss such topics as national security, international relations, public affairs, health and safety, and career advancement. Club members are not limited to number, nor classified as to occupations. The more than 90 members represent every phase of business, professional, clerical, or retired women of the community.

The American Legion. On November 22, 1919 some 65 men who had seen service in World War I met at the City Hall to organize a local Post of the American Legion. Paul Curtis was the temporary chairman. Attorney Archer Bowden of San Jose was present to explain the principles of the Legion. The following officers were chosen to hold office for three months: Paul Curtis, President; D. F. Williams, 1st Vice-President; Eldon Hatch, 2nd Vice-President; E. H. Melvin, Secretary; and Herbert Roberts, Sergeant-at-arms. The first Directors were H. O. Smith, Oliver Nino, Neal McGrady, Edward Yocco and Happy Phelps. The dues were set at 20 cents a month, and no initiation fee was to be charged.[17]

The Los Gatos Post 158 of the American Legion was chartered on December 26, 1919. Meetings were held in the City Hall and in the IOOF Hall until a permanent home was built. In 1926 a site was purchased on Park Avenue facing Memorial Park and a meeting hall was built. The building was dedicated in October 1926.

The local Post early became vocal in its opposition to "slackers." On August 2, 1920 a San Francisco newspaper, the *Call,* printed an editorial that called for amnesty for draft evaders. The local Legion adopted a resolution condemning the *Call,* saying that such "unpatriotic and un-American propaganda tends to encourage slackerism, desertion and other traitorous acts" and further that "such anarchistic and revolutionary utterances" were wholly unfair and disloyal to "the millions of American patriots who recently defended their country in time of peril."[18]

The local Legion, following the policy of the national organization, encouraged the establishment of adult evening classes in Americanization for the foreign-born. The first such class had 37 adults with two teachers from the high school. From this the Adult School program in Los Gatos developed. In February 1932 the Drum and Bugle Corps was organized with Harry Boone as the First Corps Commander.

After World War II the local Post outgrew the frame building on Park Avenue. In 1946 a parcel of land at 123 East Main Street was purchased from the Methodist Church for $4,500. The church specified that no intoxicating liquor was to be sold on the premises and that the proposed building be completed within two years. If either or both of these conditions were not met, the church could redeem the property and reimburse the Post for the amount originally paid.

The legionnaires all pitched in to complete their new building. Louis Klindt was the general overseer, taking time out from his business for this

Mrs. Ida Bruegge, one of the founders of the Los Gatos Business and Professional Women's Club and leader in many civic activities. *(Photo courtesy Mrs. Bruegge)*

work. Much of the labor was contributed by the members of the Post. The building was completed in September 1949, and on the 28th of that month a corporation was formed known as the Los Gatos Post 158, American Legion Memorial Building.

When the Carnegie Library on University Avenue was condemned, the town looked around for a new site for the library. The Legion Memorial Building, just across from the City Hall, was a logical location. In April 1954 the town purchased the building from the Legion and remodeled it for use as a library. The Legion met at the First National Bank building until its new home on Dell Avenue in Campbell was completed.

In 1956 the Campbell Post, consisting of some 80 members, merged with the Los Gatos Post 158 to form the West Valley Post 158. A building on the old Los Gatos Skeet and Gun Club property was moved to the Dell Avenue site and remodeled. This then became the home of the combined Legion Posts.[19]

One of the significant activities sponsored by the Legion is the annual oratorical contest on subjects related to the Federal Constitution. National recognition was accorded the local Post 158 in 1946 when the Los Gatos High School representative, William Wollin Yabroff, won the highest honors in the nation, winning first place over 5000 contestants from all over America.

From Floral Society to Garden Club. One of the early organizations that was interested in civic improvement was the Los Gatos Floral Society. It held its first meeting on December 29, 1892 with Mr. William McManus presiding. Mr. Eugene Pierce acted as Secretary. The chairman stated that the object of the society was to learn "the best methods of floriculture adapted to the resources of Los Gatos with a view to general improvement of the appearance of the town, that it may be made more attractive as a place of residence to the people of refined and cultured taste."[20]

142

At this first meeting Mrs. J. S. Briggs regretted that the water supply of the past had not been equal to the demands for fine flower gardens in Los Gatos, but she hoped that rains would soon come to give relief.

The Floral Society held the first of its many Festivals on May 26 and 27, 1893. For this occasion the Society urged people for miles around "to decorate with either wild or cultivated flowers, any and every conceivable sort of conveyance and drive into Los Gatos on the morning of the Gala Day and form a part of Flora's procession."

Of this fete the Los Gatos *News* reported later, "The Gem of the Foothills never shone with a purer luster, nor created wider-spread admiration than on the morning of the 26th ult." The Marshal of the day was Chas. W. Gertridge of the Los Gatos Hotel. Although the Marshal was a married man, "Many were the glances of admiration cast upon him by the feminine persuasion." The town band of 14 members looked good in their uniforms. "H. F. Schomberg, of our piano factory, wrote the finale, played on a floral harp---one of the most artistic features of the parade."[21]

With such a beginning and holding such affairs every year, it would seem that the organization would last a long time. However, it seemed to disappear and nothing was heard of it after 1900. But its principles and purposes were revived in 1923 in the form of the Los Gatos Flower Lovers' Club. This grew and became popular. In 1927 Mr. Frank Ring became President and Mrs. Ida Mansfield Vice-President; Mrs. Bessie Henderson, Secretary; and Mrs. Bert Fresher, Treasurer. In 1929 the Flower Lovers' Club planted shrubs on the banks of the Park and flowers in various places in town to make the town more beautiful. Along with other Flower Lovers' Clubs, the local group fought to clean up unsightly places along roadsides---they were ecologists. They also fought to preserve our redwood trees.

The Flower Lovers' Club gradually disappeared, but another group developed to take its place. In 1952 the Newcomer's Club was organized. After one year it became the West Valley Women's Club. This split, and one section became the West Valley Garden Club, with Mrs. George Williamson as President.

One of the projects undertaken by the West Valley Garden Club was to provide hanging baskets for light posts in the downtown area of Los Gatos. These were redwood baskets with beautiful flowers in them. They were nice for a while, but the problem of who was to maintain them arose. There was the matter of pruning, soiling and watering, jobs which were too great for the city Street

Fourth of July parade 1900 as it crosses the old wooden bridge on Main Street. *(Library Collection)*

Department to handle. A hanging basket committee of members from the Garden Club, the Home Owners' Association and the Park Commission could not agree on the solution. The hanging baskets were removed and nothing more was done.

The club has undertaken an educational program through the local press. Mrs. Juanita Lynde wrote a series of articles in 1969 for the Los Gatos *Times-Observer* on gardening. This series was popular with local amateur gardeners. The club continues to be active in the beautification program for our town.[22]

FOOTNOTES

1. Letter from the U.S. Postal Dept. dated November 22, 1880 to Alley and Bowen Co. Quoted in their *History of Santa Clara County*, p. 141.
2. Los Gatos Weekly *News*. Nov. 26, 1886.
3. Library *Collection*, Bk. 7.
4. Town Board *Minutes*, Bk. V, p. 257.
5. *Ibid.*, Bk. IV, p. 477.
6. *Mail-News*, Sept. 25, 1920.
7. *Ibid.*, Jan. 27, 1918.
8. Weekly *News*, May 20, 1887.
9. *Ibid.*, April 26, 1895.
10. Town Board *Minutes*, Bk. IV, p. 41.
11. Los Gatos *Mail*, June 15, 1911.
12. *Mail-News*, March 7, 1924.
13. *Ibid.*, March 24, 1928.
14. Material supplied by Dick Wall Jr., Secretary to Lions in 1970.
15. *Mail-News*, April 18, 1907.
16. *History of Los Gatos History Club*, 1907–1968 by Mary Corbus, D. Corbin, and M. Robertson.
17. *Mail-News*, Nov. 15, 1919.
18. *Ibid.*, August 19, 1920.
19. Adjutant M. Nimerick supplied some material.
20. Los Gatos *Mail*, Jan. 6, 1893.
21. *Ibid.*, June 2, 1893.
22. Information supplied by Mrs. Juanita Lynde of the West Valley Garden Club.

Crowd at Bunker Hill Park in the early 1900's. *(Museum Collection)*

Memorial Park picnic area. Park name was changed in 1920. It was destroyed when Highway 17 went through Los Gatos in 1954. *(Courtesy Charles Torrey)*

CHAPTER XIII

Parks and Recreation

Public Parks

MANY "old-timers" today recall with nostalgia the scores of town picnics and community celebrations held in the park below the Main Street bridge where Highway 17 now winds up the gap toward Santa Cruz. This ideal park site, in the midst of massive oak trees and beside the Los Gatos Creek, was the pride of the town from 1897 until it was eliminated to make way for the freeway in 1954.

But there was no public park in Los Gatos before 1897. On August 25, 1893, the Weekly *News* proudly announced that Herman Sund "with characteristic liberality" had offered to donate 3½ acres on the west side of Oak Hill for a public park. The *News* felt that, with a small outlay, this spot "might be a delightful place of resort." It suggested that the Floral Society might care for the park. The Los Gatos *Mail* also lamented the lack of a public park in its issue of August 16, 1894. "Los Gatos ought to have a park," it said. "It needs one, and we think it would be a good scheme and a paying investment for the city to purchase a suitable tract of ground and put it in proper shape for the public." It felt that a tract near the El Monte Hotel on East Main Street was best suited.

Many thought that Shore's Picnic Ground below the Main Street bridge was a good location for a park. It had shade; the creek ran through it and it was accessible. W. C. Shore owned extensive property in the area and had used some of it as a private picnic ground. Shore dedicated some of this land to the town for a park. This small piece of ground became the nucleus for the town park. It was dedicated as a public park on June 17, 1897, the 122nd anniversary of the Battle of Bunker Hill in the American Revolution. What could be more appropriate than to name the park Bunker Hill Park? A grand celebration was planned for the dedication on June 17, 1897.

The Weekly *News* reported the events of the day in great detail. Los Gatos had never seen such a big event. Preparations had been made for weeks in advance. When the great day came, everybody was on hand to celebrate. "Before noon the streets were lined with people. Two trains from San Francisco brought 2000 people to the Gem City for the Day." Many patriotic organizations were represented, including the Bunker Hill Association, the Sons of Michigan, Sons of Veterans, California Society of Sons of the American Revolution, and the Order of Patriotic Sons of America of Los Gatos. "Flags fluttered over every house and building in town."[1]

In commemoration of the anniversary, some earth had been brought to Los Gatos from the spot where General Warren fell on the battlefield at Bunker's Hill near Boston. This was symbolically sprinkled on the ground and the park named Bunker Hill. The main speaker of the day was Judge Edward A. Belcher, of San Francisco, who closed his ringing patriotic address with "accordingly, in commemoration of that eventful day, and by this symbol---the sifting upon it of earth taken from the spot where Warren fell upon that famous battlefield---this park is now dedicated and shall henceforth be known as Bunker Hill Park. May its name never become an empty sound."[2]

The Clar Schumann quartette of San Francisco sang the "Star Spangled Banner" and George O. Kinney, editor and publisher of the Saratoga *Item*, read an original patriotic poem, the closing lines of which went:

> "Quietly and peacefully rest,
> Columbia's noblest and the best;
> Over their dust do not weep!
> Honor'd dead in peace they sleep.
> Gave they freedom's brightest ray,
> Ours to keep and guard for aye;
> Gave they our banner, true as free,
> Flag of Columbia, gem of the sea,
> Gave they for generations yet unborn,
> A glad awakening, a glorious morn,
> Left they then to guard from foes;
> Calm they rest, as saints repose."

Alfred Wilkie, the noted soloist, sang "The Sword of Bunker Hill."[3] After more patriotic music and readings, and games for young and old, the people danced until 5 p.m., when the trains left for San Francisco. The great celebration was at an end, and Los Gatos had the Bunker Hill Park south of the old Main Street bridge.

Swimming Pool Memorial Park 1951. *(Courtesy Geo. Lagomarsino)*

For a number of years after this the Bunker Hill Association sponsored a celebration "for that first fight for liberty on June 17th." The Los Gatos *News* reported that this celebration always brought a "good quiet crowd of respectable people, fine singers, bands, orators, and they present programs of interest."[4]

But the park was not to be "Bunker Hill Park" forever. After World War I a number of people hoped to have a memorial to the boys who fought and died in that great conflict. Additional land was added to the park from time to time. In July 1920 Raymond Hicks donated land to the town to be added to the park as a memorial park. In September 1920 the J. D. Farwell family, which had purchased land in the area from W. C. Shore, gave another parcel to the town to be added to the park. On January 28, 1921 Mr. and Mrs. A. E. Falch donated another parcel on the east side of the creek, and this too was to be added to the park.

Thus, in 1920, the name of the enlarged park was changed to Memorial Park. In April 1931 the town paid $800 to the Norton-Phelps Lumber Company for additional park land, and in May of that year the J. D. Farwell family donated another piece of land to the town for the Memorial Park.[5]

Memorial Park immediately became the center of community picnics, celebrations and recreational activities. Picnic tables, a refreshment stand, a dance platform and skating platform were all a part of the park. On March 23, 1925 the Town Board passed a resolution that public interest required that a swimming pool be constructed in Memorial Park. The Board proposed a bond

issue of $22,500.[6] The election was held on April 6, 1925 and the bonds passed by a vote of 399 to 160. Mr. Eldon J. Hatch was made superintendent of the pool at a salary of $125 a month. A lifeguard for the summer season was paid $70 a month, the locker boys $15 and the matron 30 cents per hour. Mrs. Maybelle Clark was the first matron.

Eldon Hatch not only supervised the swimming pool but he directed the activities at the skating platform. He was an excellent skater himself and made skating a popular part of the recreation program at the park.

But the Memorial Park disappeared in 1954 with the coming of the freeway through our town. Highway 17 went along the creek, requiring the diversion of the Los Gatos Creek and a fill to raise the highway. A new and wider bridge was built across the freeway where once a picturesque bridge crossed a creek. A new park had to be found. After considerable discussion a parcel of land was purchased from Mr. and Mrs. Pietro Denevi along the Creek at Blossom Hill Road and University Avenue---land that was used as a dump for some time. This was developed into a park in several stages. A Citizens Park Development Committee was appointed, composed of Mrs. Ida Bruegge, Mrs. Ruth Fremont, Bernard Hardwicke, John D. Smart, and Nick M. Starry. This committee approved the Master Plan for the development of the Oak Meadow Park in April 1958.

Donald H. Smith was appointed the landscape artist for the park. Parking areas were provided, as well as picnic areas, a horseshoe court, Bocci Ball court, baseball diamond, bandstand and children's playground. Practically all of the playground equipment was donated by various organizations such as service clubs and the Junior Chamber of Commerce.

Play area of Oak Meadow Park. *(Photo by the author)*

Scene at Vasona Lake and Park, a popular recreation center all the year around.

Today Oak Meadow Park is the gathering place for family picnics, Fourth of July celebrations, and just plain everyday outings. The Los Gatos Creek runs through the park and its gentle flow is the delight of children the year around. Although Oak Meadow Park lacks the tradition and does not have the memories of the old Memorial Park, it better suits our growing community. It is a town park, the one place large enough for major town gatherings.

The nearness of Oak Meadow to Vasona Lake and Park enhances its value to the people. Walks and trails connect the two, and the Billy Jones Wildcat Railroad starts at Oak Meadow and runs to Vasona and back. Vasona is a county park that is patronized every day and crowded on weekends and holidays. It is a pleasant sight, on a Sunday or holiday, to see the numerous sailboats on the lake, with their multi-colored sails silhouetted against the blue sky. Indeed, Los Gatos is very fortunate in its parks and recreation areas.

There are other parks in Los Gatos besides Oak Meadow and Vasona. In 1965 the people approved, by a vote of 1669 to 753, a park bond issue in the amount of $750,000, the money to be used for the purchase and development of neighborhood parks. The Federal Government paid 30% of the total cost of the program. John D. Smart was chairman of the successful park bond drive. In March 1965, a Park Commission was established with Seymour

Some sailboats on Vasona Lake. These can be seen almost any day and especially on weekends in this county park. *(This and above photo by the author)*

147

Abrahams, Dr. Hugh Schade, Roland Perry, Dr. E. F. Colvin, Oscar Sohns, Mrs. Hugh Warner, and R. J. Fisher as members. (Smart declined the appointment and Mrs. Warner took his place.) In 1970, in line with the general trend, two teenagers were appointed to the Park Commission. Those selected were Nann Newbury, daughter of Mr. and Mrs. Donald D. Newbury, and Mark Dreesen, son of Mr. and Mrs. Robert E. Dakon.

The Park Commission drew up a proposed ordinance for the regulation of the parks and submitted this to the Town Council. The ordinance was approved on March 8, 1966. William Blocker was appointed to serve as the first Parks Director. He resigned in 1968, and Mr. Robert Bryant was selected to take his place.

The Billy Jones Wildcat Railroad. Railroading was Billy Jones' life for more than 71 years. Born in 1884 near Ben Lomond in the Santa Cruz Mountains, the son of a lumberjack, he left school at the age of 13 to work for the Southern Pacific Railroad. He started as a roundhouse hustler, earning $40 a month, his job being to keep the switch engines in fuel and in steam. By the time he was 21 he had become a regular engineer, and for the rest of his life he kept to the cab of an engine. His assignments included the Peninsula and the Coast run, taking passenger trains between San Francisco and Los Angeles. But he never lost his love for the Santa Cruz Mountains and Los Gatos. In 1917 he purchased a nine-acre tract of land on the corner of Daves Avenue and Winchester Road, which he called "The Ranch." In 1918 he married Geraldine McGrady, a school teacher at Wrights Station.

Billy Jones and his steam locomotive at the turntable on his ranch, Vineland and Santa Cruz Avenues. *(All photos courtesy Billy Jones Wildcat Railroad)*

In 1939, while on a trip to San Francisco, he retrieved an old 1905 engine made by Johnson Locomotive Works of Philadelphia, which was about to be shipped overseas as junk. He had it brought to his ranch, and that was the beginning of the Wildcat Railroad. This narrow-gauge prairie-type 2-6-2 locomotive became the first engine for his miniature railroad. With the help of friends he put tracks in a loop around his orchard. By 1947 the trains, the cars, and the tracks were ready to put into operation.

Some of the helpers in laying the track for the Billy Jones Wildcat Railroad in 1970. Pictured here are Al Guiliani (hands on knees), Allen Lanzo, Wilcox High School student, Bob Langevin, Los Gatos Electronics Engineer, Ray Collins (back to camera in white construction hat), a veteran of 35 years as Southern Pacific Track Foreman from Hollister.

Billy Jones operated his railroad on weekends for the children of the entire valley. There was no charge but contributions could be left, all of which were given to charity. The cars could carry 90 passengers, and some Sundays Billy Jones made as many as 50 trips around the loop, much to the pleasure of children and adults alike.

In 1967, at the age of 83, Billy Jones died. What was now to become of the little railroad? His only two sons had been killed in World War II, and his two daughters were married and had their own interests. W. E. (Bill) Mason, a local businessman, could not see the little Wildcat Railroad end. He wrote a letter to the local newspaper, proposing that the Billy Jones Wildcat Railroad be purchased for the children of this area as a tribute to the Los Gatos railroader. The community responded to this plan. A proposal to re-locate the tracks between Vasona and Oak Meadow Park was made and a non-profit corporation was formed. It purchased the equipment from the heirs and began a fund-raising campaign to complete the project.

Everyone supported the undertaking. Old-timers, Boy Scouts, Girl Scouts, service clubs, organized labor, realtors, lawyers---everyone---put shoulders to the wheel and helped raise the necessary funds to build the Billy Jones Wildcat Railroad. Architects drew up plans, engineers surveyed the new layout at Oak Meadow and Vasona. Volunteer labor came forth, and before long the turntable, the "round house," the depot and tracks were completed. A flat car was purchased to bridge the Los Gatos Creek. On the afternoon of July 26, 1970 the ceremony of the pounding of the "golden spike" was held, and the Billy Jones Wildcat Railroad began to run again for the people, young and old, of the Los Gatos area. What a wonderful tribute to the man who loved

Billy Jones Wildcat Railroad train moving out of the "depot" with a full load, crossing the Los Gatos Creek to Vasona Park, 1970.

the railroad and who loved children! It is a tribute also to Bill Mason, who conceived the idea and who led the project to its successful conclusion.

Youth Activities

Boys' Club. Early in 1907 a meeting was held in the office of John's and McMurtry's to form a permanent Boys' Improvement Club. Outstanding local business and civic leaders were present. W. C. Short was elected President; G. E. Williams, Secretary; and T. E. Johns, Treasurer. Members of the Board included D. P. Simons, W. C. Short, T. E. Johns, Henry Crall, Will Walbridge, G. E. Williams, Theo. Flint, and J. D. Shore. The meetings of the

More volunteer laborers working on the tracks for the Billy Jones Wildcat Railroad between Oak Meadow and Vasona Parks, 1970.

Watching and taking pictures is part of the fun on Billy Jones Wildcat Railroad, 1971.

club were the first Monday of each month, and Board meetings were held the first Tuesday evening of every other month.

Members had to be voted in, and there were two classes of membership: juniors from 12 to 15 years, and seniors from 15 to 20 years. Dues were 25 cents a month. Six black balls were necessary for rejection of any boy. A two-thirds vote was necessary to expel a member. Money for the club came from donations and from the 25 cents a month dues. In March 1907 George Hooke gave $25 to the club and offered the use of 50 chairs. The club gave entertainments in the form of gymnastic performances to raise money for equipment. The Ladies Auxiliary of the club and the Los Gatos History Club presented an operetta under the direction of Andrew Bogart for the benefit of the club.

Originally the club met in a building near the old wooden bridge below Main Street. A retired English navy man, Mr. Cathcart, acted as director of gymnastics. Exercises on the bars, dumbbells, and other equipment and boxing were a part of the program. When the hall below Main Street became too small, the club met in a hall on the second floor of the Bogart building---now the Los Gatos Variety Store building. A pool table was installed here along with the other gymnastic equipment.

Nothing is recorded about the club after 1911, and Henry C. Crall, one of the original members, recalls that it just gradually disappeared.[7]

The Youth Center. Nothing of significance was done for the youth of Los Gatos after the demise of the Boys' Improvement Club until the Scout movement and the Youth Council. In the early 1930's Sewall Brown, June Sohst, and Mrs. Billy Jones urged the establishment of a Youth Council in Los Gatos. Such a council was organized, and it brought under its guidance all of the youth activities, including the Scouts and other youth groups.

The Youth Council took the initiative in getting a Youth Center for Los Gatos. Sewall Brown, representing the Youth Council, asked permission from the Town Council, on June 17, 1940 to erect a Youth Center Building. The building was to be a log cabin on the pageant grounds, with a meeting hall, kitchen and locker rooms. Brown told the city fathers that the Youth Council had $660 that could be used for this purpose. The rest was to come from volunteer labor and donations.[8]

The Town Council gave permission to erect a building on the east end of the pageant grounds, next to the property owned by Mrs. Sarah Rowly. W. W. Clark, Secretary of the Chamber of Commerce, said he had been promised enough redwood logs for the building and for fencing the grounds.

First section of the Youth Center building, completed in 1941. *(Photo by Youth Commission)*

The building was completed in May 1941. All labor was donated, as was much of the material. It was an inspiring sight to see businessmen, teachers, lawyers, carpenters, plumbers etc. working evenings and Saturdays putting up the log building.

By 1952 it was necessary to add on to the Youth Center building. A drive to raise $25,000 was headed by Fran Adams. The addition was a memorial to Sewall S. Brown. Mrs. Dorothy Sanders was chairman of the ceremonies marking the beginning of the addition. Ground was broken in June 1952.

To assist in raising the needed money, Yehudi Menuhin, the famous violinist, gave a concert on December 20, 1952 for the benefit of the Youth Center. Mrs. Stanley Sanders and Mrs. J. W. Ostle were responsible for getting Mr. Menuhin, who lived in Los Gatos, to give the concert at the high school auditorium.

The addition was completed in November 1953, and plans were laid for a full-time Director of the Youth Center. For a while the financial picture looked gloomy. But Admiral Charles Lockwood and Bob Hamsher put new life into it. Admiral Lockwood and Hamsher took charge of a new financial drive and raised more than $7000.

In order to avoid constant drives for funds, the Youth Council hoped that it would soon become a part of a larger Recreation District, perhaps financed through taxation. By 1955 the very existence of the Youth Center was threatened. The High School Board finally agreed to the creation of a Recreation Commission in 1955. The Commission that was appointed consisted of John D. Smart, Chairman, Harold Sontag, Mrs. Harold Ely, Ellis Crosby, and Art Thimann. In May of that year, Mr. Hugh Welch was appointed Town Recreation Director.

In December 1955 approval was given to a formal agreement among the Los Gatos Union Elementary School District, the Saratoga Ele-

Starting the second section of the Youth Center in 1952. Workers are (l. to r.) Eliot Underhill, Young Mott, George Bruntz, Lyman Feathers, and contractor Ed Mathews. *(Youth Commission photo)*

mentary School District and the Los Gatos Union High School District for the creation of a unified Recreation District. Each of the three school districts was to have a representative on the Youth Council. John Doolittle, Assistant San Mateo City Recreation Director, was hired as Director on February 6, 1956. Mr. Doolittle resigned on June 4, 1957 and Phil Ward, Principal of Fruitvale School, took his place from July 1 to September 1. Gene Goldberg, who had been Recreation Supervisor at Sunnyvale, was employed to fill the position on October 1, 1957.

The Recreation District is under the control of a Recreation Board. In 1971 the Board consisted of Baker McGinnis, President; Gordon Goesch, Vice-President; Dr. Henry Weston, Secretary; Roy Stair from Los Gatos Union High School District; and Dr. Everett McNicholas, Superintendent of the Saratoga Union Elementary School District.

The first office of the Recreation District was at the rear of the old Los Gatos High School Gymnasium. In 1964 it moved to temporary quarters at Villa Way on Town Center property. In 1967 it moved to its permanent headquarters in the former Legion-Library building on Main Street across from the Civic Center. From this headquarters building Gene Goldberg and his staff direct a recreation and adult program that includes everything from volleyball classes to knitting and yoga classes. Some estimate of the value of the department can be gathered from the statistics of visitations. More

Bill Oakes and Eliot Underhill, who supervised the work on the second section of the Youth Center building. *(Courtesy Youth Commission)*

than 500,000 visitations to the many activities of the Los Gatos-Saratoga Recreation Department were recorded for 1970.

Y.M.C.A. The Young Men's Christian Association occupied a prominent place in the early days of Los Gatos. The Los Gatos Y.M.C.A. was organized on October 23, 1882. W. S. Mansell was the Secretary in 1885. The group met in the rear of the Baptist Church, which then occupied a building on the north side of West Main Street.

At the annual meeting of the Y.M.C.A. on Monday, October 5, 1885, Mr. J. S. Waterbury was elected President; F. M. Reed, Vice-President; George R. Reed, Secretary; and Dan Parks, Treasurer. The *News* reported that "The society is in prosperous condition and embraces in its members many of our best citizens."[9]

On October 1, 1892 the Y.M.C.A. county work began, and Los Gatos was chosen the headquarters for the county activities. The Barnes Bowling Alley was leased for a year and a county Secretary directed the work. On Friday July 20, 1894 the Ladies Central Committee of the Y.M.C.A. gave a reception attended by 125 people. An exhibition of calisthenics and a gymnasium review followed a literary and musical program.

In 1894 the Y.M.C.A. moved to new quarters on Hotel Street, to the building formerly occupied by Watkins and Skinkle Drug Store. The County Secretary, Mr. C. W. Jones, helped to dedicate the new quarters. A reading room was provided which was open evenings and contained late issues of newspapers and magazines. The gymnasium was open on Monday and Thursday evenings. More than 40 people a night practiced tumbling, calisthenics, and gymnastics on bars, rings, and dumbbells. Mr. John Gugel was the gymnastic instructor. The County Secretary hoped that larger quarters could be found to meet the growing attendance.[10]

151

Lynn Smith, Al Brennon, Bob Harris and Jim Griffith help with the second section 1952. *(Courtesy Youth Commission)*

Some more workers on Youth Center. J. Penniman, Stanley Sanders, Brook Zoller, Dad Zoller.

After 1900 the Y.M.C.A. seemed to have lost ground in Los Gatos. This was due to lack of money and lack of a good meeting place. In the 1930's the San Jose Y.M.C.A. sent workers to outlying areas to direct some recreational activities, and Los Gatos had a regular "Y" leader who met with groups of young people in various churches.

It was not until the 1950's that the Metropolitan Y.M.C.A. in San Jose conducted regular "Y" programs in the West Valley. Land for a building was purchased at 16500 Mozart Avenue, and a $245,000 building program undertaken. A beautiful and functional building on a five-acre tract was dedicated on December 5, 1970. The new Southwest Y.M.C.A. building serves more than 4,000 young people in the West Valley Area. Mr. L. A. Christensen is the Director, and he has two program directors---Gary Wayman and Howard L. Brooks Jr.

Rinconada Golf Club. On September 6, 1901 the Los Gatos *News* advocated the organization of a country club in Los Gatos. Such a club, it said, should have room for "a tennis court, golf links, ball ground, possibly a race track" and other outdoor sports. The editor felt that a suitable clubhouse could be built where social events could be held. Such a club "would supply the one thing needed for the entertainment of summer visitors" and would induce more visitors to come to Los Gatos. All interested persons were to contact the *News* office or Mr. Charles H. Sawyer of Glenridge.[11]

On January 5, 1905 the Lomita Golf Club, which had been in the process of formation for several months, was said to have 80 members. The property was near Austin Corners, adjacent to the Nippon Mura acreage. The course opened on May 20, 1905. However, the interest lagged and in a short while the club disbanded.

The "Indispensables" who helped in building the second section of the Youth building. Left to right are G. Leibfritz, John Flores, Earl Leisener, and Al Montano. *(Youth Commission photo)*

In the spring of 1926, W. B. Maxwell acquired property near Vasona Junction and quietly started working on a golf course, mostly with his own money. In February 1928 W. C. Sprague, retired Standard Oil executive, and a committee of Los Gatos men, began looking for a place to locate a golf club. W. B. Maxwell offered to sell them his property for $75,000. Their purchase of this land was the beginning of La Rinconada Country Club.

Mr. Sprague and his committee opened membership in the club at $500 each. More than 50 signed up the first few weeks, but they needed 100 members to assure the club. By March 24, 1928 they had secured 103 members and the club was assured. The following officers were elected: W. S. Sprague, President; J. U. Higginbotham, 1st Vice-President; Sanborn Young, 2nd Vice-President; Wendell Thomas, 3rd Vice-President; I. D. Mabie, Treasurer. L. H. Neuman and I. D. Mabie were the first to make the rounds of the new La Rinconada Golf Course, playing all 18 holes early in May 1929.

The first professional golfer at La Rinconada was Phil Jefferson, a professional golfer from

152

The Southwest Y.M.C.A. building on Mozart Avenue.

Washington. He held this post from 1929 until his death in 1946.

In September 1945 Dr. S. J. Leider, a dentist from San Francisco, became the owner of La Rinconada Golf Club. He purchased it from Capital Company for $80,000.[12] In 1951 the course ceased being a public course and became a private course open to members exclusively.

La Rinconada has become widely known as a good tournament club. Its beautiful clubhouse, overlooking the hills and the valley, and its large swimming pool make it a popular recreational center for its many members and their families.

Other Groups. Los Gatos has always supported the Boy Scout movement. On February 18, 1918 a meeting was called to discuss a Boy Scout Council for the town. Rev. H. H. Gillies had organized the first Scout Troop in 1917, and he felt that a Scout Council was needed to direct the work of other troops that could be organized. Besides, he was anxious to turn his troop over to such a council since his responsibilities for a church in Saratoga and the one in Los Gatos took most of his time.[13]

Scout troops were sponsored by many local organizations. Practically all of the Service Clubs took over responsibility for a troop. Most of the churches sponsored troops. Some of the leading

Admiral Chas. Lockwood, who spearheaded many a community activity for the youth of Los Gatos. *(Youth Commission photo)*

citizens who acted as Scout Masters included Sewall Brown, Ken Robinson, Lyndon Farwell, Marc Vertin and Claude Smith. Today there are seven Cub Packs in the area, 9 Scout Troops and 4 Explorer Posts, for a total of 647 boys involved in some form of scouting in Los Gatos.

Horse enthusiasts also organized. In November 1940 some 23 people met at the Town Hall to organize the Los Gatos Gymkhana Association. Ralph Phillips was elected President; Leo Frank, Vice-President; Carl Hubbell, Secretary; and Stanley Hopper, Treasurer. The purpose of the organization was to increase interest in, and enthusiasm for, owning and training horses for showing as well as for pleasure. Charter members were limited to 50.

The group held monthly dances and used the money to fix up an arena along the Los Gatos Creek, and fence it in. Here they held periodic horse shows that drew large crowds.

Because the State took the land by Forbes Mill for the Freeway, the P.G.& E. Substation had to be moved from that location. The most suitable place for a new substation was on the grounds of the Gymkhana. In 1953 the town sold this to the P.G.& E., and that left the horsemen without a meeting place. The result was that the Gymkhana Association phased out as a horsemen's group. However, many of its members joined the Red Shirts, a group of horsemen that had a large arena in the Almaden area.

FOOTNOTES

1. *Los Gatos Weekly News,* June 18, 1897.
2. *Ibid.,* June 19. The Battlefield was also known as Breed's Hill.
3. *Ibid.*
4. *Ibid.* June 13, 1904.
5. From the file *Memorial Park* in Office of City Clerk, Town of Los Gatos.
6. Town Board *Minutes,* March 23, 1925.
7. Most of the information obtained from an interview with Henry Crall.
8. Town Board *Minutes,* June 17, 1940.
9. *Weekly News,* October 9, 1885.
10. *Ibid.,* April 10, 1894.
11. *Ibid.,* Sept. 6, 1901.
12. Los Gatos *Mail,* February 14, 1918.

Friday, December 4, 1942   LOS GATOS, CALIFORNIA   LOS GATOS TIMES   SANTA CLARA COUNTY   Page Three

FOOTHILL RESIDENTS RALLY TO SUPPORT WAR EFFORT

It Happens To Me...
(JUST PRIVATE THINKS)
By L.E.S.

VOLUNTEERS GET IN BIG VOLUME OF WAR SCRAP

Local Red Cross Sets Enviable War Record
By SEWALL BROWN, Chairman

WOMEN GIVE MANY HOURS PRODUCING R. C. SUPPLIES
By MRS. WALTER BECKER, Chairman Volunteer Services

Civilian Defense Setup Prepared For Emergency
By DR. GEORGE G. BRUNTZ

SARATOGA R. C. HAS NUMEROUS WORKERS MAKING SUPPLIES
By MISS ZOE ACKERMAN, Secretary

Part of a page from the Los Gatos *Times* for December 4, 1942, telling about Los Gatos' war effort.

Page, right, from the Los Gatos *Times* December 1, 1942, showing how people could help in the war effort. *(Original copy courtesy publisher Lloyd E. Smith)*

Red Cross class of 1914. Mrs. C. A. Cosgrave, Instructor. Front row L to R, Margaret Case, Dorothy Harwood, Estelle McMurtry, Olive Knowles, Mrs. E. H. Blakey. *(Courtesy William Balch)*

CHAPTER XIV

Two World Wars and After

Some New Town Problems

DURING World War I and thereafter the Town Board faced numerous "ordinary" problems. The usual amount of vandalism had to be dealt with when, for instance, the expensive stained glass windows of the Presbyterian Church were broken three times within a short period of time. New problems also arose with the increased use of the automobile. Traffic on the corner of Main Street and Santa Cruz Avenue presented a challenge as early as 1915. In September of that year the Town Board wrestled with ways and means of regulating the congested traffic on that corner. "The Marshall spent a good deal of his time Sunday, September 20," complained the press, "compelling vehicles to turn square corners." Because of corner "cutting," vehicles often met the Peninsula Railroad cars and an accident resulted. Mrs. George Green was hit by the 5:20 Peninsula Car on Sunday afternoon September 20, 1915, with the result that her automobile "suffered fender and step damages."[1]

Late in 1916 the Town Council passed Ordinance #181 making it unlawful to permit minors---under 21 years of age---in pool rooms and billiard halls. Violators were to have their license revoked. Evidently the ordinance was not heeded for on February 19, 1917 the W.C.T.U. complained that minors were frequenting these establishments. Again, on November 18, 1918, the Town Board heard the complaint of J. Barber against A. Carson for violating this ordinance. The Board held Carson guilty and revoked his permit to do business in Los Gatos. On December 29, 1930 Police Chief Noble brought a charge against Robert Gilmore, proprietor of the Los Gatos Cigar Store, that minors were allowed in the pool room and that liquor could be had there. Lyman Feathers and Mr. Alvin Chapin supported the charge. The Board revoked the license of Gilmore as of February 1, 1931.

On February 7, 1921 the residents of Market Street presented a petition to the Town Board asking that the name be changed to Loma Alta Avenue. At the same time the residents of Johnson Avenue protested the changing of its name to El Monte Avenue. The Board changed the name of Market Street to Loma Alta Avenue, and kept the name of Johnson Avenue, as requested.[2]

Another matter the Town Board dealt with was the transportation problem. In May 1918 the Curtis brothers (George and Floyd) asked for permission to operate an automobile passenger service between Los Gatos and Santa Cruz and intermediate points. The Town Board granted this permission on May 6 for a period of five years. Their daily schedule, as published in the local newspaper, indicated that cars left from Watson's Pharmacy "across from the post office."

On May 20, 1918 the Auto Transit Company of San Francisco was granted permission to establish passenger service between San Francisco and Santa Cruz. The service was to pass through Los Gatos. The fare was $1 from Los Gatos to Santa Cruz and $1.50 from Los Gatos to San Francisco.

An important development came in 1924 when the Town Board took steps to keep the town from developing in a hodge-podge manner. It created the town Planning Commission and appointed George Green, Dr. E. M. Miller, Dr. A. E. Osborne, Zedd Riggs and Leland Walker as the first members. This Commission held its first meeting on May 7, 1924. Dr. E. M. Miller was elected Chairman and Leland Walker was chosen as Secretary.

Among the first recommendations of the commission were: That the town should be properly zoned; that the P.G.& E. poles and telephone poles should be put underground; that certain streets should be paved; that the Peninsula Railway cars should come in on the Southern Pacific tracks rather than down Santa Cruz Avenue.

It was not until late in March 1931 that the Town Council "in one of the greatest steps taken in years toward a more beautiful Los Gatos," called for the removal of the unsightly poles in the downtown section.[3] In February 1934 George Shaner, local realtor, asked the Town Council to have all poles removed from the business district, and electroliers erected. The Council took the matter under advisement.

It is of interest to note that Los Gatos had a radio broadcasting studio in 1927. The Whitlock Studio, located at 271 San Jose Avenue, opened in the early part of 1927. Mr. A. A. Whitlock stated that the "Voice of the Santa Cruz Mountains" would be heard "all over the country." He invited local talent to appear for performances. He also used a new electrola.[4]

Los Gatos kept in time with national and State Politics. Governor Hiram Johnson made his bid for votes for United States Senator in 1916. He came through Los Gatos on November 1, 1916 and spoke at the Ford Opera House. The *Mail News* reported on November 2 that those familiar with Governor Johnson's style of speechmaking "agreed that yesterday's effort was one of the most eloquent and brilliant that they have heard," and then it concluded, "Governor Johnson was enthusiastically received here and his address was listened to attentively from beginning to end." Attorney D. T. Jenkins presided at the Johnson rally and introduced the Governor. As a postscript we should add that Governor Hiram Johnson, a Republican, won his seat in the United States Senate as a Republican, but California voters helped give the Democrat, Woodrow Wilson, his second term as President.

Recall Election of 1928. Perhaps one of the most unusual recall elections in the annals of local government took place in Los Gatos in 1928. The Town Council had planned to pave certain streets in the residential area. The engineer recommended that the streets be paved with cement. A Durite Company in San Jose persuaded some of the residents in the area scheduled for paving that asphalt was cheaper and more durable than cement. About 40% of the residents signed a petition asking the Council to pave with Durite instead of cement.

On January 12, 1928 the *Mail News* reported that Councilman George Green—who was Mayor at the time—said, in regard to the paving dispute, "We understand that one of the patented asphalt paving companies is in here circulating a petition among the property owners, asking us to put down their pavement. This is in defiance of our policy of using Portland Cement, which we regard as the best kind, as well as the cheapest pavement we can use."

The Town Council rejected the petition, saying "The Council feels that dollar for dollar the people are getting more from a concrete than an asphalt pavement." The battle of the pavements raged for several months. Two "pro-Durite" candidates—H. A. Wilder and J. D. B. Manning—entered the April election for the Town Council and were elected. But a number of "anti-Durite" people were also heard from. Hiram Blanchard, who owned 130 feet of frontage on Bean Avenue, requested concrete and not asphalt pavement in front of his property. In a statement, reported in the *Mail News* on March 29, 1928 he said, "Asphalt is the refuse of

oil after the gasoline and other beneficial products are extracted."

After Wilder and Manning were elected, the new Council met and chose A. H. Bell as Mayor. During that first meeting, Councilman Green introduced a Resolution that a recall election should be held on May 22 for A. H. Bell and George Green. His hope was that the people would decide the issue and thus quiet the harassment of the Council.

The recall election resulted in an overwhelming victory for both Bell and Green—the former by 804 to 252 and the latter by 813 to 225.[5]

But the opposition was not to be quieted. S. W. Rice, a truck driver for the Sporleder Transfer Company and a property owner on Bean and Tait Avenues, sought an injunction against the town to stop the pavement program. The Hanrahan Paving Company and the Town were ordered to appear in Superior Court Number 3 on June 15 at 10 A.M. to hear the motion for an injunction to stop the paving program. The town stood to lose more than $1000 already spent on the program if the injunction were issued. This was serious, especially since the town was already in acute financial straits. On June 23 the Court decided in favor of the town and Los Gatos was able to proceed with its $80,000 paving program.

Garbage Disposal

There was no garbage collection in Los Gatos until after 1921. The town dump was used as a place to leave garbage, a practice which greatly disturbed the Town Board of Health. In 1923 Mr. John Zinardi began to collect garbage for pigs which belonged to a Mr. Crossetti at the Sewer Farm. This gradually developed into a garbage collection business which extended to the village of Campbell. The Los Gatos Scavenger Company set the rate at 50 cents a month for 30 gallons; 75 cents a month for 30 to 50 gallons; and $1.00 a month for 50 to 100 gallons. Garbage was collected weekly.

On October 18, 1926 attorney Leland Walker appeared before the Town Board to ask if his client, Mr. P. Agressi, could have permission to collect the slops from Los Gatos hotels and restaurants and use the private right-of-way on the town sewer farm. He intended to haul slops to hogs he expected to buy from the Scavenger contractors. Agressi had entered into an agreement to purchase 140 to 150 hogs from the garbage contractor, and they had given him the privilege of collecting the slops, while the company collected the garbage.

City Attorney Jenkins pointed out that the town held a contract with the Scavenger Company

Rare picture of George and Mrs. McMurtry. McMurtry was born in Lexington and was a life-long resident of the town. Served as Treasurer of Los Gatos for over 40 years—1887 to 1894 and 1914 to 1948. Active in the real estate and insurance business with A. H. Bell. *(Courtesy William Balch)*

S. D. Balch, long time banker and civic leader. Was chairman of the Town Board ("Mayor") from 1914 to 1918. *(Courtesy William Balch)*

R. R. Bell, early merchant and judge in Los Gatos. Member of the Town Board 1906 and 1910 to 1914. Long-time judge of the Los Gatos Municipal Court—a position later held by his son, A. H. Bell. *(Courtesy Mrs. Sewall Brown)*

and would hold them to that contract. "The city does not want to divide the contract."[6]

The Scavenger Company was dumping garbage they had collected from outside the town limits at the Los Gatos dump. On November 18, 1926, the Town Board asked the company to pay for this privilege. The town asked $100 a month. On December 19, 1938 the Zinardis were given a contract by the Town Council to remove garbage in the town.[7] In 1970 the Los Gatos Scavenger Company became the Green Valley Disposal Company.

One of the major problems that has faced the garbage collectors has been the disposal of the refuse. In 1955 the Scavenger Company asked permission to use land in Lime Kiln Canyon as a dump. This created a stir among the mountain residents, and the County Planning Commission denied a use permit in October 1955. Finally the company used its Guadalupe hillside land for a dump.

Although the garbage company used the fill-and-cover system, the problem of space was always a challenge. This is a serious problem in the entire Bay Area. In October 1967 Mr. James Hickey, the Planning Director for the Association of Bay Area Governments, estimated that our county will be producing an average of one and two-thirds million tons of refuse per annum by the year 2000.

The Sira System. One of the interesting developments regarding garbage disposal has been the Sira System. Mr. Gianni Siracuse developed a unique method of disposing of garbage, and it has been put into operation in Los Gatos. The system separates the metals, glass and salvageable mater-

ials. The remainder is pulverized and exploded in a 2,500 degree furnace. It is estimated that 5 tons of garbage can be incinerated into less than a bucket of residue. There is no odor since the entire process is done inside. The Green Valley Disposal Company signed an agreement in September 1967 whereby the disposal company provides 3 acres of land for the Sira System. The Food Machinery Corporation of San Jose has developed the machinery under contract to the Sira Corporation. The system went into operation in 1968 and if its prospects are as promising as they seem, the Sira System should prove a boon to the cities plagued with the problem of garbage disposal. And Los Gatos will again have a "first" to its credit.

World War I

Like other towns in America, Los Gatos felt no effects of the great war in Europe between 1914 and 1917. Life went on as usual. The big event in 1915 was the visit to Los Gatos of Henry Ford and Thomas A. Edison. Both of these men spent the day and night of October 22, 1915 in our town. The Edisons were guests in the home of Dr. and Mrs. Thomas Addison on Glenridge Woods at the end of Bachman Avenue. Dr. Addison was General Manager of the Pacific Electric Company. Mr. Ford was the guest of Mr. C. B. Gilbert, also of Glenridge Avenue. Mr. Gilbert had been manager of the electric light station in Detroit in 1889 and had given Henry Ford—then a "tramp engineer"—a job. Mr. Ford was also taken up to the Montezuma School for Boys and was impressed with that institution.

When the United States entered World War I, Los Gatos became active in the support of all war efforts. On May 8, 1917, Sheriff Langford and Mr. Chase addressed the Town Board concerning "the need for Home Guards and the planting of gardens." They also stressed the need for frugality, saying it was "a patriotic measure."[8] On May 10, 1917 the Los Gatos Chapter of the American Red Cross was organized. Mr. Herbert Smith was the first chairman. On May 17, 1917 the Los Gatos *Mail News* reported that more than 40 men had signed up for the Home Guard. This was a part of the State Home Guard organization and was open to any man between 18 and 60 years of age.

On June 11, 1917, the Town Board passed a resolution stating that since the President of the United States "did on May 10, 1917, create within the Red Cross, a War Council to which will be entrusted the duty of responding to the extra-ordinary demands which the present War will make upon the service of the Red Cross, both in the field and in civilian life," and since the President had proclaimed the week of June 18 as Red Cross Week, during which a financial drive for its support was to take place, the Board hoped that all would "give generously and in a spirit of patriotic sacrifice for the work of the Red Cross."[9]

On June 20, 1918 Mr. J. J. Stanfield, Chairman of the Town Trustees, published a notice in the *Mail News* asking people to buy War Savings Bonds.

> "Friday, June 28, 1918, is officially designated War Savings Day by the Secretary of the Treasury and the Governor of this state. All loyal citizens of this community will accordingly devote the day to subscribing for War Savings Stamps and otherwise promoting their sale in large amounts. All who are able should pledge themselves to save and invest to the limit allowed by law."

Los Gatos did its share for relief projects. On September 3, 1918 Mrs. H. G. Shirley, on behalf of the Eastern Star, asked the Town Board for permission to use the "Town Hall and Town Hall Park from Sixth Street to Mill Street, for an indoor-outdoor entertainment," for the benefit of the Belgium Relief Fund. The event was to take place on Saturday night, September 14, 1918. Permission was granted on condition that "one dollar be paid for lights."[10]

The great influenza epidemic that struck all of the country the last half of 1918 affected our town also. On November 11, 1918, the Town Board adopted Ordinance #182, requiring the wearing of masks in all public places.

Los Gatans willingly restricted their use of flour, sugar, and other necessities for the war effort. Women not only performed war work at home but some served in Europe. Miss Ruth Seeley, daughter of Dr. William B. Seeley, and sister of Mrs. R. D. Robertson, went to Europe with a contingent from Stanford University. She was in Paris during the final days of the war. When she returned to Los Gatos in the early part of 1919, she was in great demand as a speaker before local clubs.

After the war the people of Los Gatos showed their gratitude to the boys who had served their country by giving a big reception and barbecue in their honor. The Chamber of Commerce and the Merchants Association joined forces for this great event, which was held at the Town Hall Park on November 11, 1919. After the 1 P.M. barbecue there were games and races for young and old. All stores were closed for the day, it being the first anniversary of the signing of the Armistice which ended World War I.

Los Gatos and The Depression

Although the Great Depression did not strike until 1929, Los Gatos was helping the "down-and-outers" as early as 1924. The Town Board and the local Red Cross Chapter "planned to cooperate in the matter of helping the needy 'down-and-outers' who may visit the city this winter." Martin LeFevre, Treasurer of the Red Cross Chapter, and chairman of the Chapter's relief committee, recommended, in October 1924, that all persons out of work and needing means of support, be referred to him and that he be permitted to send them to the Street Superintendent, Mr. Sullivan, who would put them to work on the streets. He also recommended that "down-and-outers" needing medical care be referred to him and he would direct them to physicians. All expenses connected with the work and the medical care were to be paid by the local Red Cross Chapter. The Town Board accepted this offer, hoping it would eliminate the degrading results of charity. "All able-bodied men will be compelled to work for the money they get—they deserve no charity."[11]

The "Feathers Hotel," mentioned in a previous chapter, gained the support of the local people. In March 1931 it provided 1026 meals to men who otherwise would have gone hungry. Sleeping accommodations were provided for 513 men. About 400 a month were cared for during the years 1930 to 1933.

When the Federal Relief programs started, Los

George Green, the first Mayor of Los Gatos. Served on Town Board from 1922 to 1942. Leader in business and civic affairs. *(Courtesy Elton Green)*

A. H. "Arch" Bell, for many years Judge of the Los Gatos Municipal Court. Was Mayor of the town from 1928 to 1930. Was judge of the local court at the time of his death in 1949. *(Courtesy Mrs. Sewall Brown)*

Martin LeFevre, prominent leader in civic and business affairs. Active in Red Cross and was chairman of the Town Planning Commission at the time of his death in 1954. *(Courtesy Martin LeFevre family)*

Ralph Duncan, long time druggist and prominent civic leader. In business in Los Gatos for over 45 years. *(Courtesy Duncan Pharmacy)*

Gatos supported these with equal enthusiasm. In January 1934 the Mayor, Marc Vertin, reported that the improvement program under C.W.A. was working satisfactorily. Mr. George Green, Inspector for C.W.A., reported that 58 men were employed on work at the high school athletic field, at street repair work, and on improvements in Memorial Park.[12]

The Home Improvement campaign, sponsored by the F.H.A., was begun with a mass meeting on February 14, 1935, at which a representative from F.H.A. explained the purpose of the Act. Sponsored by the Rotary Club, a great parade was held on Friday, February 15 to promote repair and improvements of homes through the Federal Housing Act. An intensive drive to bring "new prosperity" to the town through loans promoted by the F.H.A. was undertaken in Los Gatos. Mr. I. D. Mabie was general chairman, and he appointed an advisory committee with J. Walter Crider as the head. Paul Curtis was in charge of the finance committee, and other chairmen included James Hudson, Publicity; Ida Bruegge, Women's Section; Ed Haller, Consultant; and R. H. Sund, Planning.

A campaign for a $75,000 home improvement program was begun. A contest for the best posters by high school students was conducted. Barbara Dickinson (now Mrs. Phillip White) won first prize in the girls' division. Her poster showed "a gorgeous landscape in green and gold, with a home pictured, and the message was, "Better housing program under the F.H.A. Borrow money, give employment, fix your home." Carl Taylor, of Saratoga, won first place in the boys' division. His poster showed the storm god blowing on a

weather-beaten house, and the message said, "Needs a new coat. See the F.H.A. Plan."

Eleven solicitors attended classes for instruction by J. O. Rogers of the F.H.A. These then contacted residents of the town to get them to agree on home improvements. By March 14, 1935 the campaign had passed the $75,000 mark. In fact, promises for improvements amounted to more than $100,000, with only three-fourths of the town canvassed. Permits amounted to more than $10,000 the first four months.

Mayor Vertin declared Saturday, June 15, 1935 Better Housing Day. "I call upon all our citizens to join with citizens of other communities throughout the land in marking the day with appropriate observances, in order that the benefits of the Better Housing Program may be brought to a still greater number of people."[13]

World War II

We have already seen that our town has never failed to give wholehearted support to patriotic endeavors. World War II was no exception. In October 1940 Mr. Norman O'Connor was appointed Clerk of the 113th District Draft Board. The Board met in the Whisenant Building on East Main Street. The space was donated by Mr. Whisenant, who was a member of the Board.

Immediately after Pearl Harbor on December 7, 1941, plans were made for civilian defense and protection. Mayor Stanley Mills called a mass meeting at the Town Hall, which resulted in the formation of a Temporary Civilian Defense Council. Representatives from the fire and police departments, the schools, the Red Cross, Chamber of Commerce, American Legion and the utilities were placed on this council. The Adult Education Department started an intensive training program for air-raid wardens, auxiliary firemen and policemen. Practice air-raid drills were held periodically. Dr. George G. Bruntz was asked to attend the Civilian Protection classes at Stanford University, and upon his return he suggested a permanent plan of organization for all civil defense units in town.

First Aid courses were given by the local Red Cross, and a Disaster Relief Committee was organized with Henry C. Crall as chairman. A Salvage for Victory Committee, under the leadership of George D. Edwards, collected scrap and junk. It collected more than 375 tons of scrap metal, rubber and rags the first few months and sold these to junk dealers for $700, which was turned over to the Red Cross. Yehudi Menuhin, the world-famous violinist and resident of Los Gatos, gave a benefit concert for the Red Cross on Friday evening May 1, 1942.

Los Gatans participated in the Pledge Victory Campaign which was waged in California the week of May 24, 1942. The pledge card, which all Californians were asked to sign, was a moral promise to buy a certain amount of War Savings Bonds and Stamps at regular intervals for the duration of the war.[14] A State Militia was organized similar to the Home Guard of World War I. All men between the ages of 16 and 63 were eligible.

In other words, every facet of civilian life was geared to the war effort. Food rationing, gasoline rationing, and other restrictions were taken in stride. More than 400 men from the Los Gatos area served in the various branches of the armed forces, and some of our finest lost their lives in the war.

Post-War Problems

Lexington Dam. The Santa Clara Valley Water Conservation District had a program of dam construction to back up water in "percolation" lakes to conserve, for the valley, the waters that came from the mountains. A large dam and lake were planned where the towns of Alma and Lexington stood. Some local leaders were concerned over the safety of a dirt dam just above the town. Mr. G. J. Gilligan, Secretary to the Chamber of Commerce, sent a letter to the Town Council on August 4, 1952 in which he raised certain questions about Lexington Dam. What steps were planned to prevent water pollution? Air pollution? Adverse aesthetic effects of such a dam? He recommended that the town call a public meeting to discuss these

The old Rogers Packing House on the corner of Almaden Road and San Jose (now Bascom) Avenue. In place of this old landmark there is now a service station. During World War II soldiers were stationed here. *(Courtesy Mary Yocco Rugh)*

matters. He felt that a committee should be appointed to consider whether an injunction should be sought to prevent the building of the dam.

Mr. Lloyd E. Smith, the publisher of the Los Gatos *Times,* addressed the Council, saying there was no question that the dam would be built. But he felt that the town should take steps to insure its safety. He also suggested that a committee be appointed, and this committee should meet with the Santa Clara Valley Water Conservation District and the State of California Division of Water Resources to find out what precautions were being taken to ensure the safety of the dam. Admiral Thomas B. Inglis was appointed chairman of this committee on September 26, 1952.

In the meantime, Mr. Smith ran editorials and items about the dam in the *Times.* Because of his insistence, the engineers made changes in the structure to ensure absolute safety. Today Lexington Dam is a beauty spot and a recreation center for the people in the area.

Annexations. Annexation threats on the part of San Jose were not confined to the 1950's and 1960's. On December 2, 1920 the *Mail News* became alarmed that "some of the prominent people of San Jose are proposing a new form of city government for the cities and towns of Santa Clara County—the borough system, which, in short, means that the cities and towns of the county outside of San Jose, be annexed to San Jose."

The editors of the local newspaper said that although the people of Los Gatos were proud of their county seat, not a single person could be found who was willing to incorporate "the Gem

The Old Town Hall, built in 1913, was torn down in 1965 to be replaced by the new Civic Center. *(Los Gatos Museum Collection)*

City with San Jose." As far as Los Gatos was concerned, "we believe the people here are desirous of maintaining the identity of Los Gatos."

Although the Borough System was not adopted, the idea of annexing outlying areas was never dropped. The danger of the growth of unregulated subdivisions was recognized by the County Planning Commission. On July 6, 1937 this Commission asked the Planning Commissions of the towns in the county to get together in the interests of better subdivision control. On the same day John Skeggs, of the State Highway Commission, stated that the subdivision on San Jose Avenue and extending to Kennedy Road, was unsatisfactory to the State Highway Commission. This led to a discussion, in the Town Council, as to who really constituted the Planning Commission for Los Gatos. Town Attorney Jenkins ruled that a new state law had abolished the old Planning Commission and therefore it no longer existed. Ordinance #245 was introduced, and it established a new Planning Commission on July 19, 1937.

When the "expansionist" San Jose City Manager, "Dutch" Hamann, came into office, he adopted a policy of growth for San Jose through annexation of outlying areas. As long as such "finger annexations" did not come too close to our town, there was no serious concern. However, by 1954 San Jose was annexing at an alarming rate, reaching its tentacles out in strip annexations that almost touched Los Gatos. In June 1954 the Town Planning Commission decided the best way to fight this expansion was to have Los Gatos beat San Jose "to the draw" and annex new territory itself. The Commission gave the green light to the Town Council for "an active and immediate annexation program."

When San Jose annexed the area of the Los Gatos Cemetery, Councilman Charles Gamble quipped, "Los Gatos should adopt the slogan 'Live in Los Gatos and be buried in San Jose'." He felt the cemetery grab would "make the old Los Gatans turn over in their graves if they knew they were being hauled into San Jose."[15]

Los Gatos planned to annex the Blossom Hill residential area, part of the Cambrian Park area and some territories east of town. The minutes of the Town Council for 1960 to 1968 are filled with annexation plans. The Planning Commission had already been instructed, in 1952, to set up plans for annexation. At that time the town feared that San Jose would "swallow up" our town from the north, and steps had to be taken to prevent that.

The result of this was that the town limits of Los Gatos were greatly expanded. Los Gatos protected itself from being taken into San Jose, but it also found new problems facing it as a result of the growth of the town. These problems were perhaps too great for the type of government the town had. The question arose: "Should a new system of local government be adopted for Los Gatos?"

Town Manager Government

In 1927 the State Legislature enacted a State law changing the name of Town Boards such as that in Los Gatos to City Council. The Trustees were to be known as Councilmen and the chairman of the Board was to be known as "Mayor." The Town Marshal was now Chief of Police. George A. Green thus became the first Mayor of Los Gatos in 1927. H. O. Baird became the first Chief of Police.

Other changes in local government were in the air. On August 9, 1927 Dr. Antrim E. Osborne, former State Senator, advocated the establishment of a City-Manager form of government for Los Gatos. He believed that it would mean greater efficiency. "When we ask businessmen to become members of the City Council," said Dr. Osborne, "one of two things is bound to happen. They cannot give full attention to both the city government and to their own business." He felt that the people had no right to demand that a man jeopardize his own affairs "in a comparatively thankless job." By hiring a manager to give full time to the city's business "we would run this corporation on a business basis."[16]

Mayor George Green felt that a city manager system would increase the cost of city government. "I have nothing against the City Manager idea," said Mayor Green, "but I do know something about city finances, and if you add the salary of a city manager to the present budget, he could not save enough to pay his cost."[17]

The Town Council discussed the City Manager system on June 6, 1935 and the members seemed favorably disposed to it. However, they wanted further discussion of the matter. Finally, on October 23, 1939 the people voted on the question of a City Manager for Los Gatos. It was defeated by more than a two to one majority—677 to 325.[18]

Nothing more was done until February 18, 1952 when the Town Council adopted a resolution to let the people vote on the matter again at the regular April election. Mayor LeRoy Wright voted against the resolution. Town Attorney J. Rainey Hancock explained that the vote would be only a "straw vote" to see if the public was interested in that form of government. In the April 8, 1952 election the people voted 649 to 676 against a City Manager system. On February 16, 1953 the Town Attorney reported to the Council that the State Government Code applicable to sixth class cities provided that the City Council can, either by ordinance or by a vote of the people, adopt the City Manager form of government. On the strength of this advice the Council on February 24, 1953 passed Ordinance #352 establishing a City Manager form of Government for Los Gatos. The Town Clerk was instructed to advertise in the *Western Cities* magazine and in the International City Managers' Association *Bulletin*—if there was no charge—for applications for the office of City Manager for Los Gatos.[19]

The 100-year old house, above, on Alpine Avenue shortly after it was acquired by Mayor and Mrs. John Lincoln. Left, part of the beautiful gardens which have been added and where the annual Tulip Festival benefit for the Los Gatos Museum is held. Also a popular "Garden Tour" stop. *(Courtesy the Lincoln family)*

The award-winning Los Gatos Civic Center. Administration on left, Police in center, and libraries on right. Completed in 1965. *(Photograph by Morley Baer of Berkeley)*

In April 1953 Mr. Karl A. Baldwin, Assistant City Manager of San Mateo, was hired as the first City Manager for our town. Mayor Charles K. Gamble said the selection was made from a list of 46 candidates. His beginning salary was $525 a month.

The town administration grew with the growth of the town, and additional space was needed. Mr. Baldwin was asked to study the costs of using the old Presbyterian Church as an annex to the City Hall. The police, Engineer and a number of other offices moved into this building.

One of the first problems faced by the City Manager was the Freeway through Los Gatos. Originally only a Lark Avenue Cloverleaf was planned. This would leave the downtown area without access to the freeway and would cause traffic jams on Santa Cruz and San Jose Avenues. A public meeting was held on January 11, 1954 to discuss a cross-town highway link connecting Saratoga Avenue with San Jose Avenue. The Town Council proposed a bond issue of $173,000 to build the town's part of the crossing---one-third of the cost. The rest would be paid by the State. The people at the mass meeting urged the Town Council to submit the bond issue to a vote at the April 1954 election.

Although every effort was made to push the bond to a favorable vote, it failed in the April 13 election. The Charles Street Crossing, as it was known, failed to get the required two-thirds majority of the votes. A new bond issue in the reduced amount of $80,000 was passed by the voters on December 6, 1955 by a 3 to 1 margin. The State agreed to pick up the tab for the remainder of the $400,000 cost of the project. Los Gatos now got its cloverleaf entrance from Highway 17 to the business part of the town.

The new bridge on Main Street across the Freeway was financed entirely by the State. It was built in 1954 by the Carl Swenson Company at a cost of $353,477.50.

The New Civic Center

In 1960 Mayor A. E. Merrill appointed a Civic Needs Committee to look into the matter of a new Civic Center. After studying the situation from all angles, the committee recommended a general obligation bond issue to finance civic improvements. In addition to the bonds, the project required $888,000 from the General Fund surplus. The final cost of the project was $1,007,465 including land purchases, landscaping, paving, etc.

The new Civic Center buildings included three separate units---City Clerk, City Manager, Council Chambers, Engineer; Police Department; and Library. This municipal complex won top award for Los Gatos in the First Annual Governor's Design Awards in 1966. The winner was picked from all new civic buildings in California, and Los Gatos was the only city to receive an award in the public building category. Councilman---later Mayor---Charles DeFreitas went to Pasadena on December 28, 1966 to accept the award in behalf of the town. Los Gatos was the winner over 52 entries in the Architectural Division.

When the plans were completed for this new Civic Center, the question of what to do with the old City Hall became a problem. Many old-timers looked at it with nostalgia. They wanted it preserved. The arguments over what to do with the 52-year-old building became heated. Some wanted it to remain "as a monument to the rich heritage of Los Gatos History whose great architectural style properly sets it apart from the modernistic municipal nerve center going up near by." Some felt that if the building could not remain on its old location, perhaps it could be moved and preserved as a museum. Indeed, the Los Gatos Museum Association, then still looking for a permanent home, would have been happy to use it as a museum building.

Then there were those who considered the old building a monolith, "a concrete ammunition depot which has no place in the landscape make-up of the new Civic Center."[20] The Town Council received letters for and against preserving the old Town Hall. Dr. William W. Johnson wrote in favor of tearing down the structure. "It is an earthquake menace among other liabilities," he wrote. "Make way for the landscaping of the new building—a quality edifice which will be another forward step in man's evolution of structures for his use."[21]

The other side countered with threats to picket the Town Council to get the old building preserved. The West Valley Garden Club sent a Resolution to the Council, written in the first person, as if the building was telling its own story. "I am the Town Hall," it said, "born in 1913 on Main Street in Los Gatos. A great many people have admired my architectural beauty and charm and would like to see me perpetuated for future generations to enjoy." Then in the resolution it asked the town to withdraw "its plan to destroy me, and preserve the building."

The Council did not act on the resolution at the August 2, 1965 meeting. Norman Stoner, from the audience, suggested that the Council appoint a committee to evaluate the Old Town Hall. Councilman Henry C. Crall stated that demolition was a part of the contract and that it had to be carried out. At the August 16 meeting the Council passed a motion asking each member to appoint one person for a committee to evaluate the old building. The committee was composed of Clayton Bruntz, President of the Junior Chamber of Commerce; Chester Root, architect; John Lochner, President of Lions Club; George Sicular, Professor of Civil Engineering at San Jose State College; and Pat Walsh, President of Rotary Club. Walsh was made chairman of the committee.

Even the Town Council was divided on the issue. Mayor John Lincoln and Councilman Egon Jensen favored the preservation, and Vice-Mayor Henry C. Crall and Councilmen A. E. Merrill and Joe Whalen favored removal. Councilman Crall pointed out the high cost of removing the old building and making it structurally secure. The debate raged for weeks.

On October 4, 1965 the Committee reported its findings and recommendation to the Council. It found the building impossible to move and a danger to keep. It recommended that it be demolished. Thus, the Old Town Hall was torn down, and a beautiful lawn and trees were planted on its site. But even as it disappeared, many old-timers watched in disbelief as the bulldozers knocked their favorite building down to make room for the new Civic Center park in front of the Memorial Library.

FOOTNOTES

1. *Mail News*, September 24, 1915.
2. Town Board *Minutes*, February 7, 1921.
3. *Mail News*, April 2, 1931.
4. *Ibid.*, January 20, 1927.
5. Town Council *Minutes*, June 4, 1928.
6. *Mail News*, October 21, 1926.
7. Town Council *Minutes*, December 29, 1938.
8. Town Board *Minutes*, May 8, 1917.
9. *Ibid.*, June 11, 1917.
10. *Mail News*, September 3, 1918.
11. *Ibid.*, October 23, 1924.
12. *Ibid.*, January 18, 1924.
13. *Ibid.*, June 13, 1935.
14. Los Gatos *Times*, May 1, 1942.
15. Los Gatos *Times-Observer*, November 2, 1954.
16. Town Council *Minutes*, Book 3 p. 58. Also *Mail News*, August 11, 1927.
17. *Ibid.*
18. *Ibid.*, Book 4, p. 26, October 30, 1939.
19. Town Council *Minutes*, February 24, 1953.
20. *Times-Observer*, July 31, 1965. (See files of this newspaper for a running account of this fight.)
21. *Ibid.*

We end, as we began, with the original Forbes Mill. Los Gatos grew around the mill, and was first called Forbestown. A portion of the mill is still standing and is a landmark in Los Gatos.
(Library Collection)

Bibliography

Addicott, J. E., *Grandad's Pioneer Stories.* Los Gatos *Times* Printing Co., Los Gatos, 1953.

Alley, Bowen & Co. Publishers, *History of Santa Clara County California.* San Francisco 1881.

Bank of Los Gatos (pamphlet) "The Legend of Los Gatos."

A. Berryman & Co. (Leaflet) "Map of California" Rand McNally Co. 1888.

Cleland, Rober Glass, *From Wilderness to Empire A History of California 1542 to 1900.* N.Y. Alfred A. Knopf, 1944.

Farquhar, Francis P. ed. *Up and Down California in 1860–1864. The Journal of William H. Brewer.* New Haven, Yale Univ. Press, 1930.

First Methodist Church, *A Century of Faith and Service, 1866–1966.*

Foote, H. C. ed., *Pen Pictures from the Garden of the World.* Chicago, Lewis Publishing Co., 1888.

Guinn, J. M. *History of the State of California* and Biographical Record of Coast Counties. Chapman Publishing Co., Chicago, 1904. 2 volumes.

Hamsher, C. F. "How Los Gatos Got its Name." Pamphlet distributed by W. R. Hamsher, Realtor, Los Gatos.

Holdredge, Helen, *Mammy Peasant's Partner.* G. P. Putnam Sons, N.Y. 1954.

Irvine, L. H. "Los Gatos, Gem City of the Foothills" *Sunset* magazine Homeseekers' Bureau of Information. San Francisco, 1915.

MacGregor, Bruce, *South Pacific Coast.* Howell North Books. Berkeley, 1968.

McCaleb, Chas. S. *The San Jose Railroads Centennial 1868–1968.* Foothill Junior College District, 1968.

Nine Men and One Hundred Years of Water History. San Jose Water Works, S.J. 1967.

Rambo, F. Ralph, *Remember When,* A Boy's Eye View of an Old Valley. Rosicrucian Press Ltd. San Jose.

Rice, Bertha, *Builders of Our Valley.* Bertha Rice, 1957.

Sawyer, Eugene T. *History of Santa Clara County.* Historic Records Co. Los Angeles, 1922.

Schweitzer, T. P., "History of Los Gatos Union High School" by the students of his three history classes 1967–1968.

Shortridge, Chas. M., *Santa Clara County and its Resources,* a souvenir of the San Jose *Mercury* 1895. San Jose *Mercury* Publishers, 1895.

Stuart, Reginald R., ed. *The Burrell Letters,* including excerpts from the Birney Burrell Diary and "Reminiscences of an Octogenarian." Reprinted from the Calif. Historical Society *Quarterly,* 1948–1950. Oakland, 1950.

Walter, Mrs. Carrie Stevens, *Central California, Santa Clara Valley,* San Jose, 1887.

White King Sewing Machine Pamphlet, "Santa Clara Valley" San Francisco, 1887.

Newspapers and Documents

Microfilmed and in Los Gatos Memorial Library.
  Los Gatos Weekly *News* 1881–1915
  Los Gatos *Mail* 1893–1915
  Los Gatos *Mail-News* 1916–1953
  Los Gatos *Times* 1936–1962.
Files of the Los Gatos *Times*–Saratoga *Observer.*
Los Gatos Town Board *Minutes,* 1887 to present.
Folder on *Parks,* Office of City Clerk, Los Gatos.
Numerous letters, small documents from Old-Timers.

Appendix

TOWN OFFICIALS
1881 to 1971

TOWN TRUSTEES AND COUNCILMEN

Palmer Perkins	1887–1888
J. W. Lyndon	1887–1892
D. D. Holland	1887–died 1888
Herman Sund	1887–1890
George Seanor	1887–1888
W. J. Parr	1888–1892
Peter Johnson	1888–1894
Chas. F. Wilcox	1888–1889
Thos. Gibson	1889–1890
F. M. Jackson	1890–1892
Fen Massol	1890–resigned 1897
D. C. Crummey	1892–resigned 1893
D. P. Simons	1892–1896
Samuel Syverson	1892–1894
J. A. Hicks	1893–1894
T. J. Davis	1894–1902
H. Schomberg	1894–1898
E. N. Davis	1894–1900
R. L. Hutchinson	1897–1898
B. M. Gregory	1898–died 1900
G. R. Lewis	1898–1902
J. H. Lyndon	1900–1904
D. C. Crummey	1900–resigned 1903
C. M. Sullivan	1900–1902
R. R. Bell	1902–1906
B. P. Shuler	1902–1906
J. H. Pearce	1902–1906
B. F. Williams	1903–1904
T. E. Johns	1904–1908
Wm. Sporleder	1904–1916
F. M. Derrickson	1906–1910
J. W. Lyndon	1906–resigned 1907
D. P. Simons	1906–died 1910
R. P. Shuler	1907–1910
J. E. Teed	1908–1910
C. H. Wheeler	1908–1912
Geo. W. Turner	1910–1914
R. P. Doolan	1910–1914
R. R. Bell	1912–resigned 1914
W. C. Short	1912–1918
S. D. Balch	1914–1918
C. W. Gertridge	1914–1922
J. J. Stanfield	1914–resigned 1919
I. D. Mabie	1918–1938
Wm. A. Riggs	1918–resigned 1920
W. M. Godfrey	1918–1920
J. Walter Crider	1919–1924
A. L. Erickson	1920–1922
L. H. Killingsworth	1920–1922
Geo. A. Green	1922–1942
By law the first *Mayor* in 1927	
L. H. Neuman	1924–1928
A. W. Templeman	1924–1928
A. W. Wilder	1928–1932
J. D. B. Manning	1918–died 1931
Marc J. Vertin	1931–1942
S. D. Balch	1931–1932
H. K. Phelps	1932–1936
Russell H. Sund	1932–1940
Paul E. Curtis	1936–1940
Carl S. Balch	1938–resigned 1940
Chas. Ricketts	1940–resigned 1943
Stanley Mills	1940–1944
C. A. Spotswood	1940–1946
Bert Fresher	1942–1946
A. G. Jacobson	1942–1946
Avel Granstrom	1943–resigned 1943
J. C. Adams	1943–1948
L. H. Wright	1944–1952
Harry Boone	1946–1958
C. A. Kirkendall	1946–1950
J. F. Thompson	1946–1958
A. E. Merrill	1948–resigned 1949
Hal Belyew	1950–1956
W. E. Mason	1950–1954
Chas. K. Gamble	1952–1956
A. E. Merrill	1954–1956
Fred Berryman	1955–1956
W. O. Graham	1956–1960
James A. Stoops	1956–1960
W. E. Mason	1958–resigned 1961
Gail Packard	1958–1962
John Lincoln	1960–1968
James Donati	1960–1964
H. C. Crall	1962–1966
Joe Whelan	1962–1966
Egon Jensen	1964–1972
J. D. Michaelsen	1962–resigned 1969
Marjorie Muttersbach	1969–1970
Roland Parry	1966–1970
Seymour Abrahams	1968–1972
Ruth Cannon	1970–1974
Mark B. DiDuca	1970–1974

MAYORS OF LOS GATOS

Note: From 1887 to 1927 the Chairman of the Board of Trustees was considered to be the "Mayor." However the legal title was not created until 1927 when the state law stipulated that the Board select a Mayor. Actually the first legal Mayor under this law was George A. Green.

Palmer Perkins	1887–1888
J. W. Lyndon	1888–1892
Peter Johnson	1892–1894
Fen Massol	1894–resigned 1897
H. Schomberg	1897–1898
E. N. Davis	1898–1902
J. H. Lyndon	1902–1904
B. P. Shuler	1904–1906
T. E. Johns	1906–1908
D. P. Simons	1908–1910
G. W. Turner	1910–1912
R. R. Bell	1912–resigned 1914
S. D. Balch	1914–1916
W. C. Short	1916–1918
J. J. Stanfield	1918–resigned 1919
Wm. F. Godfrey	1919–1920
C. W. Gertridge	1920–1922
J. Walter Crider	1922–1924
I. D. Mabie	1924–1926
Geo. A. Green	1926–1927
First legal Mayor	
A. H. Bell	1928–1930
I. D. Mabie	1930–1932
Marc Vertin	1932–1940
Carl S. Balch	1940–resigned 1940
Stanley Mills	1940–1944
C. B. Spotswood	1944–1946
J. C. Adams	1946–1948
Jas. F. Thompson	1948–resigned 1951
L. H. Wright	1951–1952
Chas. K. Gamble	1952–1954
A. E. Merrill	1954–1962
John Lincoln	1962–1966
Egon Jensen	1966–1968
John Michaelsen	1968–1969
Roland Perry	1969–1970
Chas. DeFreitas	1970–1971
Seymour Abrahams	1971–1972

TOWN CLERKS

A. E. Wilder	1887–1888
J. D. Mason	1888–1890
J. W. Riddle	1890–1892
Geo. A. Butler	1892–1898
Geo. A. Walker	1898–1902
J. F. Henderson	1902–1904
K. H. Erickson	1904–1906
Eli Winning	1906–resigned 1914
Donna Winning	1914–1940
Ruth Blake Crichton	1940–1952
Beverly H. Blatnick	1952–1964
Jo Leibfritz	1964 to present

TOWN TREASURERS

Geo. S. McMurtry	1887–1894
J. J. Stanfield	1894–1896
B. W. Pearce	1896–1898
F. F. Watkins	1898–1908
Zedd Riggs	1908–1914
Geo. S. McMurtry	1914–1948
W. R. Hamsher	1948–1964
Nogah Bethlahmy	1964–resigned 1966
James Stoops	1966 to present

TOWN MARSHALS

J. L. Gellatt	1887–1888
A. M. Howell	1888–1890
L. E. Hamilton	1890–1892
J. L. Gelatt	1892–1894
M. F. Blank	1894–1898
E. E. Springer	1900–1908
J. D. Shore	1908–1912
J. Barber	1912–1921
H. O. Baird	1921–1926

CHIEFS OF POLICE

H. O. Baird	1926–1928
Henry C. Noble	1928–1939
Lyman Feathers	1939–1943
Ralph Phillips	1943–1970
Harold Johnson	1970 to present

Index

12/97 ∅